MW01382766

TALES
OF THE
PROFITABLE TRADER

The User's Guide to Modern Price Action
From Theory to Practice

JAMES HARRIS

Copyright

To request permissions, contact the publisher at: contact@smartuncle.com

ISBN Hardcover: 979-8-9873913-1-0
ISBN Paperback: 979-8-9873913-4-1
ISBN Ebook: 979-8-9873913-7-2

Join our mailing list! Sign up to receive book announcements, gifts, perks, special promotions and more.

Disclaimer

It must be understood that a very high degree of risk is involved in trading securities. The Company, the authors, the publisher and the affiliates of the Company assume no responsibility or liability for trading and investment results. Statements on the Company's website and in its publications are made as of the date stated and are subject to change without notice. The author and SmartUncle.com ("the Company"), including its employees, contractors, shareholders and affiliates, are NOT an investment advisory service, a registered investment advisor or a broker- dealer and do not undertake to advise clients on which securities they should buy or sell for themselves. Readers must make their own decisions about trading and investments. All information contained on the company's website is provided for informational purposes only, is general in nature, does not constitute investment advice, nor is it an offer or solicitation to buy or sell any security. While we believe the information provided herein is reliable, we do not warrant its accuracy or completeness. Past performance does not guarantee future results. There is risk of loss in all trading and investing activities. Nothing contained herein should be construed as a recommendation by the Company or its affiliates to buy, hold or sell any security issues mentioned herein. This document may not be copied without permission from SmartUncle.com. By reading this book you agree to these terms: Investor accepts all risks inherent with investing, including total loss of capital; author and Smart Uncle LLC does not provide investment advice; nothing contained herein shall be construed as an offer or solicitation to buy or sell any securities; Investor accesses content at own risk; Investor releases author and Smart Uncle LLC from all liability due to use of content; Investor agrees terms may change at anytime without notice based on changes in conditions beyond our control. Please consult a licensed financial advisor prior to making any financial decisions. These products are for informational and educational purposes only and should not be construed as investment advice. The indicators, strategies, rules and all other features of the Company's products are provided for informational and educational purposes only. Examples presented are for educational purposes only. Readers should not rely solely on the Information in making any trades or investments. This is not a recommendation to buy or sell any security, and this does not take into account the investment objectives, risk tolerance or financial situation of any particular investor. Please consult your broker or financial advisor to determine if trading in securities is right for you. Past performance is not indicative of future results. Stock market trading may result in losses that exceed your deposits. Therefore, you should not invest or risk money that you cannot afford to lose. Before deciding to trade any products offered by Smart Uncle LLC you should carefully consider your objectives, financial situation, needs and level of experience. You acknowledge that you have read the "Disclaimer" prior to trading in order to be aware of the risks involved.

Acknowledgement

To my dad, who always knew my true worth.
The one person who has always seen my potential, even
when I couldn't see it myself.

To my mom, who helped me to become an entrepreneur.
Who showed me that it's never too late to start something new.

To my sister, who is always there for me when I need
her. Who believed in me even when no one else did.

To all the other important people in my life who have
helped me to get where I am today, thank you. You know
who you are.

And finally, to my future self, I promise to never give up
on my dreams. And to always believe in myself, even
when no one else does.

I want to say thank you for everything.

Contents

Preface

It is never too late to be a trader, but it is always too soon to jump into the wrong trade. I learned this the hard way when I embarked on my journey of trading. You see, most traders start just like me—they see an opportunity to make money somehow and go for it blindly without having any idea of what they're doing or why they're doing it other than pure greed. Trading can be risky. Sometimes these people succeed.

You might not walk out with tons of money, but you could lose a lot! I can't tell you how many times I've heard people say that the vast majority of traders lose their money. They might be right, but we'll never know for sure since there is little research to back up this statistic. Most traders do it long enough to make some profits before they quit altogether—only a few continue and become successful in trading.

In a study by Ryan Garvey and Anthony Murphy, they studied traders who made a profit and those who lost. They found that about 65% of traders were in the red after commissions, while a smaller percentage of 35% profited. The most profitable trader made more than $197k and the least profitable lost more than $748k. The average gross profit for each profitable trader was almost $8k, but losing traders averaged a net loss of $775. The transaction costs of trading stocks means that it can be hard to make a profit when you trade. With free-commission online brokers, this is no longer a problem.

Trading is not usually profitable for most people. However, it can still be good for some. There are ways to reduce risk by limiting the downside potential, such as always using stop losses, and never trading around earnings. It is worth following these rules and hoping for success—there are no guarantees of what the future holds.

For me, trading was never something for which I planned in life; but in hindsight, this is the greatest thing I have done. Conversely, looking back now, there are so many more things that I could have done with all the time spent researching and trading stocks. However, at least one good thing came out of all this, a skill that can never be taken away.

Chapter by Chapter

This four-part book will explain price action trading in the stock market. In fact, trading can be exciting and rewarding, but you need to know the different methods and techniques before you start.

In Part I, I will teach you the basics of stock trading, including what stocks are, how they work, and how to make money from them. Once you understand stocks, you can move on to part two, which will teach you how to apply that knowledge in the real world.

» **PART I : The Journey**

» **Chapter 1, "Introduction."** Tale of the market crash of 2020. The technical approach to trading is learning how to trade stocks effectively. This means learning the market language and understanding what moves the markets. It's also important to understand the risks versus rewards and whether or not becoming a trader is worth it for you.

» **Chapter 2, "Stock Market Investing."** Tale of Michael Burry's "Big Short." When you invest in the stock, you are taking co-ownership, with equity, in a company. There are ways to becoming a sophisticated investor and minimize your risk. One way is to practice with a paper-trading account. Another way to reduce your risk is to start small with a cash management account. The final way is to go all-in with a margin account.

» **Chapter 3, "Trading Tactics."** Tale of Ray Dalio. There are many different trading tactics that can be employed to make a profit in the market. Some traders focus on short-term methods, such as intraday trading, while others take a longer-term approach and focus on swing trading. While each trader will have their own preferred method, there are some general tips that can be followed in order to improve your chances of success.

In Part II, you will learn about the different tools and strategies that are available to traders. You will also learn how to execute trades and which market instruments are best suited for your trading style. By the end of this section, you should have a basic understanding of how the stock market works and be ready to start trading stocks yourself.

» **PART II : Trading Platform**

» **Chapter 4, "Trading Tools."** Tale of Peter Lynch. Trading tools are important for any trader, whether a beginner or experienced. One of the most important trading tools is charting. Another important tool for traders is technical indicators. Most trading platforms already offer their execution tools. These tools allow you to place trades quickly and easily. If you want to be successful at trading, it is important to learn about all of the different trading tools available.

» **Chapter 5, "Trade Execution."** Tale of the Navinder Sarao. A market order is an order to buy or sell at the best available price. A limit order is an order to buy or sell at a specified price or better. A stop order is an order to buy or sell when it reaches a specified price, and a trailing stop order is an order to buy or sell when it reaches a specified price that is trailing the market price by a specified amount. One-cancels-the-other orders, also known as OCO orders, are two orders that are linked together such that if one order is executed, the other is automatically canceled. This can be helpful in managing your risk, as it allows you to place a stop loss and take profit at the same time.

» **Chapter 6, "Market Instruments."** Tale of Aristotle and Thales. A market instrument is a tradable financial asset of any kind. Financial assets include stocks, bonds, options, futures, and currency. Most market instruments are traded on exchanges, which provide a centralized marketplace for buyers and sellers. Exchange-traded funds are one type of market instrument that has become increasingly popular in recent years. Futures contracts are another type of popular market instrument. Foreign currency is yet another type of market instrument. Cryptocurrency is a relatively new type of market instrument that is based on blockchain technology.

In Part III, you will learn about technical analysis. Technical analysis is a method of analyzing stocks using past data to predict future movements. You will learn how to read charts and interpret indicators to make informed trading decisions. Additionally, you will learn about different trading strategies that can be used to capitalize on market trends. By the end of this section, you should understand how to trade stocks using technical analysis.

» **PART III : Modern Price Action**

» **Chapter 7, "Technical Analysis."** Tale of Robert Edwards and John Magee. Technical analysis is the examination of past market data to identify patterns and predict future price movements. Price action refers to the movement of prices on a chart. Consolidation patterns occur when the price of an asset remains within a certain range for an extended period. Momentum patterns indicate whether the current trend is likely to continue or reverse. Reversal patterns signal a potential change in direction. Retracement patterns show temporary pauses in an ongoing trend. Gap patterns emerge when there is a significant disparity between the prices at the start and end of a trading session or period. Volume is the number of shares (or contracts) traded over a certain period.

» **Chapter 8, "Trend Analysis."** Tale of William Delbert Gann. By understanding and identifying trends, traders can make better decisions on when to enter and exit positions. There are various methods of trend analysis, but one of the most popular is using moving averages. Another popular method of trend analysis is a trend following. This involves riding the current trend until it reverses. Finally, it is also important to be aware of consolidation patterns. These occurrences occur when the market is range-bound and prices are not trending in any particular direction; the consolidation is a result of a temporary equilibrium between supply and demand. Consolidation can often lead to breakout moves, so it is important to be aware of these periods. By understanding trend analysis, traders can better identify opportunities in the markets.

» **Chapter 9, "Market Cycles."** Tale of Charles Dow and Edward Jones. The market cycle is the natural rise and fall of market prices in response to the forces of supply and demand. The market cycle is often described in terms of four stages: expansion, peak, contraction, and trough. Market cycles can be further subdivided into sub-phases, each of which represents a distinct stage in the overall cycle. Consumers and businesses alike must be aware of market cycles. A basic understanding of market cycles can help individuals and firms weather economic downturns and prosper during periods of growth.

In Part IV, you will learn about risk management and trading psychology. You will learn how to manage your risk exposure and protect your portfolio from unnecessary losses. Additionally, you will learn about the importance of discipline and psychology in successful trading. By the end of this section, you should have a basic knowledge of how to trade stocks while minimizing risk. You will learn about different ways to improve your trading skills and increase your chances of success. Additionally, you will learn about how to set realistic goals and stay motivated in the face of adversity. Finally, you will learn about ways to become more profitable in stock trading.

» **CONCLUSION.** Tale of Warren Buffett. Closing this book with a powerful and inspirational message to investors and traders alike.

PART I

THE JOURNEY

One question needs to be asked: "Is trading success a result of luck?" This is not a book to disparage anybody's belief system, but rather a book to highlight the differences among trading styles and show that you need to consider these differences in order to make better trades. With a variety of factors and strategies from which to choose, trading in the stock market is no small task. This book presents many different strategies for trading success.

There are two main routes you can take. One is a buy-and-hold strategy where the investor holds onto stocks for an extended period of time regardless of market conditions. The other option is momentum or short term trading, which involves buying at low prices in anticipation that they will rise again soon afterward.There are many different strategies that traders use to be successful in the financial markets. And there is no one "God" strategy. Some of these strategies may include buying stocks identified by fundamental analysis, finding stocks with the best growth potential for an investment, or buying shares in areas where there is a liquidity shortage. The choice of strategy will depend on the trader, and it is up to them to find one that suits their personality best.

I trade exclusively on price action, so many of the ideas in this book are related to identifying price movements and finding opportunities. There are price levels where the sentiment of the stock may change, resulting in a knee-jerk reaction. A buyer or seller frenzy may follow as a result of it. Identifying these areas on a price chart are imperative to being a profitable trader. If you are able to identify these levels, then you will be able to profit from the changes in price behaviors that follow. For instance, there must be at least two losers for every winner. When the first person is selling in fear, I buy their shares; and when the second person is buying in greed, I sell shares to them. After the smoke clears, I have a profit, and other participants may have a loss. This is how I profit in the stock market.

Take a peek at the Advanced Micro Devices (AMD) chart (See Figure 0.1). Even if you don't have the trained eye now, you'll have one 12 chapters from now. There are strange things happening with AMD that even the novice can spot, such as the price activity at item A. The chart for AMD shows some very unusual activity before its

fiscal second quarter report. I followed the chart's signal and purchased shares at A and B before the sharp rise in price, and selling at
C. It is this type of action, using the chart to make decisions on individual stock, that you will learn. After reading this book, go back to
this page to discover why buying stocks at item A and B and then
selling at item C was a good trade opportunity.

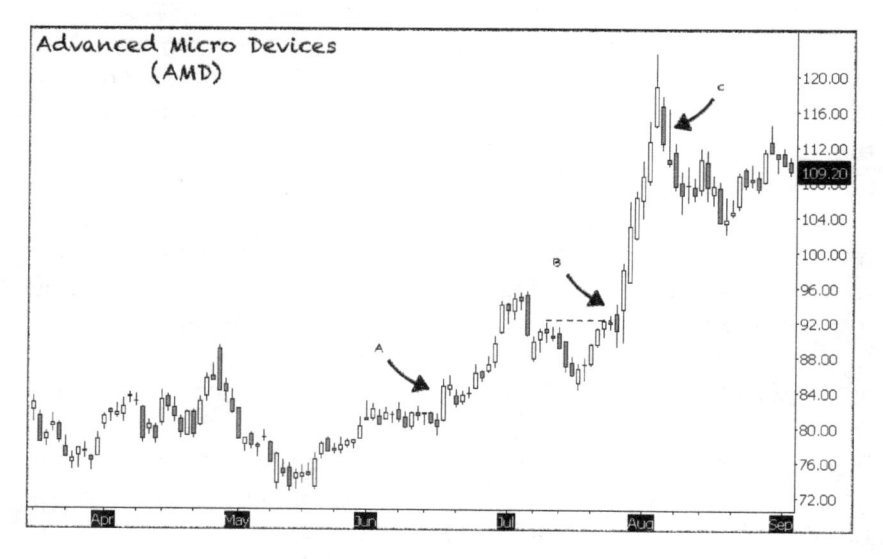

Figure 0.1: Advanced Micro Devices

You will learn how to identify these opportunities by using such
simple technical analysis tools as support/resistance levels, moving
averages, and trend lines that will allow you to find these potential
moves before they happen. It does not require that you have any
previous knowledge of financial markets or trading strategies. With
just some basic knowledge of how to read charts, which I'll teach you,
anyone can become an expert trader like me. This book contains
many examples, which includes real-life screenshots from my actual
trades. It also includes step-by-step instructions on how to implement each strategy into your own personal trading style. Your only
responsibility is to understand the different trading styles and
choose a style that best suits you.

1 Introduction

Chapter Overview

- » Understanding the technical approach to trading.

- » Speaking the market language.

- » Acquiring the appropriate knowledge, mindset, and expectations.

Tale of the market crash of 2020

In March 2020, the Dow Jones Industrial Average (DJIA) suffered its largest percentage drop in US history, signaling the beginning of the market downturn. Only two other days in American history have ever seen such a market crash on the same day, Black Monday in October 1987 and the Great Depression in January 1930. The sharp decline in global stock prices was prompted by a fear of the coronavirus spreading, and the prospect of a recession. The disease has been classified by the World Health Organization as a pandemic. Many were concerned that their government authorities were not doing enough to slow the virus' spread.

Who could have predicted that 2020 would be the year of the market crash? Not the investors who were caught off guard. The resulting shutdown of several companies and industries sent shockwaves through the economy. Layoffs were still being announced, and the unemployment rate continued to rise. Millions of people lost their homes and their savings. Consequently, the decrease in purchasing power has exacerbated market conditions for the worst. While it remains to be seen how long this market downturn will last, one thing is certain—it will go down in history as the year of the crash.

The market crash of 2020 was a harrowing experience for investors. In the span of a few months which caused many investors to lose a lot of money. Surprisingly, the market recovered within eight months (See Figure 1.1). This eight-month period was the shortest time on record for the market to rebound. Also, this was a remarkable feat, considering that many sectors of the US economy were still struggling. Despite the struggles of many sectors of the US economy, the market saw a comeback. This crash showed the resilience of the US economy and the strength of the stock market. Losses from this record-breaking fall were entirely recovered in the same year, about five months after the market bottomed.

Although, this was a dramatic event, it did not last long. For months afterward, the news was filled with stories of businesses shutting down and people losing their life savings. But in the last few months, there's been a lot of good news on the vaccine front, and, as a result, the market has been rising steadily. In fact, at the time of this writing, it's trading higher than its pre-crash high.

The market crash of 2020 ultimately proved to be a relatively brief and minor setback. I'm still not fully recovered, but things are certainly looking up. At first, I was really confused; but after doing some research, I realized that the crash wasn't as bad as I thought it was going to be. In fact, it actually gave me an opportunity to buy some stocks at a lower price. As of now, I'm still monitoring the market closely, but I'm not as worried as I was before. It took me a little over a year to get over the crash. And slowly but surely, I began to rebuild what I had lost.

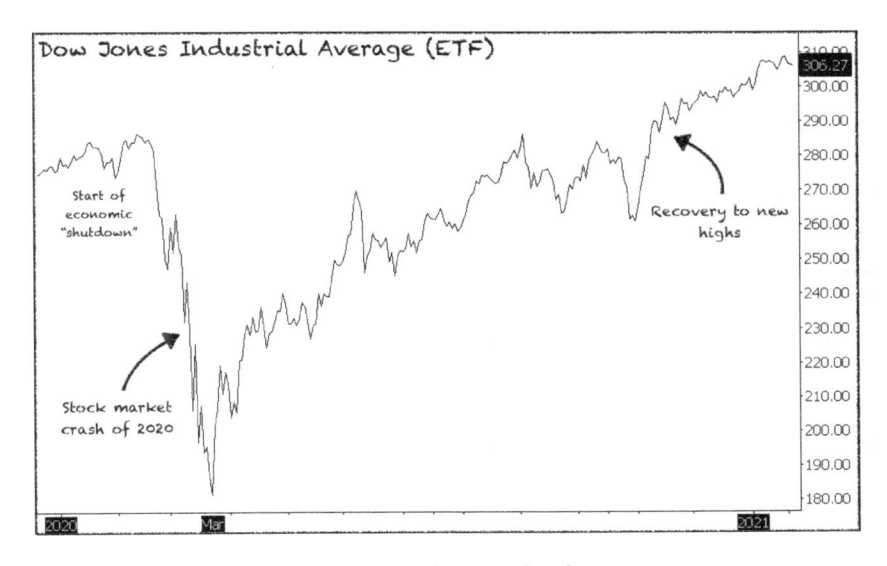

Figure 1.1: Market crash of 2020.

We learned from our mistakes, and we moved forward stronger than ever before. It was an incredibly difficult time for everyone involved. But, as they say, time heals all wounds. For many Americans, it was a reminder that the economy is not as stable as we would like to believe. For others, it was an opportunity to buy stocks at bargain prices. Regardless of how you felt about the crash, it's important to understand what caused it and how it could affect your investments going forward. Here's a look at the market crash of 2020 and what investors should know. The market is slowly starting to rebound, and I believe that it will only continue to grow in the years to come.

In the next chapter, I'll share some short tales from my life and famous traders that will hopefully provide some insights. Novices will definitely relate to my experiences of making mistakes and learning from them. But ultimately, what it takes to be successful is perseverance and a willingness to keep learning. So, here's to a prosperous future for all of us!

LET'S GET STARTED

I was not always a profitable trader, but I loved it so much at the time that I did not care. When I first started, my family did not believe in the stock market and thought that it was too risky for someone with so much to lose as myself. My Dad made fun of me since he thought that it was nothing more than a way to gamble because he never understood the profits that could be made after some practice. I was not about to give up on my love of trading because it gave me the freedom and creativity that I had always wanted.

He was almost right because my first few years as a trader were very frustrating—lots of losses and not seeing light at the end of the tunnel. Then one day it happened—it all clicked into place, and everything changed. When I became profitable, I felt like I had reached the pinnacle of success. Of course, it was not easy getting there. Once he saw how good of a job I was doing at trading, he no longer teased me, and now we are very close because he is proud of what his son has accomplished.

Through my experiences of losses, I learned what worked and what didn't work. It may seem like an insurmountable task for those who don't know much about trading before they begin. The truth of the matter is that it doesn't matter how much you know, if a trader lacks experience, they can fall short. In the stock market, it's not a question of if you will lose money, but when—it is about how we handle adversity that determines our success.

If you're looking for a way to get ahead with your trading journey, then look no further than this book. I'll teach you everything you need to know about modern price action so that, by the end of this book, you will be able to make better trading decisions using powerful techniques. I will answer the question of how to be a profitable trader from theory to practice.

THE TECHNICAL APPROACH TO TRADING

Trading can be a very profitable endeavor, but it's also incredibly risky. Many traders lose money, and the reason is because they don't have a solid trading strategy. A lot of people think that trading is a get-rich-quick scheme. But the reality is that it's a skilled profession that takes years of practice and hard work to master. It's hard to make a profit in the stock market if you don't have a firm understanding. That's where technical analysis enters. You may also feel overwhelmed and intimidated by charts and trend lines. It doesn't have to be difficult or scary. In fact, this book will teach you everything you need to know to start using technical analysis for your own investments.

Technical analysis is the process of interpreting historical data to forecast future prices, but it doesn't tell you why it occurred. Many people are also turned off by the notion of having to learn something new to trade successfully. To be clear, this is not a precise science, and it can be difficult to understand how technical analysts arrive at their conclusions. It's the key to becoming a successful trader. With it, you can trade any market and time frame with confidence. You'll know when to buy and sell, so you can maximize your profits while minimizing your risk.

Why should you learn technical analysis? It is a method of evaluating price action with charts and other indicators to determine how prices move over time. Technical analysts believe that the collective actions of all market participants, such as buying and selling pressure, ultimately determine prices. As a result, technical analysis can be used to identify potential signals—moments when buying or selling pressure is present in the market and may be anticipated again in the near future. Analysts also examine price data to identify patterns that may repeat themselves in the future. By doing so, they seek to gain an edge in the market and achieve higher returns. While technical analysis has its critics, there is no denying that it can be a useful tool for traders who know how to use it correctly.

How do you use technical analysis in the stock market? It is the process of looking at charts and making decisions based on what you see. More experienced traders tend to find trading signals through pattern of human behavior—what pattern are telling you with their actions (news)—as well as patterns (price patterns) that show up over time. There are a variety of ways to do technical analysis, but some of the most common methods include looking at support and resistance levels and moving averages. It can be used on any time frame, but I would recommend less experienced traders to look at longer-term charts.

Is it possible to have success with a purely technical approach to trading? Yes. Technical trading is an approach to trading that is based on finding patterns in the movement of price and trading according to those patterns. Technical traders advocate taking more calculated risks when we know things ahead of time, instead of picking individual stocks blindly by following trends and just guessing what will happen next. It can be used to identify trend reversals and price targets for trades. However, it is not without its critics. Some traders argue that technical analysis does not take into consideration fundamental factors, such as the financial health of a company or any news about it. Others who do not advocate technical trading often advise that it may not be wise for anyone new to trading to try and time the market. It is a complex field, and there is no one-size-fits-all approach to trading. Ultimately, it is up to each individual trader to decide whether or not they believe technical analysis can help them achieve their investment goals.

What advantages does a purely technical approach offers? It is the most popular approach to trading because it minimizes risk and maximizes profit. Unlike investors who use fundamental analysis, who base their decisions on what the current value and fiscal condition of the company, technicians don't care if a company is performing well nor fiscally sound. Neither care if they are making widgets for sale or experimental machines for a university lab. All they want is solid timing information that will help them buy low and sell high, or in the case of a short sell at the high to cover at the low. Your emotions, which play such an important role in determining how you make your trades, must factor into your trading portfolio's holdings, can be managed much more easily and quickly through technical analysis than through any other approach readily available. It's a great way to avoid the mistakes of trading from fear and greed.

You need to have an edge over the market to make money, and that's not easy to do. Even if you're not interested in learning about technical analysis, you probably know that it's important to do so if you want to be successful in the market. In fact, it is a proven way to obtain profit. It's been used by professional traders for years. Most traders rely on technical analysis, while most investors utilize fundamental analysis to try and get an edge over the market, but both of these approaches have their flaws. Technical analysis can be subjective, and fundamental analysis can take a long time to develop.

The first approach is reading charts to identify market structure in price movements. By reading charts and identifying key formations, you can get a quick understanding of where the market is going.

SPEAKING THE MARKET LANGUAGE

Do you want to be successful in the market? Of course, who doesn't? Trading can be confusing, and it's hard to know where to start. And one of the most important steps is understanding the language of the market. Since there are a lot of technical terms used in trading and investing, it can be hard to keep track of them all. That's where I come in—with this handy guide listing all the most important terms you need to know. This terminology section will help you understand the most important market terms. With this knowledge, you'll be able to follow along with my strategies more easily. Don't let this lack of knowledge hold you back any longer. After reading this section, you'll have everything you need to begin and become a market wizard in no time at all.

Understanding the fundamental elements of my techniques is also learning the terms I'll use often to explain them. The chart below will help you understand those elements of price action that I will use to describe significant price events and movements (See Figure 1.2). You don't have to be an analyst wizard to understand, and you've probably heard some of them before. But you might not be completely clear on what they mean. Also, how will you understand my strategies if we don't speak the same language? As a result, I've included a quick summary for both new traders and seasoned technicians. So review the chart and familiarize yourself with the market terminology. It will pay off in the end!

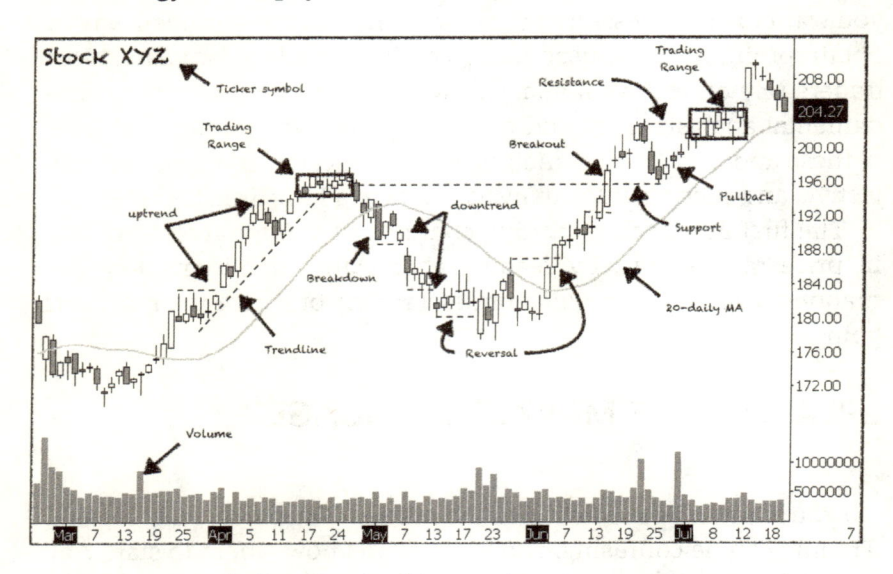

Figure 1.2: Labeling the significant price events and movements

Once again, the market has its own language, and before we can chart a successful future, we must first learn the terminology. Therefore, before completing this chapter, it is critical that you grasp what each phrase means. Make a note of this list and save it for future use. Meanwhile, take some time to study and thoroughly review each item on the list. If you carefully follow my advice, this book will become easy to understand and extremely beneficial to you. You may also refer to this chapter later if you need to refresh your memory. I won't go over these terms in alphabetical order since some basic concepts must be taught first before the following term can be fully comprehended. This will look to many of you to be similar to learning a new language. However, if you carefully read this list, it will make sense later in the book. Let's start with the foundations before moving on to more technical jargon. So, let's take a look at each term individually to see how it's used in this book and what it means.

Support. It can be hard to know when to buy a stock, and even harder to know when to sell. Most people buy stocks when the price is going up, but this is actually the worst time to do so. The best time to buy a stock is when it's at its lowest point, because this is when you'll get the most value for your money. The support level is the price at which a stock does not fall below for a certain length of time. It's like your safety net when the market gets rough. When prices start to drop, buyers will flock to this level and help prop up the stock, preventing it from falling any further. The selling pressure is removed, more buyers return to the market, and confidence returns.

Use the support level to your advantage by buying stocks when they reach this point. You'll be confident knowing that the stock has some stability and is less likely to fall any further. Plus, you can always sell it later when the price goes back up. When the stock falls below this price, it may indicate that there is selling pressure and could lead to further declines. A breach of the support level could also lead to a change in trend from bullish to bearish.

Are there any benefits to knowing the support level for a stock? Yes, there are plenty of benefits! If you know that a stock has strong support at a certain level, you'll be more likely to buy it when it dips to that level, confident that it is unlikely to fall much further. Conversely, if you know that a stock has weak support at a certain level, you may choose to sell it before it drops any lower. Additionally, even if you're not planning on buying or selling any stocks in the near future, knowing the support levels can still be helpful in understanding market fluctuations and trends.

Resistance. It's hard to know when a stock has reached its peak level and when to sell. Most people wait until price drops sharply before selling, but this can lead to large losses if the stock price falls after the breakdown. The resistance level is important to watch because when the resistance level is reached, buying pressure may diminish and selling pressure will increase. The resistance movement is usually psychological because a stock price has an emotional effect on its traders. This can lead to a stock price decline. When a stock breaks out through the resistance level, it means that the stock is now trading at a higher price than it has in the recent past. This can attract new investors to the stock, which can drive up the price even more. The resistance level is like a ceiling; once the stock breaks through it, there can be no stopping it.

Trading Range. Trader's see a stock that's just below support and think it's a good time to sell, or they see a stock that's just above resistance and think it's a good time to buy. This can go wrong when traders step in at the last minute and force prices in the opposite direction.

The trading range is a space where stock prices fluctuate between the highest and lowest prices over a given period of time. This area is typically shown on a chart using support and resistance lines (See Figure 1.3). The price of a stock will often bounce off the upper and lower limits, which reflects an effort to move it back in one direction or another.

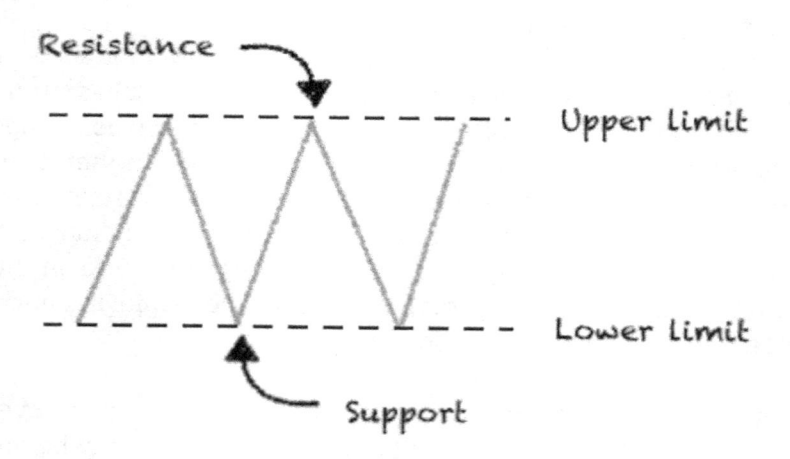

Figure 1.3: Trading range between support and resistance

An area like this can represent a price trap for aggressive bears who see a just-below-support supported sell opportunity. This can also go wrong when sellers step in at the last minute but price forces higher before they can be bought out. The same is true for aggressive bulls who see a long-awaited chance to buy, only to find themselves in the same situation where sellers stepping-in, forcing prices lower. In either case, it's important to be aware of trading ranges so you don't get caught in a price trap!

How do you know if a stock is in its trading range? A stock is in its trading range when it is bouncing between a support and a resistance level. The support level is the price at which buyers are thought to be strong enough to buy and keep the stock from dropping any lower. The resistance level is the price at which sellers are thought to be strong enough to sell and keep the stock from rising any higher. When a stock breaks out of its trading range, it usually means that the buyers or sellers have gained control of the market.

There are a number of benefits to trading within a stock's range. First, it can help you manage risk and limit your losses. When you know the range in which a stock is trading, you can buy if a stock is trading lower and tests support near the bottom of its trading range; scoop up some shares knowing that there's a good chance it will bounce back up. Conversely, by selling short near the top of a stock's trading range, you can take profits before the stock reverses and heads lower. Another benefit of trading within a range is that it can help you boost your profits by taking advantage of small price movements. Those who trade breakout strategies generally only profit when prices move sharply outside of their predetermined ranges.

When a stock price goes near its trading range limit, this can be an indication that the stock is overbought or oversold. If the price goes too far outside of the range, this could also signal a potential breakout or breakdown.

Uptrend. If you're looking at a chart and see a sequence of gradually higher peaks and troughs, that's an uptrend, also known as a bull trend. It is when the price is moving in an upward direction. When there's an uptrend, each successive peak is higher than the previous, and each trough is also higher than the one before it (See Figure 1.4).

This continued rise indicates that buyers are willing to pay more and more, and that demand is outstripping supply. Ultimately, it is a sign that the market is healthy and that prices are likely to continue rising.

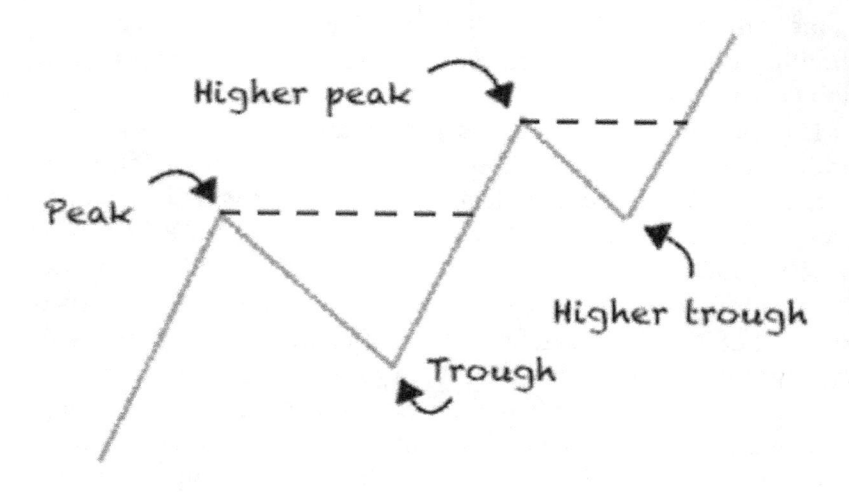

Figure 1.4: Uptrend is higher peaks and troughs.

Investing in stocks during an uptrend can be very profitable. For instance, if you're able to identify an uptrend and invest in a stock before it peaks, you could see significant gains. However, it's important to remember that stock prices can go down as well as up, so always do your research.

How do you know when an uptrend is over? It is typically over when prices can't seem to make any higher highs and/or lower lows (See Figure 1.5). This typically signifies that the bulls are getting tired and that there's not much buying pressure at support left. It also indicates that there's been too much bullish sentiment in the market, and that a reversal could be imminent.

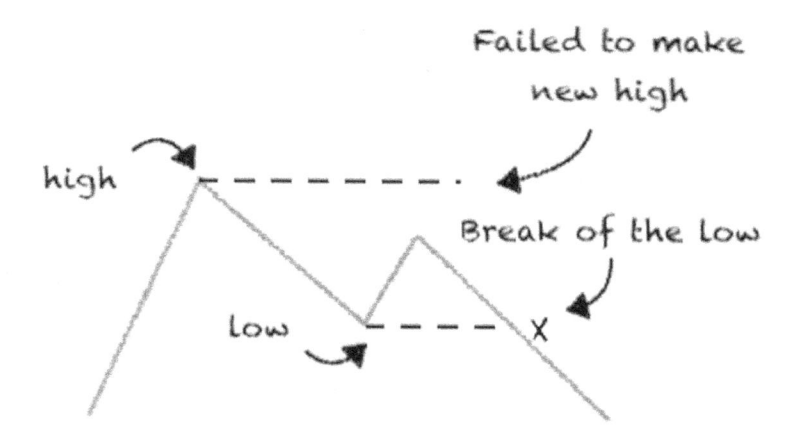

Figure 1.5: Uptrend is over after failing to make new high.

Downtrend. There are many advantages to being aware of market trends. In times where stocks and other financial instruments trend down, it can often be an excellent time for buying on sale because you'll know that these assets will soon reverse their course (i. e., go up). Market sentiment changes quickly; however, without understanding what caused the downtrends—such as fear or greed—it may prove difficult predicting when exactly another turnaround might occur.

A downtrend is the opposite of an uptrend. When a stock, or even the entire market, goes from being generally up to being generally down, then that is a downtrend. In short, they're rare because people tend to buy stocks as they go down in price. However, when you're investing, it's always important not to fall prey to biases and know what the situation looks like objectively, so you don't get surprised by a crash in price.Downtrends can happen for all sorts of reasons—maybe there's been a change in sentiment about the company, or news comes out that there's going to be a big dip in earnings next quarter. Whatever the reason, it's critical to be aware of downtrends to make sound trades.

Is there a way to make money in a downtrend? Yes, there are a few ways to make money during a downtrend. The most obvious way is to short the market by short selling stocks that you believe will go down in price. This can be a risky strategy, so it's important to do your research before entering into any short positions. Another way to make money during a downtrend is to look for companies that are trading at a discount and invest in those companies.

Reversal. It is when the present trend is shifting and new trades arrive from the other side, causing the trend to come to a halt before continuing in a different direction. Reversals during market peaks are referred to as distribution patterns, while the ones that occur near market bottoms are known as accumulation patterns.

Figuring out when a reversal is going to happen can be tough, especially if you're not familiar with all the technical analysis. Not only is it difficult to predict when a reversal will happen, but it can also be risky to trade against the current trend. If you're not careful, you could easily end up losing money. When a reversal occurs, it means that the trend has changed. In other words, what was once up is now down, or vice versa.

There are many reasons why a reversal might occur. For example, it could be due to a change in the economy (e. g., people start spending more money), a change in the political landscape (e. g., new policies are enacted that affect how businesses operate), or even a natural disaster (e. g., a hurricane hits and causes widespread damage). It's important to note that reversals don't always mean that something is wrong. In many cases, they can be simply due to random chance or fluctuations in the market.

Breakout. You're interested in trading stocks, but you don't know how to spot a breakout. It can be a sign that a stock is about to make a big move, so it's important to pay attention to it. However, most people don't know how to spot them.

NOTE

The term refers to both strong uptrends (i. e., up breakouts) and weak downturns (i. e., down breakouts, are also referred to as breakdowns.").

A breakout is the rapid movement of a stock price through trend lines that are acting as resistance or support. They represent an important indicator of underlying investor sentiment because they relate directly to levels at which traders have been unwilling to sell. Because most traders place their stop orders in relation to these dynamic points, sudden bursts of activity often occur in the vicinity of breakout points where market participants do not want to risk holding for fear of prices moving against their position.

Breakouts are often those that have been consolidating for a while and then suddenly make a move higher or lower. This can be due to some sort of news event or development that gets investors excited or worried about the stock. Either way, they are worth paying attention to because they can offer the biggest opportunity—but only if you're quick! So, keep your eyes peeled for them and you could be in for a windfall.

Breakout-trading is a type of trading strategy that tries to take advantage of a sharp price move that occurs outside of the normal range of prices. For example, a breakout trader will enter into a new position when the price moves above or below the high or low of the previous day, depending on which direction the breakout is taking place. The best way to trade them is to use technical analysis tools, such as trend lines and moving averages, to help you identify potential trades. You should also use stop orders to enter into new positions, as this will help you get into trades at better prices (See Figure 1.6). Finally, make sure you have a tight stop loss in place in case they fail.

How can you tell when a breakout is fake? There are a few things for which you can look to help you tell whether it is real or fake. First, see if the volume of trading activity is high. A genuine breakout will usually be accompanied by heavy volume as investors rush to buy (or sell). If the volume is low, it could be a sign that it isn't real. Another thing to look at is the price action before and after the breakout. If prices soared very quickly and then just as quickly fell back below the level, it's likely that it was not real.

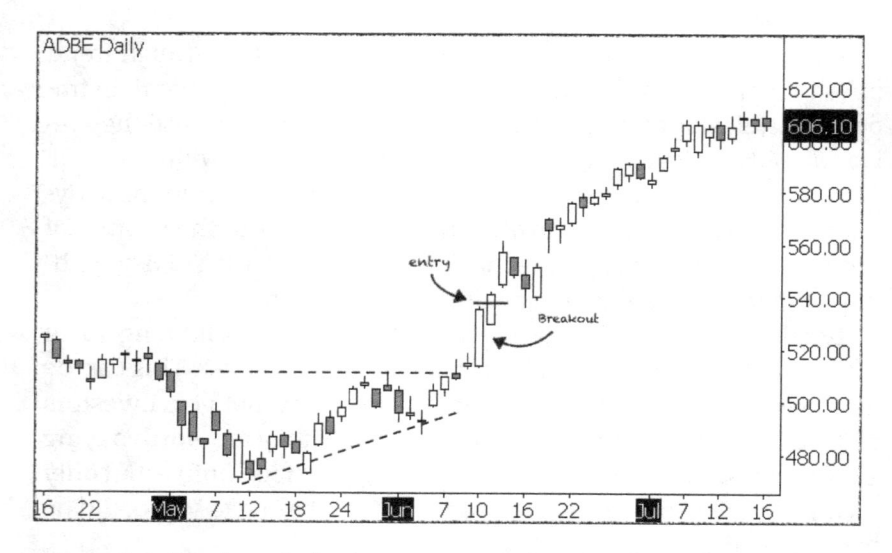

Figure 1.6: Breakout is the increase surge in price through trend lines.

Short Selling. This can be a risky trading strategy that can lead to substantial losses if the stock price increases. Many inexperienced traders shy away from short selling because of the risks involved. However, when done correctly, it can be a very profitable trading strategy. At its core, it is simply betting against the market. And as we all know, there's always money to be made when the market goes down.

Short selling is a strategy that can be employed when an trader believes that a stock is overpriced and likely to decrease in price. To short sell, the trader borrows the stock (or contract). The short seller will then sell the shares and hold the money in the margin account as collateral. Short sellers earn from the difference between the price of the stock sold on margin and the lower stock price paid later if the stock price falls. If the market goes up, however, the buyback price may surpass the initial sale price, requiring the short seller to cover their borrowed shares as soon as possible to avoid further losses. In other words, shorting is a risky endeavor that should only be undertaken by experienced traders who are prepared to lose money. Nevertheless, for those who are willing to take on the risk, shorting can be profitable.

I don't really have an opinion about people who make a living by betting against the market because I don't fully understand what that means. I'm not opposed to short selling in general because I short the market all the time, but I think it's important to remember that it's a risky strategy. If the stock price goes up instead of down, you could end up losing money.

Short "Squeeze." A short squeeze is a trading term that describes what happens when a stock that is heavily shorted receives favorable news or another event that draws a significant number of new buyers. When this occurs, the stock is bought up and shorts are forced to cover their positions (being squeezed out), resulting in more purchasing, which can cause a stock to climb rapidly and significantly.

In January 2021, one of the biggest short squeezes in history started on Reddit, when hundreds of thousands of retail traders teamed together to drive the price of GameStop shares up to an all-time high of around $500. Before the surge, GameStop's stock was worth $17.25. At the time, almost 140 percent of GameStop's public float had been sold short, so when the rally gained traction, short sellers were obliged to cover their positions by buying as much stock as they could, adding to the price increase (See Figure 1.7).

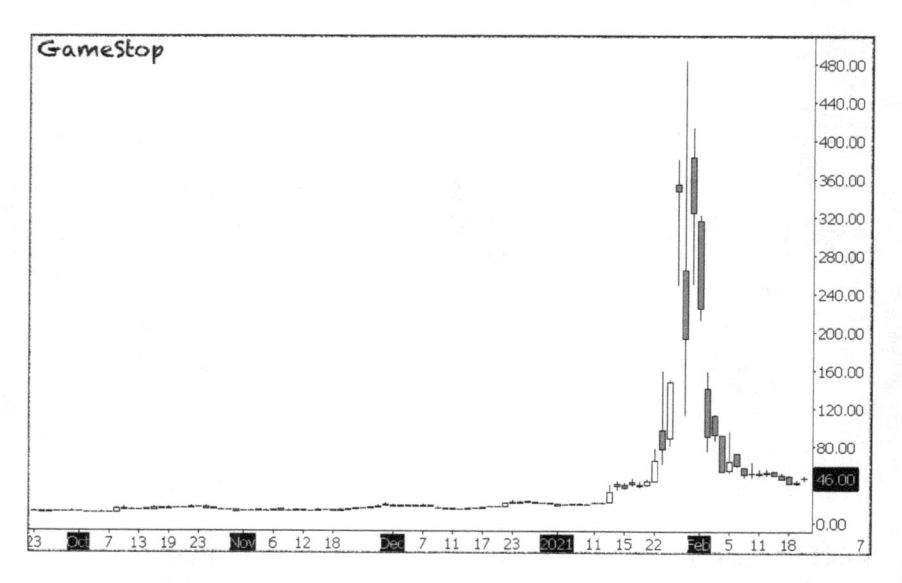

Figure 1.7: GameStop's massive, short squeeze

Breakdown. By utilizing tools such as moving averages, trend lines, and chart patterns, traders can identify potential price points where they may occur. Breakdowns usually signal the start of a downward trend, and by understanding how to identify them, traders can take advantage of market conditions and make profits.

A drop below crucial support levels should be accompanied by a surge in volume, suggesting that the downward trend is being maintained. When price falls below a support level, technical traders may either cancel any existing long positions or short sell them, since this is a clear indicator that the bears have gained control and that further selling pressure is on the way.

Pull back. Why are prices dropping? I don't understand what's going on with the stock market. A price drop could be caused by a variety of factors, but most commonly it is the result of a "pull back." A "pull back" occurs when there has been a consistent upward movement in prices and some sellers take advantage of the higher prices to sell their inventory. This causes an overall decrease in demand, which results in lower prices. Pull backs are not only normal during economic cycles, but they are also beneficial to the market because they provide opportunities to "buy low." So, if you see a price drop, don't panic! It could be just the market doing its thing.

NOTE There are also certain technical indicators that can help you determine when a pullback is over. For example, one popular technical indicator, called the "stochastic oscillator," can be used to identify when a pullback has ended and the price is ready to resume its previous trend

A pullback is typically over when the price resumes its previous trend. In other words, if the price was trending upward before it pulled back, it will resume trending upward after the pullback is over.

Trend line. By extending the chart's low points or high points over time, traders can create a trend line that will indicate whether the market is in an uptrend, downtrend, or sideways trend. By identifying these lines, traders can make better decisions about when to enter and exit trades.

A trend line is a tool that traders use to help them identify the direction of the market. In an uptrend, the line will be slanted upward, indicating that the price is making higher lows and higher highs. In a downward trend, the line will be slanted downward, indicating that the price is making lower highs and lower lows. In a sideways trend, the line will be horizontal, indicating that the price is remaining in a relatively tight range.

Moving Average. You're looking at a stock chart and you see that the price has been moving up and down, but you don't know what to make of it. It can be tough to make sense of all the movement in the markets, especially when prices are bouncing around all over the place. A moving average can help you visualize the trend. When price crosses above the moving average, it is said to be in an uptrend, and when price crosses below the moving average, it is said to be in a downtrend.

A moving average is a technical indicator that smooths out a price series, filtering out noise and enhances visualizing the trend. The period (also called "length") of the moving average dictates how far back in time the calculation includes. A shorter period will look more jagged while a longer period will be smoother with less volatility.

Again, when price and moving average cross each other price is said to have "changed direction." Some traders use this crossing in combination with other indicators to help judge where prices may be headed next. Moving averages can be used on any time frame from 5 minutes to monthly charts. Moving averages work best in trending markets; they are not as useful in choppy or range-bound markets. Moving averages lag price; they do not predict it. There are many different types of moving averages, the most common are simple, exponential, and weighted. Moving averages can also be used as support and resistance levels in some scenarios.

Relative Strength. It is a stock market indicator that indicates overbought and oversold positions of a certain stock. It is a stock market indicator that measures the strength of stocks over time. It goes up when stocks are advancing and falls when prices are declining. Overbought refers to when the relative strength is above a defined upper level, and oversold refers to when the relative strength is below a defined lower level. It is not an indicator that tells whether the general market is trending up or down. Instead, it tells us the price trend.

Trader. A trader is a person who buys and sells stocks, bonds, contracts or commodities for a living. This can be a very stressful occupation. A trader typically has a broker who facilitates the trade by buying and selling stocks on behalf of the trader. The trader usually has a brokerage account, with each trade producing fees for the brokerage firm. A successful trader might spend most days glued to their screens analyzing research, watching live news events, or placing orders with brokers to buy or sell over the phone.

Investor. Investing in stocks can be a very profitable venture, but it's also risky. As any investor knows, stock investing is all about timing. You need to buy when a stock's price is low and sell when it is high. But it's not just a simple matter of buying and selling—you also need to have a good understanding of both the markets and the companies in which you're investing.That means keeping up with economic data and current events that could affect your investments. It can be a full-time job, and it can also be very rewarding. After all, there's nothing like seeing your investment portfolio grow. So, if you're thinking of becoming an investor, make sure you're prepared to do your homework. It might just pay off in the end.

Short Term. Short-term trading can be incredibly profitable, but it's also incredibly risky. It's a great way to make money quickly, as long as you're aware of the risks and are able to stay cool under pressure.

A Short-Term Trader is a person who buys and sells stocks, within the frame of hours or days (or months) according to market signals, speculatively in hope of a quick gain. Another example would be day trading—when you buy and sell within the same trading day.

Long Term. A long-term investor is someone who holds positions for months, or years to take advantage of longer-term price trends. Some people are more interested in buying low and selling high while others would rather wait until they can get it right then jump into something quickly. Long-term investors usually have a plan and are patient enough to wait for the perfect moment to enter or exit an investment. They know that markets go through cycles and prices always come back around, so they're willing to hold on for the long haul. Many long-term investors also use fundamental and technical analysis to identify patterns that can indicate where prices are headed. If you're thinking about becoming a long-term investor, remember that it takes patience and discipline to be successful.But if you're willing to put in the work, long-term trading can be a great way to make money in the markets!

Return to Figure 1.2 and take another look now that you've gone over each term and have at least a basic grasp of them. It shouldn't take you long to understand them. Return to this section if you forget or are uncertain what a term in the following chapter means.

IS IT WORTH BECOMING A TRADER

I will never forget the first time I placed a trade. Oh, and it didn't require me to call a broker; instead of that nonsense, all I needed was my smartphone and computer. Now I can easily control my own financial future with a few mouse clicks. Although the stock market is a place of excitement, opportunity, and reward, it's also one that can make you quite rich—or put your entire life savings in the hole. Let's look at some of the most frequently asked questions that new traders may have.

Is becoming a trader right for you? Only you can answer that question, but there are some important factors to consider before taking the plunge.

First, do you have the time to devote to trading? The stock market is open around the clock, so if you're not prepared to commit to constant monitoring, it's probably not a good idea to get involved. Second, do you have the temperament to deal with the highs and lows of the market? Trading can be an emotionally charged activity, and if you're not able to maintain a cool head in the face of losses, it's best to steer clear.

Let's ask this question, why do you want to trade stocks? It's a great way to make money on the side, and it doesn't require a lot of time or effort. Plus, with the advent of online trading, it's easier than ever to get started. It doesn't matter what your background, education level, or location might be—trading can provide an opportunity that suits anyone! All you need is a computer or mobile phone, and you can send buy orders for shares to the exchanges almost instantly. This comes with many benefits, including instant access and the ability to trade from anywhere in the world. So, if you're looking for a way to make some extra cash, trading stocks might be the perfect solution for you.

What does it take to become a trader? Trading stocks is hard work—there's no denying that. But what many people don't realize is that the key to success in stock trading isn't avoiding risk, it's managing it. The fact is, there are so many things that can go wrong when you're trading stocks that the only way to be successful is to take the right risks and manage them well. Of course, this isn't easy. But if you're consistent and you have a good risk management strategy, then success will be yours!

How to become a profitable trader? In the world of trading, it's often said that you need an edge to be successful. And while that may be true, the reality is that most trading strategies don't actually have any real advantages. That's because most market trends are random. So as profitable traders, our goal is to find methods that work at specific moments. What many traders forget, however, is that the stock market is where other traders come with their strategies—no matter man or machine. The stock market is not a mechanism that is divined by destiny or events predefined. Instead, it's more like a sporting event where participants are fighting for position to get in and liquidity to get out. So, if you want to be a successful trader, remember that you're not just up against the market—you're up against other traders as well.

How to find trading opportunities? The stock market is a lot like combat. All the participants are trying to win by profiting off the back of others. There are sometimes causalities, though they're common in volatile markets. For example, a person may gamble it all and lose it all after a margin call. Other traders take advantage of this by trading against them. Personally, I look at the stock market as if it's an interactive video game with rules that can be learned. But most people don't even know these rules exist until someone reveals them. This book will reveal those rules so that you can also play this game at the same level.

Finally, do you have the financial resources to commit to trading? Unlike other forms of profit generating endeavors, trading requires a significant amount of capital. So, if you're not prepared to risk a substantial amount of money, it's probably not the right choice for you. Ultimately, only you can decide whether or not becoming a trader is right for you. But if you're willing to put in the time and effort, it can be an exciting and lucrative way to take control of your financial future.

Constantly changing your strategies in search of the perfect one will only lead to losses. Instead, you should focus on finding a few solid setups which you feel confident about and stick with them for the long haul. If you can do these things, you'll be well on your way to making money in the market.

ACQUIRING THE APPROPRIATE KNOWLEDGE

There is a broader category of trading strategies that relies on many different methods to try and pinpoint the best trading signals. The three most popular approaches are (1) reading chart patterns; (2) studying the order flow of market trends, like price levels and trade volumes; and (3) trading indicators. These can be used to identify opportunities in all markets and time frames, but it is most effective when the market makes a clear trend.

Reading chart patterns. Most traders spend hours analyzing data and charts, trying to predict future price movements. This can be incredibly time consuming and frustrating, especially if you're not seeing the results that you want. And by watching for order flow at important price levels, you can confirm in which direction the market is moving.

Studying the order flow of market trends. The second approach entails studying the order flow in markets using price levels of significant importance. Order flow trading can help take the guesswork out of trading. By understanding how much of the market is being traded at different price levels, you can more easily predict which way the market is moving and make more profitable trades. This is typically observed through watching for peaks, valleys, and areas of consolidation to confirm if momentum is trending in a particular direction (which can be used to predict future price movements). With this knowledge, you'll be able to enter and exit trades with confidence, knowing that the odds are in your favor.

Trading indicators. The third approach is less effective than reading charts, but most traders use a bit of both. Trading indicators are mathematical calculations that traders use to determine when a particular stock is likely to increase or decrease in value. Trading indicators can be confusing and difficult to understand, especially if you are new to trading. Using a combination of both reading charts and indicators is often more effective than just reading charts. Trading indicators can be useful in identifying patterns and trends, but they should not be the only factor considered when making a trade. Ultimately, it is up to the individual trader to decide what approach works best for them.

In the case of making decisions, there are a lot of different factors that you can take into consideration. You could concentrate on reading charts, or you could focus on the order flow. You might even consider some trading indicators. But what is most important in determining your choice of approach is which factors you consider to be the most important. If you place a high value on reading charts, then that will likely be the deciding factor for you. However, if you think that order flow is more important, then that will probably be what determines your approach. Ultimately, it all comes down to your own individual preferences and priorities. There are many potential profit-making opportunities waiting for you in the stock market! Your ability to act quickly and think on your feet can be the difference between a profitable trade or one that ends in disaster. To do this, you need the discipline to follow through with trading plans and remain calm at all times.

THE TRADER'S MINDSET AND EXPECTATIONS

Trading can be difficult, and you need to expect the unexpected. But if you are well-prepared for what trading really entails before starting, then it will make your experience much more enjoyable with less chance of mistakes being made! It's important to align your expectations with the trading approach that will work best for you. When traders spend years chasing unrealistic goals and gains, they often forsake their journey in the process. Make sure to think about what motivates your actions so you can make changes if necessary. The trader's mindset is amongst the most important skills in trading and can determine success or failure. It takes a lot more than luck to win at this game; it requires sound judgment, experience with risk management, discipline, and control over your emotions. The trade-off between fearlessness and greediness is necessary—the emotional balance that we call "fearless but not greedy."

Fear is a natural reaction to an anticipated threat. But when traders get bad news about specific stocks or the economy, they liquidate their accounts into cash and refrain from taking more risks. Quantifying fear might be helpful—so you can evaluate what you are afraid of and why you're afraid of it! Greed is a difficult emotion to resist. It's often based on the intuition that we can do better, and make more profit. You should learn how to identify this sentiment and develop trading plans with practical ways to circumvent this behavior. This book discusses in later chapters how understanding trader psychology can actually prepare you for your trades.

You can't let the stock market fool you into abandoning good trading discipline. Be patient, wait for the perfect opportunity when it arises, and be confident in your trades. Recording each trade as it happens helps to keep track of what went wrong with a certain trade so that one may learn from their mistakes quickly and efficiently by reviewing these records every day or week. This book discusses in a later chapter how to record trades into a trading journal.

Technical analysis helps traders have an idea of where the market is moving and what impact any given event will have on prices. Risk management strategies help make sure that your portfolio is protected, so you can increase the probability of success over time. Good trade opportunities are not worth it if they don't provide a favorable low-risk entry point. It's better to not trade and wait for a better opportunity to materialize.

 **NOTE** It is often difficult to keep up with the fast-paced world of Wall Street. Knowing when to adjust your strategy can be challenging for even the most seasoned professional traders, but it's important that you develop an instinctive feel for the market.

Discipline and patience are two vital related skills that every trader needs. Without them, it is very difficult to stay in a game that will cost you no matter what. Some traders make the mistake of trading when there are no genuine opportunities in sight; such actions virtually always do not end well. To be a good trader, it's important to commit at least some time to studying technical analysis and fundamental analysis so that you can make smarter trading decisions. This book also discusses how to use risk management to protect yourself in later chapters.

Stay away from scam trading signals or indicators if you want to remain competitive and profitable over the long term. Your unrealistic expectations may turn into a loss even if you use appropriate techniques to perfectly time your entry or exit. Also, unrealistic expectations will likely lead them astray compared with those who are more knowledgeable in this field but have realistic ideals for what is possible in terms of profits made from trades combined with risks taken. These people know not only how profitable it can be sometimes, but also its limitations, largely because there's always an opportunity cost associated with any action we take! This book discusses how to become a profitable trader in a later chapter.

It's no secret that the stock market is a volatile place. Prices go up and down all the time, and it can be hard to keep track of what's taking place. However, there are some basic principles that drive the market, and if you understand them, you'll be better equipped to make money. The most important thing to remember is that the stock market is driven by emotion. People buy stocks when they're feeling optimistic about the future, and they sell them when they're worried. As a result, prices are constantly fluctuating based on how people are feeling. If you can stay ahead of the emotional curve, you'll be in a good position to profit from the stock market. Another important thing to remember is that demand drives prices up, while supply drives them down. If more people are interested in buying a stock than there are shares available, the price will go up. On the other hand, if there are more sellers than buyers, the price will go down. Understanding this basic principle can help you anticipate changes in the market and make money accordingly.

2 Stock Market Investing

Tale of Michael Burry's "Big Short"

You want to know about the Michael Burry story and how he achieved success as a fund manager? Most people don't achieve anything close to the level of success that Michael has. He is a renowned trader with a remarkable history. In this section, I am going to share with you everything you need to know about Michael Burry. I will discuss his career, investments, and more. So, if you're interested in learning from one of the best in the business, keep reading. Michael Burry's story is one of grit and determination. He started out as a young man with a dream and a plan. He worked hard, and he achieved success.

He was born in 1971 in San Jose, California. At the age of two, Michael lost the left eye to a condition called retinoblastoma. He attended the University of California for economics and pre-med. Afterward, he got his medical degree from Vanderbilt University School of Medicine. Michael worked as a doctor for some time before starting his firm. While he started in the medical career, finance and businesses seemed to be among the hobbies that Burry enjoyed and wanted to do. Even though he had shed his medical occupation early, his brilliant mind has indeed thought of enigmatic ideas that broke through in the financial world.

Some people may believe that working in different industries may water down one's capabilities; but for Burry, it seems like it has only broadened his perspectives and fueled his intuitions even more. Who could have thought that a man with an ocular disability would be one of the most successful finance investors? Nothing is impossible if you set your heart to it—not even making seemingly outlandish predictions that later turn out to be true! Burry has been quoted saying, "You don't have to be smarter than everyone else; you just have to be more disciplined." We couldn't agree more. After all, it is often those who are able to stick to their guns (or in this case, strategy) who come out on top. Burry is a man of many talents. Not only is he an expert in financial investments, but he's also skilled in deriving business models and predicting the financial markets.

In 2000, Burry established Scion Capital, a hedge fund that made him one of the earliest prominent investors to bet against the US housing market, which was one of his most successful bets. Thanks to his bold thinking, Burry was able to achieve great success as an investor. He famously anticipated the subprime mortgage crisis. Over the years, he has made significant progress with investments and trade, which makes him among the notable traders. Burry noticed that the housing market was artificially inflated and was due for a crash. He took positions against the market by investing in credit default swaps. He correctly predicted that the market would collapse, and he made a fortune by shorting subprime mortgages.

By 2004, Burry's business had raked over $600 million—all thanks to his savvy value approach to business management. Clearly, Burry is a man with whom to be reckoned with. His skills in finance are unrivaled, and his quick thinking has made him a fortune. We can all learn a thing or two from this remarkable individual. He made his fortune by thinking outside the box. Unlike other investors, who focused on the stock market, Burry looked for opportunities in niche markets that were often overlooked by the mainstream. As a result, he was able to generate high returns for his investors.

By 2009, Burry had made over one billion dollars from his investments, largely due to his prescient call on the housing market. Burry's success is attributed to his unique approach to investing, which focuses on identifying undervalued assets and companies with strong prospects for future growth. He has also been an early investor in some of the most successful tech companies, including Tesla and Alibaba. Given his track record of success, it is no surprise that Burry is widely considered to be one of the best investors of his generation.

In March 2020, we had a similar crash because of an economic shutdown related to a health crisis. No one saw this coming nor predicted that the coronavirus pandemic would trigger a financial crisis similar to the subprime mortgage crisis of 2008. Many investors underestimated how bad the virus could get and overestimated how much the government could do to help the economy.

INTRODUCTION TO MARKET INVESTING

The stock market is one of the best places to buy and sell stocks, but did you know that there are some similarities between brokerage and wholesaler. When I was a child, my mom had a store selling figurines and collectibles, and she often goes to wholesalers to buy products to restock her shelves. She can get her products for much cheaper than she would if she bought retail. She would mark up the prices on each product and sell them to her customers. This way, she makes more profit off each sale. When she ran out, we are back to the wholesalers. On occasion, my mom added new products to her store that she only bought in bulk if they flew off the shelves quickly enough. If not, we are back to the wholesalers again searching for more products. The stock market is just like the story of my mom's business: she buys at a wholesaler to resell in her store. An online brokerage is also a place where traders can buy stocks at bargain prices to resell them for profit.

Although the stock market is an exciting place to be, and there's plenty of opportunity for making a profit, a detailed understanding of online brokerage and the services they offer is a must to make headway. You can trade with confidence when you have an in-depth knowledge of which brokerage is right for you, which means that you don't fear them! In this chapter, we'll talk about online brokerages, pattern day-trading rules, and what you need to know about cash and margin accounts. Also, a paper trading account has a rich history, and it's come to mean something different in today's stock market. You can't overlook this tool that will help you become better at trading. Before we talk about brokerages, let's discuss what exactly is the stock market and discuss what owning equity of a company as an investor really means.

BECOMING A SOPHISTICATED INVESTOR

Investing in the stock market is one of the best ways to make your money grow, but it's not without risk—no matter how sophisticated you are and no matter how much information you know. The attitudes of individual investors toward their investments are complex and dynamic for many reasons, including their psychological makeup (i.e., personality), situation (i.e., financial position), risk tolerance level, and time horizon; and our own understanding of markets in general, thus leading some people to pass on investing altogether. However, if you're the type of person who is able to take a measured approach to risk and you're comfortable with the potential ups and downs of the market, then investing can be a great way to help you reach your financial goals.

 Just remember that no return is guaranteed, and that past performance is never a guarantee of future results. So do your homework, build a diversified portfolio, and always focus on your long-term goals. With patience and discipline, you can be a successful investor.

You can go the traditional route and put your money into savings bonds or CDs. Or you could take a risk and invest in the stock market.

If you're looking to make more than the average return, stocks are a great option. The stock market has a long history of outperforming other investments, such as bonds and cash. In the last five years, it has averaged a 17.04% annual return according to the S&P annual returns from 2017 to 2021. And if you invest in an index fund of the S&P 500, you're investing in the top companies in the country, big and small, successful or floundering. Investing is one of the best ways to plan for your future with long-term goals like retirement or a child's education expenses.

You can also put your money in bonds, or debentures. You can invest in commodities like gold or oil. Or you can stuff your mattress with cash and hope for the best. But what's the difference among all of these options? And more importantly, which one is the right choice for you? Let's start with shares. When you buy shares in a company on the stock market, you become a part owner of that company. This gives you a claim on future profits and access to any dividends that the company may declare. Stocks are attractive investments because they have the potential to generate a lot of revenue. However, they're also risky because companies can go bankrupt or experience other unforeseen circumstances.

When you invest in a company, one of the things you can buy is called a share from the equity market. Shares signify ownership in a company and entitles the shareholder to a portion of the company's profits or assets. With online brokerages, it has become easier than ever to buy and sell shares quickly and easily. You can be as sophisticated or unsophisticated as you choose. There's no shame in being unsophisticated. In fact, some might even say that it's a popular choice in today's society. Let's just take a moment to appreciate the sophisticated among us. After all, without them, we wouldn't have anything to which to aspire. Thank you, sophisticated people. We salute you.

SHARING CO-OWNERSHIP WITH EQUITY

There's a lot of money to be made in owning a piece of a company, but it's not always easy to understand exactly how it works. In simple terms, owning a share of a company means that you co-own that corporation and are entitled to a portion of its profits and assets. A company's shares can be publicly traded on securities exchanges like the New York Stock Exchange (NYSE) or National Association of Securities Dealers Automated Quotations (NASDAQ), or they can be privately owned and managed by institutions like private equity firms and hedge funds. And while public companies are owned by many different people, private companies are usually only owned by a few. To get in on the ground floor of a potential goldmine, your best bet is to find a good private equity firm in which to invest. But whatever route you choose, just remember that there's always some risk involved in any investment. So don't put all your eggs in one basket!

"Going public." It's a phrase that conjures up images of sold-out initial public offerings (IPO) shares and savvy investors cashing in on the next big thing. But what exactly is an IPO? An IPO is the first time that members of the public can purchase shares in a company that has previously been privately owned. In essence, it's when a company sells pieces of its ownership to raise money by selling shares. Private companies may need to do an IPO for a few reasons, such as needing more funds or not being able to find any outside funding. Whatever the reason, going public is a huge step for any company, and one that comes with a whole host of challenges. From valuation and pricing to regulatory compliance, there's a lot to think about before going public. For those companies that make it through the process successfully, an IPO can be a hugely lucrative way to raise capital and take their business to the next level.

On the subject of investing, there are two main camps: those who are in it for the capital gains, and those who prefer to as passion income via dividends. A dividend is basically a financial return on your investment in a company, most often in the form of equity. It's how businesses pay their shareholders back for investing their hard-earned money into the company. And since dividends often indicate future earnings potential or stable share prices, they're a huge incentive for people to save up and invest their money. So, if you're ever on the fence about whether or not to invest in a certain company, just ask yourself: do you want to make some quick money, or do you want to get paid just for owning a chunk of the business? The choice is yours!

To trade or invest in stocks, you're going to have to open an account with a broker and make a deposit. Thankfully, there are various types of brokerages that provide access to the stock exchanges. Online brokerages typically charge lower fees than traditional brokerages, making them an attractive option for cost-conscious investors. The next section will identify a couple of these online brokerages and list the pros and cons of each.

MODERNIZATION OF BROKERAGE

The stock market is a fast-paced, unpredictable game of chance. You can't participate without your broker by your side. But nowadays, you don't have to meet them in person or call them. Thanks to the convenience and accessibility of online brokerages. In the past, when someone wanted to sell a stock or make changes to their portfolio, they had to call their broker. Today, with smartphones, there's no need for that—anybody has the opportunity to succeed because they're now able to take advantage of online brokerage like never before. They allow you to trade in the stock market and offer research tools that make trading easier. For example, I can pull up my brokerage account and start flipping through the different stocks. When I need to buy more of a stock, I do; but if I am unsure, I can research more companies using their platform. The power of online brokerage is at your fingertips. So, don't be afraid to go online and find a broker that best suits your needs.

Let's quickly discuss the differences between full-service and discount brokers. Full-service brokers are an old way of investing in the stock market, but you would be surprised by how many people still opt for them rain or shine. Even though full-service brokers seem outdated, nearly everyone who trades stocks these days is capable of controlling their money and has enough knowledge to trade in the stock markets without professional advice. On the other hand, discount brokers charge much lower commission rates while still providing essential services, such as order execution and account management. For most people, discount brokers are a more attractive option.

You might be wondering whether to go with a full-service broker or a discount broker. Full-service brokers offer a more personal service, which can be helpful if you're new to the market and don't have time to do your own research. However, they also come with higher commission rates. Discount brokers, on the other hand, offer low-cost trades and access to analytical tools and accurate news about stocks. So, which is the better option? It really depends on your needs and preferences. If you're looking for personal guidance, a full-service broker might be the way to go. But if you're comfortable doing your own research and want to save on costs, a discount broker could be a better choice. Whichever route you decide to take, make sure you shop around and compare different. And because there are more competitors in this type of brokerage than in full-service brokers, you can find some fantastic deals!

There are a few things you'll need. First, you'll need a strong internet connection—after all, you can't trade if you can't connect to the internet. Second, you'll need a device that can access the internet. And third, you'll need to find a broker that's right for you. Once you have all three of those things sorted out, simply sign up with your chosen broker and start trading. Of course, not everyone has the time or inclination to trade stocks themselves. For those people, full-service brokers are a great option.

NEW AGE OF DISCOUNT BROKERAGE

There are a good number of brokers from which to choose, and it's important to find one tailored to your needs; but don't expect too much out of any single one—they won't always have everything for which you're looking. Always do adequate research before settling down with any broker. We've discussed the types of brokers, which are full-service and discount. Below, we will discuss four popular brokers for accessing the stock market. In the case of choosing a broker, the options may seem endless. However, it's important to find one that tailors to your needs and expectations. That being said, don't become too attached to any single broker. They won't always have everything for which you're looking.

Charles Schwab is a popular full-service broker that offers a wide range of services, including investment advice, guidance, and research. It has branches in all 50 states and is known for its customer service. Interactive Brokers is a popular online discount broker that offers commission-free trading on stocks, funds, and options. It is known for its sophisticated trading platform and easy-to-use mobile app. TD Ameritrade is another popular online discount broker that offers commission-free trading on stocks, ETFs, and options. It is known for its robust platform with sophisticated tools and their customer service. E*TRADE is a discount broker that offers online and mobile trading platforms. It offers competitive pricing, making it a good choice for people who are just starting out in the stock market.

It's important to remember that the cheapest option isn't always the best option. While a low-cost broker may seem like a good deal at first, you could end up paying hidden fees or commissions that eat into your profits. Once again, it's important to do your research and make sure your chosen online brokerage offers all the research tools and resources you need without any hidden costs. For example, the Robinhood broker is an organization that offers very low rates for trades. However, one common drawback with low-cost brokers is their lack of customer service options; it can take days to get in touch with someone at times because it doesn't have phone lines open 24 hours.

Let's revisit Interactive Brokers, which is an American multinational brokerage firm that operates the largest electronic trading platform in the US by number of daily average revenue trades. It offers a variety of services to individuals who want to trade securities, including stocks, options, futures, FOREX, bonds, and funds. Interactive Brokers also clears transactions for every stock that's listed on the exchanges. Customers can trade with Interactive Brokers by purchasing stocks through its proprietary software, Trader Workstation (TWS), which provides customers with direct access to trading floors and allows them to route their own orders directly to market makers or specialists for execution. In addition, Interactive Brokers' sophisticated order management capabilities allow customers to monitor and modify their positions in real time. As a result, Interactive Brokers is an excellent choice for those who want to participate in high-volume market trading.

On the topic of brokerage accounts, there are two main options: cash or margin. A cash account is the simplest type of account and is best suited for beginner investors or those who want to limit their risk. It's important to know exactly what type of brokerage account you have because different accounts offer different capabilities.

UNDERSTANDING MARGIN ACCOUNTS

If you're like most people, you probably think of the stock market as a place where you can either make a lot of money or lose everything you've put in. And while it's true that the stock market can be risky, there are also opportunities to make a great return on your investment using leverage. One way to do this is by opening a margin account. A margin account is an account that allows you to borrow against your stock portfolio and cash in your account to finance trades and add leverage when purchasing assets.

There's nothing quite like having leverage. With a margin account, you can trade with borrowed money, which can help you amplify your gains (or losses). But it's not all fun and games. Margin accounts come with a few strings attached. For one thing, you'll need to maintain a minimum in cash assets. And if you create a margin balance, you'll be subject to interest rates. These rates are based on the current prime rate plus an additional amount charged by the lending firm. So, if you're thinking of borrowing big, be prepared for some high interest. Finally, the margin requirement for any given trade is set by the brokerage and can vary from day to day. So, before you trade on margin, be sure to do your research. Most brokers set the maintenance margin at 50% of the purchase price. Thus, for a $1,000 security, the investor would need to use $500 in cash to buy it on margin.

When you trade with a margin account, you're essentially playing with house money. And as anyone who's ever gambled knows, that can lead to some pretty big wins—or losses. So, what happens if the market takes a turn for the worse and you find yourself on the losing end? Well, if you're not careful, you could end up owing your broker a lot of money. That's why it's important to understand the rules governing margin accounts before you start trading. The Financial Industry Regulatory Authority (FINRA) has a set of regulations that must be followed by anyone who wants to trade on margin. These regulations include those with $25 thousand or more who trade with their brokerage account. So, if you're planning on levering up your account to make some trades, make sure you have the cash available to cover your losses—just in case. FINRA requires this because traders need time to adjust positions as market conditions change, but not over-extend themselves too often, which would drive them into bankruptcy! That sounds reasonable, right?

Have you ever had one of those days where everything seems to be going wrong? You're in the middle of a huge trade and you realize that you don't have enough money in your account to cover the margin. Suddenly, your broker is demanding that you add more money to your account or risk losing your positions. Don't let a margin call ruin your day. To make sure you never get a margin call, deposit more money into your account before it's too late. Brokers use notification systems to alert you when your account falls below the required margin level, so you can take action and avoid any potential losses. By following this simple advice, you can protect yourself from the devastating effects of a margin call.

Margin interest rates can be very confusing for newcomers. For starters, let's take a look at what margin is. In investment terms, margin is the amount of collateral that an investor has to put up in order to borrow money from a broker to buy. The loaned funds are used as collateral for the securities purchased with the intention of the investor paying back the loan plus interest to the lender (broker). As for margin interest rates specifically, these are set by brokers and can vary depending on which one you use. They also may change, depending on market conditions. But generally speaking, they're usually between 3% and 6%.

NOTE Leverage is often thought of as a "double-edged sword." On one hand, it can be used to magnify profits. On the other hand, it can also magnify losses. But what exactly is leverage? In financial terms, leverage refers to the use of debt to acquire assets. Leverage can be a powerful tool, but it's important to understand how it works before using it. When used properly, leverage can provide investors with the ability to control large positions with minimal risks on capital. If the stock price goes up, the investor will make money on their investment. However, if the stock price goes down, the investment will lose money. Leveraging can thus help investors increase their returns while trading using the minimum margin requirements.

When the stock market crashes, everyone panics. But for savvy investors, a bear market is an opportunity to make some serious profits. One way to take advantage of a bear market is by shorting stocks. Short selling is a financial trading strategy where you borrow shares of a stock from somebody else, sell the stock, and then buy it back at a lower price so you can return the shares to the person and/or firm from whom you borrowed and pocket the difference. It's essentially betting that a stock will go down in value. Short selling can trade be done through a margin account, which means you can invest your money with borrowing power to increase your potential rewards—but you'll also increase your potential losses. So, if you're thinking about shorting stocks, tread carefully. But if you know what you're doing, it can be profitable.

In summary, a margin account allows you to borrow money from your broker to buy stocks. This can be a useful tool for experienced investors who are looking to maximize their returns. However, it also comes with a higher degree of risk. In the next section, we'll cover cash account advantages and disadvantages.

BENEFITS OF CASH MANAGEMENT ACCOUNTS

While a margin account can be a great investment tool, there are a few key reasons why traders may want to use a cash account instead. First, margin accounts can be risky. Because traders are borrowing money to trade, they can end up in debt if the stock market takes a turn for the worse. Second, margin accounts can be expensive. The interest rates that brokers charge for margin accounts can be quite high, and this can eat into profits. Finally, margin accounts can be difficult to manage. It can be easy to get carried away when borrowing to invest, and investors may end up with more stocks than they can afford to hold. For these reasons, cash accounts may be the better choice for some.

There are two main camps: those who prefer the simplicity of a cash account and those who prefer the flexibility of a margin account. Cash account investors are limited to using only available cash or existing long positions to make trades. This can be seen as a downside by some, as it limits your ability to short in a down market. However, others view it as a way to enforce fiscal discipline and avoid taking on too much risk. Margin account investors, on the other hand, can borrow money against cash or the value of assets in their account. Long term investors typically use cash accounts to avoid interest accrued over time, while short term traders typically use margin accounts to take advantage of higher leverage. Ultimately, the decision of which type of account to use comes down to a matter of personal preference.

There are some rules and regulations if you want to do trading through a cash account. The Federal Reserve Board regulates what types of transactions can be completed. The most common violation is cash liquidation. This kind of violation occurs when a customer buys and pays the cost by selling another on the same purchase date. This is considered a violation because the customer needs to have settled cash in their account before making the new purchase. The settlement period for a trade usually takes two to three days, but may take longer.

If you make too many cash liquidations from your account in a 12-month period, your brokerage firm might restrict your account. You will only be able to buy if you have enough cash in your account to cover the purchase. This restriction will be in place for 90 days. Cash liquidation violations are taken seriously by brokerage firms. Currently, modern brokerage systems will automatically prevent their users from triggering a cash liquidation violation. Purchasing is only possible when you have enough settled cash in your account. This is not the only violation, and there are other violations that I will briefly outline, so as to avoid them.

Free riding is when you trade stocks without having the money to cover the trade. If you sell a stock you bought with unsettled funds in your cash account, it's called a free-riding violation. In a cash account, you must pay for the stock before you can sell it. If you buy and sell a stock before you pay for it, you are stealing, which is illegal. If you don't pay your broker, they will freeze your account. If someone is buying and selling a lot of stocks very quickly, they might get a "free-riding violation." If you don't pay attention to how free riding works, you could face severe penalties. It's important to understand how this type of stock trading works before you get involved. There are no concerns with modern broker systems because free-riding is avoided. As a safety measure, there are usually two days between when someone buys something and when they have to pay for it. During this time, the buyer has a secured credit that they can use until the funds from the purchase settle.

Although it may be done with good intentions (or faith), remember that settling funds violations can have serious consequences. If you're found to be in violation of the rules, you could be subject to a number of penalties, including fines and suspension of trading privileges. So, if you're going to use a cash account, be sure to only use settled funds to buy. And if you're thinking of selling anything, make sure you are paid-in-full before doing so. By following these simple rules, you can help avoid any potential problems down the road.

THE PATTERN DAY TRADING RULE

Contrary to what some people may think, day trading is not illegal. There are only these rules that apply to it, which restrict how traders can operate. I recommend everyone contact their brokers to find out if they fall into the category of pattern day traders or not. If you're not a pattern day trader, you're in the clear! However, if you are classified as a pattern day trader, there are a few things about which you need to be aware.

First, you must maintain a minimum equity of $25,000 on any given day. If not, you can only make three round-trip day trades within a five-business-day period. Finally, if you violate any of these rules, you may be subject to a Pattern Day Trade call, which will restrict your trading privileges. But don't worry, there are still ways to trade without being subject to these rules.

If you're looking to get started in the world of online stock trading, but don't want to commit to a minimum deposit of $25,000, don't worry—you can still register for an offshore brokerage account. Offshore brokerage accounts offer the same services as regular online accounts, but without the hefty minimum deposit. So, whether you're a seasoned investor, trader, or a complete novice, an offshore account could be the perfect way to get started. This book does not cover offshore online brokerages, but, with a simple search, you can find many great brokerage options.

Some people like to trade safely, but others want more action. You can have a cash account or a margin account, so there's nothing stopping you from using either one! It just depends on your trading style and the amount of risk you are willing to take. Paper trading accounts are always available for some people who want to practice trading before moving to a live account. The next section is about the advantages of using a paper-trading account and how using one can actually help you become a better trader.

PRACTICE WITH PAPER TRADING ACCOUNT

In the old days, if you wanted to get into the stock market but were too chicken to actually put your money where your mouth was, you would do what's called pen-with-paper trading. You would write down your predictions of what was going to happen in the market, and then see how you did compared to reality. These days, paper trading has become a lot more popular, mainly because it's now done through demo accounts. These are accounts that give investors, and traders the chance to test their investment skills before they put any real money on the line. That way, if they lose money, it's not real money that they're losing. New investors and traders can begin by paper trading, and then once they've developed a feel for how the market works, they can start investing and trading for real. So, if you're thinking about getting into the stock market but don't want to risk any of your own money, paper trading is a great way to get started.

A paper-trading account is a kind of brokerage account where the investor and trader selects stocks, then checks their expected return with different investment strategies. It is a mock or practice account that allows the investor and trader to find the strategy that works best before launching into a live account. This assurance is possible because there is no risk of losing your original capital. However, it is important to remember that a paper trading account does not always provide the same results as a live account. This is because market conditions are constantly changing and a paper account does not take these changes into account. Nevertheless, a paper trading account is still a useful tool for learning about different investment and trading strategies and testing new ideas.

 Paper traders are not considered to be investors because they had no money invested, so it was important that they differentiated themselves from those who spent real dollars. Now, paper trading is done entirely electronically. So, if you're thinking about opening a paper-trading account,

Many people view paper trading as a way to learn about the stock market without putting any of their hard-earned money at risk. However, paper trading can actually be quite dangerous. Since there is no real money at stake, paper traders are often more reckless than they would be if they were trading with real money. This can lead to them making poor trades that could cost them a lot of money if they were trading with real money. In addition, paper trading can give people a false sense of security. They may think that they are better traders than they actually are and take on too much risk when they start trading with real money. This can lead to them losing all of their money very quickly. Paper trading is a fantastic way to learn about the stock market, but it is important to remember that it is not real life. Trading with real money is a very different experience and requires a much more cautious approach.

For those just starting out in the world of trading, a paper-trading account can be an invaluable tool and, if you're the type of person who likes to do their homework before making a financial commitment, a paper-trading account gives you the perfect opportunity to research different stocks and track their performance over time.In short, a paper-trading account provides new investors with an ideal way to learn the ropes without incurring any real losses. Every good trader knows that the key to success is practice, practice, and more practice. But what's the best way to practice? Some say that the best way to learn is by doing, and there's certainly some truth to that. So, if you're looking to up your game as a trader, be sure to paper trade first and perfect your strategies before going live.

In conclusion, there are many various strategies for investors and traders to employ in an attempt to profit in the stock market. Some people buy stocks and hold onto them for years, patiently waiting for the company to grow and the stock price to rise. Others trade stocks rapidly, buying and selling multiple times in the same day in an attempt to take advantage of small fluctuations in the market. And then there are those who short stocks, betting that the price will go down so that they can buy it back at a lower price and pocket the difference. Shorting stocks is definitely a riskier strategy than simply buying and holding, but it can also be very profitable if done correctly. Of course, as with any type of investing or trading, there is always the potential for loss, which is why it's important to understand the risks before making any trades. In the next chapter, we will discuss short-term and long-term trading.

3 Trading Tactics

Chapter Overview

- » Who are short and long-term investors?

- » Beginner's guide to fundamental analysis.

Tale of Ray Dalio

Raymond T. Dalio is an American billionaire investor and hedge fund manager who has a net worth of $18.4 billion dollars as of 2021. He is the founder of Bridgewater Associates, a global macroeconomic consulting firm. He is widely considered to be one of the most innovative investors, having come up with such financial innovations as global inflation-indexed bond risk parity, currency overlay management, and portable alpha management. In addition to his stellar career in finance, he is also a committed philanthropist, having given away millions of dollars to various causes over the years. He is truly a remarkable individual who has made an indelible mark on the world of finance.

Dalio's investment strategy is a unique blend of conventional diversification with wagers on or against markets around the world. His strategy allows both leverage and external diversification. His exact investment portfolios are kept secret from the outside world and only a few people in his firm understand. Nevertheless, his experience and ability to forecast market trends has made him one of the most successful investors in the world. He had a long and successful career on Wall Street before attending college, starting out as a futures trader and broker at Shearson Hayden Stone in 1974. In fact, he had a bit of a tough time when it came to finding a college. During this time, he continued to buy and sell stocks, but was mostly in commodities futures. He got a job as a clerk in the New York Stock Exchange. He later worked as director of commodities at Dominick's and Dominick. Throughout his career, he has witnessed some pretty major economic events. It was there he witnessed Nixon's decision to take the United States off the gold standard.

Dalio was later admitted to Harvard Business School—not too shabby for someone who initially had some trouble getting into college! After graduating from Harvard, he moved to Wilton, where he lived with his family. He continued to trade commodities futures at the floor of the New York Stock Exchange. His clients trusted him and continued to allow him to manage their portfolio, even after he left the firm in 1975 to start Bridgewater Associates—a wealth advisory firm that serviced corporate clients, mostly those he had retained from his previous job.

There are a variety of different approaches that can be taken. Some people invest for the short term, others invest for the long term. Some investors focus on individual stocks, while others take a more holistic approach. However, there is one investment firm that takes a truly unique approach to investing. Bridgewater is a global macro firm, which means that it invests in economic trends such as exchange rates, inflation, and gap growth. Dalio has divided his holdings into beta and alpha investments. His goal is to structure portfolios with correlated investment returns based on risk allocations, instead of asset allocations. He eventually implemented his market insights into algorithms. His big break came when he signed McDonald's as a client in 1987, and he became well known outside of Wall Street after turning a profit from the stock market crash of 1987. He later signed other larger clients, such as the pension funds of Eastman Kodak and the World Bank.

By 2005, Bridgewater Associates became the largest hedge fund in the world. The fund grew rapidly by using the standard hedge fund model, which charges a management fee of the yearly profits accrued from using the investment system. During this year, Bridgewater managed enormous sums of money for entities including the Pennsylvania state employee's retirement system and the California public employee's retirement system. In 2007, Bridgewater was hit hard by the global financial crisis. However, Bridgewater's clients were better prepared for the market crash than most other investors and weathered the storm relatively well. During the year, the firm's total assets under management increased from $33 billion to $50 billion.

Dalio is known for his bold predictions, and it seems that he may have been onto something with his 2008 forecast about the Federal Reserve printing money. According to researchers at the firm, the world's largest financial entity has had an estimated future liability related to bad debt totaling a trillion dollars. However, these concerns were dismissed by the US Treasury Department and White House Economic Advisors. In 2011, he published his principles on investment and corporate management. It seems that Dalio's predictions should be taken seriously—after all, he has a pretty good track record.

His stake in Bridgewater Intermediate Holding was purchased for $250 million. In 2017, Dalio announced he would step down as company's CEO. Since then, the company has been managed by Jon Rubinstein. Dalio has associated his character of being a hyper realist as being able to understand mechanisms that world functions on without adding any abstract value judgment. However, some have accused him of being too cynical and not seeing the beauty in life. Regardless, there is no denying that he is among the most influential people in the world today.

INTRODUCTION TO TRADING TACTICS

My interest in the card game "Magic: The Gathering" as a youngster sparked my awareness of strategy, style, and tactics, which readily transferred over to how I approached the stock market. Magic is a card game with thousands of different cards from which to choose, with each one representing a different spell and ability. This makes for an amazing amount of strategy when playing the game—you can be anything from aggressive, with the goal to control the board by quickly getting rid of your opponent's creatures, or maybe you're a good old-fashioned beatdown creature player who dominates in numbers with brute force attacks. Whatever your style, there's something that will lead the way to victory.

Playing the game was challenging enough, but I really wanted to win. The best way to win was through strategy and patience. As I played against other players, it became evident that everyone had their own strategy and would adapt accordingly if they lost a few games in a row. One of my friends always used fast-paced strategies because he didn't want to play for hours on end like some people did. He also tended to play cards that exploited his opponent's weaknesses rather than just using brute strength with every card he drew or acquired from a purchase. Me? I preferred slow-paced strategies and trying to get as many cards out onto the field as possible so that when my opponent tried to attack me, all their resources would be spent before mine.

So, how is my story similar to the stock market? The stock market is a fast-paced industry and lots of things are happening every moment. There are thousands of transactions happening every second, as some investors succeed and others are unlucky. It's important to know how the stock market works. The more knowledge investors have of what they're doing, the better their chances of success. If you are a serious trader, then it is worth paying attention to trends and adjusting your strategy accordingly.

There are many types of popular tactics, and, interestingly, these different tactics can be classified as short-term or long-term. In this chapter, we will explore the common trading tactics that can help you find your own perfect style. Building knowledge of these tactics could be a source of inspiration to try until you find one that is right for you.

I believe swing trading, a form of short-term trading, is a better approach to the market, and there are different kinds of strategies that one might use. The duration of a trade is one distinguishing feature. I can hold a trade for days or seconds. Personally, I primarily focus on swing trading, particularly technical analysis, instead of the asset's fundamentals.

 Technical analysis refers to a series of statistical techniques that traders believe can be used to identify and predict trends in the prices of financial assets. Fundamental analysis is a methodology for evaluating an asset's value by looking at company data or market factors.

Along your journey, you may make some trades that turn out to be very profitable and others that are not so successful. It takes time to learn how to see the best opportunities for trading to avoid losing on bad trades. Without further ado, here are the things you need to know about trading stocks.

SHORT-TERM TRADING METHODS

Many people think that in order to trade stocks, you need to have a lot of free time on your hands to do research and watch the market carefully. But that's not necessarily true—short-term trading only requires quick timing and an understanding of what's going on in the economy. You don't need to worry about the underlying value of assets, but rather speculate on the rise and fall of prices. This can be done while holding down a regular job, which makes it perfect for many people. So, if you're looking to get into trading but don't have a lot of time to dedicate to it, short-term trading may be the perfect solution.

In the world of financial trading, there are three main types of short-term strategies—intraday trading, swing trading, and scalping. Intraday traders are most active during the regular market hours when the markets are open. Day trading is also a form of intra-day trading in which large amounts of shares are bought and sold within the span of one day. Swing trading is when a trader holds a position for longer than one day but less than a few weeks. And scalping is when a trader opens and closes multiple positions within a day.

Each of these strategies has its own advantages and disadvantages, and traders need to carefully consider which one is right for them. Here's a quick rundown of the pros and cons of each strategy. The main advantage of day trading is that it allows traders to take advantage of short-term market movements. The downside is that it can be very stressful and time-consuming, as traders need to be constantly monitoring the markets. Swing trading is less stressful than day trading, as positions are held overnight. However, it can also be more difficult to profit from small market movements. Scalping is the most fast-paced and stressful type of short-term trading. However, it can also be the most profitable, if done correctly.

To be a successful trader, one must first consider what type of trader they wish to be. There are many different markets available to trade, and each has its own benefits and risks. A short-term trader will likely have different constraints than a long-term trader. For example, a short-term trader may be more concerned with managing risk, while a long-term trader may be more concerned with time constraints. Intraday trading is a great way to take advantage of the movements in the market, and swing trading allows for a longer time frame to make profits. Both of these strategies can be profitable if executed properly. In this book, we will not go over any scalping strategies, but instead we will cover some benefits of intraday and swing trading.

INTRADAY TRADING STYLES

For the uninitiated, intraday trading can seem like a confusing and dangerous way to make money. After all, isn't it better to just buy and sell and wait for the perfect moment to do so? But for those who are willing to take on the challenge, intraday trading can be a highly profitable way to earn money in the stock market. And there are a few things that you should know before you start. As a means to day trade in stocks, day traders need to have a fast computer and high-speed internet connection so that trades can be made quickly. These reduce a lot of uncertainty, so traders are required to manage and reduce risk as quickly as possible.

First, intraday trading is also referred to as "day trading." This simply means that you're only looking at stocks that will be traded during the day. You're not holding any positions overnight, which means you don't have to worry about the volatility that can occur while the markets are closed. Second, day traders are always attentive to the market. They're constantly looking for opportunities to buy low and sell high. And because they're only looking at stocks that are traded during the day, they can make use of the fluctuations between closing and opening hours. Finally, they usually have a number of open positions over the course of the day.

Day traders are cautious about quick market changes, so they develop thoroughly planned strategies to cope with these sudden developments. They are also aware of the resistance, support levels, and price trends that took place during trading hours. The benefits of day trading are endless, and one great benefit is that it allows you to take advantage of volatility in the markets for a quick profit. It can also be considered a full-time profession for some individuals.

Anyone who's ever played the stock market knows that there is always a risk involved. Every investment comes with the potential for loss, and even the most experienced traders can't always predict which way the market will go. However, day trading—buying and selling within the same day—can help to mitigate some of the risks associated with the stock market. Because these trades typically last less than four hours, they are less likely to be affected by unexpected changes in the market. Additionally, day traders can use stop-loss orders to limit their losses if a trade doesn't go as planned. Of course, day trading is not without its risks, but by understanding the risks and taking steps to minimize them, traders can help to ensure a more successful experience.

Intraday trading may be right for you. Just be sure to do your research and understand the risks before you start. Let's summarize below the benefits of day trading. Day trading is the act of opening and closing transactions during the same day, with no open trades going after hours. By day trading, investors can take advantage of opportunities that may present themselves during the course of the day, while also avoiding the risks associated with holding positions overnight. Day trading can be a successful strategy for mitigating volatility risk, but it requires a high degree of vigilance and discipline. Investors who are not prepared to closely monitor their positions may be better off employing a buy-and-hold strategy.

INTRODUCTION TO SWING-TRADING TACTICS

It's hard to find reliable information about swing trading strategies. Most people have no idea how it works and they're missing out on the opportunity in front of them. If you want to learn more about the swing trading method, then keep reading this book! I'm going to explain everything that you need to know about these tactics.

Swing trading is a bit like going on a roller coaster. You strap yourself in, hold on tight, and some hope for the best. But unlike a roller coaster, you can actually make money doing it. It is all about timing. You have to buy low and sell high, and you have to do it within days or weeks. That can be tough to do if you're not in tune with the market. But if you are, it can be an extremely profitable way to trade. So, if you're thinking of giving this style a try, make sure you know what you're doing. Otherwise, it could be a very costly mistake.

For instance, let's say you're a swing trader and you've just heard some good news that the industry will experience growth soon. You can take advantage of stocks that are about to rebound and increase in value following an expected sell-off to be able to profit on the way up. However, if you don't act fast enough, you run the risk of the market taking off without you.

If you're the kind of person who gets anxious at the thought of missing out on a potential profit, swing trading might be for you. Swing traders only place buy orders when they believe the price will go up in the near future. They're essentially opportunists, capitalizing on fluctuations in market prices to make a profit. So as to be successful at this style of trading, you should be able to identify price action and other characteristics of individual stocks to define support and resistance points. Minimizing the risk of overnight market volatility is also important to remember. So, if you're looking to get in on the action and make some quick profits, this style might be right up your alley.

Let's summarize below the benefits of swing trading. Another great benefit of this style of trading is that it offers flexibility in your schedule. You can choose when you want to work since there are no set hours, like with traditional jobs. If you only want to work for a couple of hours each day or even just a few days each week, that's completely up to you! This is perfect for stay-at-home parents or anyone who doesn't want the commitment of a full-time job. Time is money, as they say, and nowhere is that more true than in the world of swing trading.

For traders who value flexibility in their time, swing trading is the perfect solution. That means they can juggle their trading around other commitments, whether it's work, family, or social obligations. Finally, it is a great way to learn about different aspects of the market and how to make money from them. If you're patient and disciplined, you can quickly become an expert trader. And if you need to take a break from trading for a few days or weeks, do so without having to worry about losing their hard-earned profits. Swing trading might just be the answer.

BEING A LONG-TERM INVESTOR

There are two main schools of thought—buy and hold, or buy and sell. The former approach is more commonly associated with long-term investment strategies, while the latter is more commonly associated with short-term speculation. However, both approaches have their merits and drawbacks. For example, buying and holding allows investors to capture the long-term upside, while also allowing them to ride out the inevitable ups and downs of the market. However, this strategy requires a great deal of patience and discipline, as well as a willingness to accept lower returns in exchange for stability. On the other hand, buying and selling provides investors with the opportunity to make quick profits, but it also exposes them to the risk of missing out on a major rally. As such, there is no "right" or "wrong" approach to trading; it simply depends on what suits your individual goals and risk tolerance.

Investing is all about playing the long game. While there may be some quick-and-easy profits to be made in the short term, the majority of gains are typically found in investments with a greater time horizon. This is due to a number of factors, such as dividends, which can help to increase an investment's overall return. Furthermore, long-term investors are less likely to be affected by short-term fluctuations in the market, such as economic cycles or changes in legislation. As a result, they are better able to ride out any bumps in the road and emerge with a profit at the end.

Have you ever wondered how those people become successful traders? The answer is simple—they analyze the market with a method called fundamental analysis, which is a way of investing that relies on economic factors, such as supply and demand, earnings per share (EPS), and the company's financial reports. Also, long-term traders put a lot of attention into what they see on their daily, weekly, monthly, and yearly charts. In the next section, we will discuss in detail how to become a fundamental trader. For example, if you are looking at a company's financial reports and you see that its earnings per share is increasing, that is a good sign that the company is doing well and its stock price will likely go up. On the other hand, if you see that the company's debt is increasing and its earnings are decreasing, that is a bad sign and you should sell the stock.

Position Trading. Also known as active management, is a long-term trading strategy. Unlike day trading or swing trading, position traders hold their position long for extended periods of time, generally ranging from several months to several years. Proficient position traders utilize both technical and fundamental analysis when evaluating the market, while also considering factors such as past performance and current trends. However, to succeed in this area requires an ability to accurately determine entry and exit points. However, this also comes with the risk that your trade will not reach your price target. Still, for those who are willing to take on this risk, position trading can be a great way to achieve long-term success in the stock market.

Dollar Cost Averaging (DCA). There's no such thing as of the perfect strategy. But if you're looking to minimize your risk, dollar cost averaging may be worth considering. The idea is simple—rather than buying all your shares at once, you spread out your purchases over time. By buying in increments, you lower your overall cost basis and reduce the potential for large losses if prices take a sudden nosedive. Of course, there is a downside to this strategy—it can tie up extra funds for long periods of time, making trading less flexible. But if minimizing risk is your top priority, dollar cost averaging may be the way to go. Also, if you're planning to hold onto your shares for a while, don't forget to review your portfolio regularly. No matter what strategy you choose, pay close attention to market trends. By keeping up with news and economic reports, you can stay ahead of the curve.

If you're looking for a lasting career in the financial markets, long-term investing is your best bet. Long-term trading has been proven to be one of the most reliable methods of successful investing due to its low-risk factor that allows investors more control over their portfolio and less volatility than other strategies. Not only does it provide a greater return on investment but also offers tax advantages and is cost-effective as well.

Below is a summary of reasons why long-term trading is better than short-term trading:

Low Volatility. Anyone who has ever watched a horror movie knows that it's always the calm before the storm. The same can be said of investments. When the markets are relatively stable, it's easy to get complacent and think that the good times will last forever. However, history has shown that periods of low volatility are often followed by sharp movement in price. That's why savvy investors know that it's important to take a long-term view to investing in stocks and other assets. By holding onto assets for the long haul, you can avoid being caught up in the panic of a market crash. And, over time, you're likely to see your investment grow, even if there are some bumps along the way. So, next time the markets seem eerily calm, remember that it might just be the calm before the storm. And if you're prepared for what comes next, you can weather any storm.

Tax Advantages. There's nothing quite like the feeling of a big win. And while we all want to make money, it's important to remember that Uncle Sam always gets his cut. For short-term traders, this can be a major bummer, as their taxes are calculated at the same rate as their regular earnings. But for long-term traders, there's a silver lining—their gains are taxed at a lower rate. So not only do they get to enjoy the fruits of their labor, but they also get to keep more of their hard-earned cash. It just goes to show that patience really is a virtue!

Cost Effective. Anyone who has ever traded stocks knows that transaction fees can eat into profits quickly. For the casual investor, these fees may not seem like a big deal. After all, what's a few dollars here and there? However, for serious traders who are buying and selling multiple times per day, fees can quickly add up. Fortunately, there is a way to avoid fees—using low commission brokerage. Most brokerages offer discounts to customers who trade frequently, and some even waive fees entirely for their most active traders. As a result, serious traders can minimize their costs and maximize their profits.

In conclusion, short-term trading is all about making quick gains, but sometimes the best gains come from taking a longer-term approach. Many experienced investors believe that buy-and-hold strategies can be the key to success in the stock market. With a buy-and-hold strategy, investors purchase shares in a company and then hold onto those shares for weeks or even months, waiting for the price to increase. There are several different types of buy-and-hold strategies, including fundamentals, position trading, and dollar-cost averaging. Each of these strategies has its own pros and cons, but all of them can potentially lead to big profits if executed correctly. So, if you're looking to take your trading to the next level, consider giving some of these long-term strategies a try.

FUNDAMENTAL ANALYSIS TRADING

The price of a stock often reflects the sentiment of the country's economy. For example, people who are feeling optimistic about America's economic health will want to invest in stocks and companies with promising future prospects. If they think the economy is doing well, so do you, so their expectation of a company can be translated into increased demand—which translates to higher prices on Wall Street. When an investor wants to buy a share of a company at $50 per share, for example, they might not be able to afford one or two whole shares but might still be interested in buying. A company may find it advantageous to do splits to decrease price and increase number of shares commensurately. Its shareholders' stakes in the individual shares of common stock remian the same. Stock splits are designed to lower the share price of a company so people can buy shares with less capital. Data shows that stocks that had a higher "initial investment threshold" (i.e., you need more money to buy their stock) tended to outperform just after the split, relative to stocks whose shares were already fairly accessible—about 2 percent better in US markets over the following year, on average.

In the financial sector, all changes in a company's share value are watched closely by people known as analysts, who are on the lookout for certain events that can cause an increase or decrease in company's value. Analyst upgrades and downgrades take place when a company's earnings or future stock price forecast changes. Analysts make predictions about what will happen in the market, so they change their opinion to either "upgrade" or "downgrade" that company. The most important thing to know about analyst upgrades is that they're often good news for the company being upgraded. After all, if you're an investor who is looking to buy stocks, wouldn't you want to buy from a broker with a positive prediction? And the most valuable thing about an upgrade is that it often signals increased enthusiasm for shares of similar companies.

EXAMPLE For example, if a company is going through some financial trouble, the trader may want to sell their shares before the stock price falls any further.

Fundamental trading is the act of stock trading without taking superficial factors into consideration. Normally, trades are done based on technical analysis, which involves following price action. However, fundamental investors will not only take statistical data, such as financial information, into account, but also consider economic factors and company-specific issues that might have an effect on a company's value in the long term. In comparison, technical analysis deals with more short-term trading opportunities, as analysts will examine graphs and charts to get an idea of where quotes are heading in the future, based on past performance. Being aware of the fundamental regulatory policies and financials of a company can give the trader an edge.

Additionally, being aware of regulatory policies can help investors avoid investing in risky companies that are most likely to fail. This can help protect their investment portfolios and minimize losses. Most fundamental investing comes from institutional investors who look at reports and financial data published by companies or financial funds with money for investing over a longer period of time.

Price-to-sales (P/S) is a method of valuing a company that measures its market capitalization (cap) per dollar of revenue. Market cap can be thought of as the price of the company, while revenue is a measure of its size. This ratio is used by investors to find companies that may be undervalued relative to their peers. To calculate P/S, divide a company's market capitalization by its total sales over the past 12 months (See Figure 3.1).

$$\text{Market Capitalization} = \text{Outstanding Share} \times \text{Share Price}$$

$$P/S = \frac{\text{Market Capitalization}}{\text{Sales}}$$

Figure 3.1: Price to sales

 For example, let's say Company A has a market cap of $1 billion and sales of $100 million over the past 12 months. Company B has a market cap of $2 billion and sales of $250 million over the past 12 months. Company C has a market cap of $3 billion and sales of $500 million over the past 12 months. In this case, Company A would have a P/S ratio of 10, Company B would have a P/S ratio of 8, and Company C would have a P/S ratio of 6. P/S can be used to compare companies within the same industry, or across different industries.

Generally speaking, a lower P/S ratio is considered better than a higher P/S ratio. This is because a lower P/S ratio indicates that a company is trading at a cheaper price relative to its sales. However, it's important to keep in mind that P/S is just one metric, and it should not be used in isolation. Investors should always consider a variety of factors before making any investment decisions.

The most common financial data used are earnings per share (EPS), revenue, and cash flow. These are all numbers about which you should be knowledgeable. EPS is a calculation used to measure the annual net income of a company based on its number of shares. It's calculated by dividing the company's net earnings (after subtracting any dividends paid) by the total number of shares outstanding during an accounting period shown in Figure 3.2.

$$\text{Earning Per Share} = \frac{\text{Net Income} - \text{Dividend Payments}}{\text{Weigthed Average Shares Outstanding}}$$

Figure 3.2: Earning per share.

Revenue, or "gross revenue," is broke down to gross revenue and net revenue. Gross revenue does not account for costs of goods sold or any other discounts or allowances. It measures the net income of a company's primary operations while disregarding things like investments, interest fees, and taxes. Cash flow is when you look at your bank account, so think about it in terms of outgoing and incoming cash flow. In terms of corporations, cash flow includes financial sources such as earnings (profit) from investments or selling other assets besides its stocks, as well as payments from creditors for debts incurred by the corporation and expenses like buying raw materials for finished goods that will be sold in the near future.

The company's cash flow, earnings report, and balance sheet can all be found in the financial section of their website. They can also include the results of financial ratios such as Return on Equity (ROE) and debt to equity (D/E). They might not seem important, but these numbers are crucial for working out a company's balance sheet. ROE is the ratio of shareholder profit over a company's net worth. It can be calculated by dividing a company's operating profit by its shareholders' equity, as shown in Figure 3.3.

$$\text{ROE} = \frac{\text{Net Income}}{\text{Average Shareholder's Equity}}$$

Figure 3.3: Return on equity.

D/E is a measure of the percentage of debt that a company uses when privately financing. Generally, D/E ratios range from 0-100%. A D/E ratio of 100% means that all capital has been financed by debt. A low ratio of less than 50% suggests that most financing was done with equity (shares). Total liabilities include short-term debt, long-term debt, and other fixed payments. Figure 3.4, debt-to-equity. D/E is a key financial ratio used to measure a company's leverage. The D/E ratio is computed by dividing a company's total liabilities by its stockholders' equity. A high D/E ratio means that a company has taken on a lot of debt and is at greater risk of bankruptcy if it can't repay its loans. A low D/E ratio means that the company has less risk of bankruptcy.

$$\text{Shareholder's Equity} = \text{Total Assets} - \text{Total Liabilities}$$

$$\text{Debt to Equity} = \frac{\text{Total Debt}}{\text{Equity}}$$

Figure 3.4: Debt to equity

You can compute the D/E ratio for an individual company or for an industry as a whole. To compute the industry average, you would need to find the total liabilities and stockholders ' equity for all the companies in the industry and then compute the average. The D/E ratio is just one tool you can use to evaluate a company's financial health.

Price-to-earnings ratio (P/E) is a measure of a company's stock price relative to its earnings. It is computed by dividing a company's share price by its earnings per share. P/E ratios can be used to value companies and to compare the relative valuations of different companies. A high P/E ratio indicates that investors are willing to pay more for a given level of earnings than they are for other companies' earnings. This may reflect optimism about the future prospects of the company, or it may simply reflect higher overall market valuations. To compute a company's P/E ratio, you divide its current share price by its earnings per share (EPS) (See Figure 3.5).

P/E ratios can be affected by a number of factors, including earnings growth, expected future earnings, and overall market conditions. For example, a company with strong earnings growth may have a higher P/E ratio than a company with slower earnings growth, all else being equal. P/E ratios can be useful in valuation. There are many other factors that affect a company's value, and P/E ratios should always be considered in the context of the larger picture.

For example, if a company's stock price is $30 and its EPS is $2, then its P/E ratio would be 15 ($30/$2).

$$P/E = \frac{Market\ Capitalization}{Earnings} \qquad P/E = \frac{Share\ Price}{EPS}$$

Figure 3.5: Price to earnings ratio

Price-to-Book (P/B) is a financial ratio used to evaluate whether a stock is undervalued or overvalued. It is calculated by dividing the market price per share by the book value per share. A stock is generally considered undervalued if the P/B ratio is less than 1.0, and overvalued if it is greater than 1.0. While there are no hard-and-fast rules, stocks with P/B ratios below 0.5 are generally seen as deep bargains, while those above 3.0 are often considered expensive. Computing P/B ratios can be done relatively easily using publicly available information from most companies' balance sheets. The market price per share can be found on most stock quote websites, while the book value per share can usually be found in the company's annual report (See Figure 3.6).

$$Book\ Value = Tangible\ Assets - Total\ Liabilities$$

$$P/B = \frac{Market\ Capitalization}{Book\ Value} \qquad P/B = \frac{Share\ Price}{Book\ Value\ Per\ Share}$$

Figure 3.6: Price to book

While P/B ratios can be a helpful tool in identifying potential bargains, it is important to remember that they are only one piece of the puzzle. So as to be successful at this style of trading, you should be able to identify price action and other characteristics of individual stocks to define support and resistance points. Profit Margin (P/M) is computed by dividing net profit by net sales. Net income is a financial measure used to assess the profitability of a company or individual (See Figure 3.7). Essentially, it represents the total amount of money earned after subtracting all expenses incurred during a specific period of time. There are a few different ways to compute net income, but the most common method is to take total revenue and subtract all expenses (including taxes, interest payments, and operating costs). This figure can then be either positive (indicating profit) or negative (indicating loss).

 A company that has net profits of $100,000 and net sales of $1,000,000 would have a profit margin of 10%.

$$\text{Net Income} = \text{Revenue} - \text{Expenses}$$

$$\text{Profit Margin} = \frac{\text{Net Income}}{\text{Sales}} \times 100\%$$

Figure 3.7: Profit margin

A low profit margin can also be a sign that the company is not efficiently using its resources, or that it is borrowing too much money. If a company's profit margin is low, it may be indicative of a number of problems. For example, the company may be overstaffed, or selling its products at too low of a price.

Current ratio is a liquidity ratio that measures a company's ability to pay short-term obligations. It is computed by dividing a company's current assets by its current liabilities. A high current ratio indicates that a company has more than enough assets to cover its short-term liabilities. This suggests that the company is in good financial shape and is unlikely to face liquidity problems. A low current ratio, on the other hand, may indicate that a company is having difficulty meeting its short-term obligations. This could be a sign of financial distress and may lead to bankruptcy if left unchecked.

Quick ratio, or liquidity ratio, measures a company's ability to meet short-term obligations. This ratio is computed by dividing a company's current assets (which includes cash, marketable securities, and accounts receivable) by its current liabilities (which include accounts payable and short-term debt), see Figure 3.8. A quick ratio of 1.0 or higher suggests that the company should be able to meet its obligations without difficulty. A lower quick ratio may indicate that the company is having trouble.

$$\text{Current Ratio} = \frac{\text{Current Assets}}{\text{Current Liabilities}} \qquad \text{Quick Ratio} = \frac{\text{Liquid Assets}}{\text{Current Liabilities}}$$

Figure 3.8: Current ratio and quick ratio

Overall, there are many factors that affect the stock market and how individual investors invest their money. By being aware of these factors, investors can maximize their returns and keep their investments safe from volatility.

PART II

TRADING PLATFORM

G et ready, because you're about to learn everything there is to know about making the most of your trading platform. Did you know that when it comes to trading, having the right tools can be the difference between being a successful trader or not? It can be difficult to figure out which tools are the best, and every trader needs to find the right trading tools for them. In this chapter, I will break down the five most popular trading tools for you, and later I will show you different ways they can be used, depending on your personal preference. We'll mention some tools that come with trading platforms by default, as well as others from third-party providers.

Charts. A chart is an essential tool for any trader, as it provides important information on price movements and other factors. The most popular type of chart is the candlestick chart, which shows the price movement over time. There are also other types of charts, such as the line chart and the bar chart. Each type of chart has its own advantages and disadvantages, so it is important to choose the right type of chart for your needs. While there are many different chart types, line charts and volume charts are also popular. These charts provide a quick visual representation of the price movement over time. The points of the line chart represent the closing prices, while the bars on the volume chart represent the volume of trading over a specific period. Volume charts, on the other hand, provide more detailed information about the price movement. In this book, we'll go over line and volume charts in greater detail. Line charts are a nice way to see the overall price trend. By looking at both line and volume charts, you can get a better understanding of how price move.

News streaming service. Did you know that some traders only rely on news to trade? Financial announcements play a vital role in market movements. And if you know the implications of a specific happening in the financial world, you can make lots of profit. A news streaming service is a type of website, radio, or television show that streams live video footage from the world of finance. These services are used to help investors stay up-to-date on the latest news and events that may affect the markets. It is critical to stay up to date on the latest news in order for them to find possible market opportunities or risks.

Technical indicators. Not every broker provides technical indicator tools. They include moving averages, the stochastic oscillator, and the relative strength index (RSI), among others. Moving averages are one of the most popular technical analysis tools used by traders. A moving average is a simple mathematical calculation that helps smooth the price data over time. This makes it easier to identify the trend. The stochastic oscillator is a technical analysis tool that uses the closing prices to help identify overbought and oversold conditions. The RSI is a similar technical analysis tool that helps measure the momentum. RSI ranges from a lower and upper bound, with lower bound representing oversold conditions and upper bound representing overbought conditions. Technical indicators will be addressed in greater depth later in the book.

Stock filters. A stock filter is a technical analysis tool used to help identify potential stocks to trade. There are many different types of stock filters, but they all have the same goal: to help you find good stocks to trade. One of the most popular types of stock filters is the market capitalization and 52 weeks new high. The phrase "52 weeks new highs" is used by traders to indicate that a stock has made a new high over the past 52 weeks. This is a bullish sign for traders and often indicates that the stock is in a bull market. Stock filter attributes and option are also discussed later in this book.

Execution platform. A stock exchange or securities exchange is a financial market where stocks, bonds, and other securities are traded. The two largest stock exchanges in the world are the NYSE and the NASDAQ. These exchanges are places where traders can buy and sell stocks. An execution platform is a set of tools for executing trades on the exchange. And as far as I know, there's no stock market execution tool specifically named "execution platform." This term is usually used in a more restrictive sense, to refer only to the electronic communication networks (ECN) that facilitate trading in financial markets.

NOTE Stock trading is an auction. The first and most important rule for successful stock trading is patience. There are times to buy low and times to sell high, but if you chase stocks as they rally or bail out as they decline, your trading career will never last. Don't let the fear of missing out get the best of you! Buying low doesn't always result in making money because there's a chance the dip will fall through, or the peak will leave you behind instead of gains on that purchase. Similarly, trying to protect yourself against a potential decline by selling low often hurts more than it helps, because while you are protecting yourself from one type of risk—a price drop, you open yourself up to additional risks—prices spiking.

The stock market is an area where in-depth knowledge and experience are necessary to thrive. Although many people lose money in the stock market, it is possible to become a successful trader. But that is if you keep your head down and learn the basics of stock trading using available market tools.

4 Trading Tools

Chapter Overview

- » Using charts and trading tools.

- » Getting the most out of execution platforms.

Tale of Peter Lynch

As anyone who is familiar with the life of Peter Lynch knows he is a man of many accomplishments. Not only is he a successful businessman, but he is also a generous philanthropist and a respected member of the Harvard Medical School community. In terms of his personal life, he married Carolyn Anne Hoff, who is a co-founder of the Lynch foundation. In terms of wealth, Boston Magazine identified his wealth at $352 million, in 2006. By 2013, the Lynch foundation was valued at $125 million, with the various donations being part of the expenses that he faces. The support for medicine, religion, and education has been part of the legacy factors that have influenced the stability of his legacy and developments. As such, it is clear that he is a man who has had a profound impact on both his own life and the lives of those around him.

Lynch is an American investor, with interests in mutual fund management and philanthropy. He was born in 1944 in Newton, Massachusetts. During his early years, his father passed due to cancer. He started off as a caddie, which helped him raise money for the family. His family value aspects seemed to have developed the sense of belonging, which influenced most of his personal and professional career goals. His drive for success can be linked back to his difficult childhood and teenage years spent working hard to support his family. This experience instilled a strong work ethic in Lynch that would serve him well throughout his career. Lynch's impressive track record as a stock picker and fund manager has made him one of the most respected names in the investment world. His book, "One Up on Wall Street," is a best-seller and is required reading for anyone interested in investing.

Lynch is a true success story, rising from humble beginnings to become one of the most respected names in finance. He is a Wall Street legend and has been called "The Investor of the Century" by Fortune magazine. He graduated from Boston College in 1965 with degrees in history, philosophy, and psychology. While at BC, he began trading shares, guided by his savings. He went on to earn a master's in business administration from the Wharton School, at University of Pennsylvania in 1968. After graduation, he took an internship at Fidelity Investments that led to a job working in the paper, publishing, and chemical industries–sectors that would prove essential to his investing success. In 1977, he was named head of Magellan Fund, where he would achieve legendary status.

Lynch is best known for his role at Magellan Fund, one of the most successful investment funds of all time. But before he made his mark on the world of finance, he had a humble beginning working in the back office of Fidelity Investments. It was there that he honed his skills as a research analyst, eventually becoming the head of research in 1974. His experience at Fidelity would prove to be invaluable when he took over as manager of Magellan. Under his leadership, the fund grew from $18 million to over $14 billion by 1990. Today, he is retired from the fund management business, but his legacy continues to influence the way investors think about the markets.

Lynch is one of the more well-known and successful investors of all time. He also had a keen eye for spotting emerging trends and companies that were poised for growth. As a result, his investment philosophy has had a profound impact on the development of different literature on investing. Three of the most influential books on investing—"Beating the Street," "One Up on Wall Street," and "Learn to Earn"—are all based on his investment philosophy. Thanks to his insights, these books have helped countless investors make more informed decisions about where to invest their money. The primary themes in both the books are developing practical principles to manage the respective markets, trading tools, and investment strategies. His primary philosophy is to invest in what you know; this comes with the understanding that people should focus their investments on companies or ventures they understand and can meet expected obligations. This advice is still relevant today and has helped many people achieve success in the stock market.

INTRODUCTION TO TRADING TOOLS

I was playing poker with four friends the night after Thanksgiving. After talking a lot of smack all year, it was now time for the showdown. The poker tournament of the century was going down in my basement. I was sitting across from our dealer, Obi, who, a former colleague of mine, has been playing poker for a long time. However, he decided not to participate in the crossfire of the onslaught of profanity and our choice of colorful language. There I was, the dealer, and three other players. I remember being dealt my first hand and feeling like this is where I should have stayed, in bed. I had two and six off suit. But, I decided to stay in and see what the flop would bring. Also, I could read their body language like an open book, and there's no chance for them to beat me.

When I started playing poker, I quickly learned that I needed to control my breathing if I wanted to be successful. I would get excited when I had a good hand, and my breathing would quicken as a result. Unfortunately, my opponents were able to pick up on this and use it against me. They could tell when I was bluffing based on the way my breathing changed. Eventually, I learned how to control my breathing and use it to my advantage. Now, when I have a weak hand, my breathing stays calm and under control. This sends a signal to my opponents that I am confident in my hand, and they are more likely to fold. As a result, controlling my breathing has become an essential part of my poker strategy.

There I was, sitting at the poker table, eyeing my opponents. I was thinking about how I could beat them all. First up! His name was Kent and he was very calm and deliberate with his movements. I could tell he wasn't going to give me anything easily. I decided to attack him early on, hoping to put some pressure on him. But he just calmly folded every hand. After a while, I started to get impatient and started betting more aggressively, trying to force him to fold. But again, he just folded every hand. What a coward! He must have been too scared to even play the game. I eventually got tired of playing with him and focused on other people at the table. I don't think I've ever seen someone so scared of playing poker.

If you've ever played poker with Jeffery, then you know that he's not the best bluffer in the world. In fact, he's pretty terrible at it. I can always tell when he's holding a weak hand because he gets really tense and uneasy. He starts to shift his weight from one foot to another. He looks really nervous. Based on his body language, it's usually pretty easy to tell when he's bluffing. So, if you're ever playing poker with him, just watch out for those telltale signs, and you should be able to take all of his money.

I have played poker with Chinedu a lot, and I must say, the guy is a real piece of work. He's one of those players who just loves to make big bets, even when he knows he's not going to win. And of course, he always tries to bluff his way out of it. Well, I decided to call his bluff on one hand. Sure enough, he showed his cards and he lost the hand. After that, I made it a point to always call his bluff. It was really easy to do because his body language was so obvious. So, if you're ever playing poker with him, he makes big bets, but he never has anything to show for it.

Then, out of nowhere, Kent sprung his trap. He bet big, and when everyone else folded, "Big Bet" Chinedu was left with no choice but to call his bet by going all in. Kent showed his cards, and it turns out he had a full house! Chinedu couldn't believe it. He had been played like a fool by Kent. Kent and I took all of Jeffery's money steadily, but sure, until it was just us. It was getting late, and we decided to go all in on the next hand. We were the last two players left at the table. Sure enough, I luckily pulled out a flush and took all of his money. It was a fantastic night.

Just like in poker, trading involves making calculated decisions based on the information you have available. In both cases, you are trying to outsmart your opponents and make money. Trading is not a game that can be mastered overnight. It takes time and practice to become successful. But if you are willing to put in the effort, you can learn how to trade and make a lot of money. There are many different indicators and sources of information that traders use to make money. Some people trade based on technical analysis, while others trade based on news events. And there are also those who trade based on their gut feeling. No matter what strategy you use, the goal is always the same: to make money.

UNDERSTANDING CHARTING TOOLS

The adage "knowledge is power" has never been more true. After all, understanding the different charting tools is essential to being a successful trader. And while it may seem like a daunting task to master all of the different tools at your disposal, rest assured that it's not as difficult as it sounds. In fact, becoming an expert in one specific tool can be the key to setting yourself apart from the competition. So, what are some of the most popular charting tools used by traders? Line graphs, candlestick charts, and volume bars are three of the most commonly used tools for analyzing the market. Each has its own distinct advantages that can be leveraged to give you an edge in the market.

Line graphs are typically used to track price over time, making them ideal for short-term analysis. Candlestick charts, on the other hand, provide a more detailed look at price action and are often used for longer-term analysis. Volume bars are typically used to measure the amount of trading activity and can be helpful in identifying trends. As you can see, each of these charting tools has its own unique benefits. By understanding how to use each one effectively, you can give yourself a significant advantage in the world of stock trading. Let's look at each one in more depth.

Line Graphs. Are easy to read. The time is on the x-axis and the price is on the y-axis. You can see at a glance the overall direction of price over time with minimal distractions or noise from other indicators. It also provides information about support levels that can help inform the trader on when might be the best time to buy/sell into a position. Figure 4.1 below displays an overall price direction, its reaction to a supported price level, and current closing price. A chart has the time and price. The timeline on a line chart goes from left to right. Price is shown on an axis or vertical scale in a series of intervals that are equally spaced at a certain distance from one another.

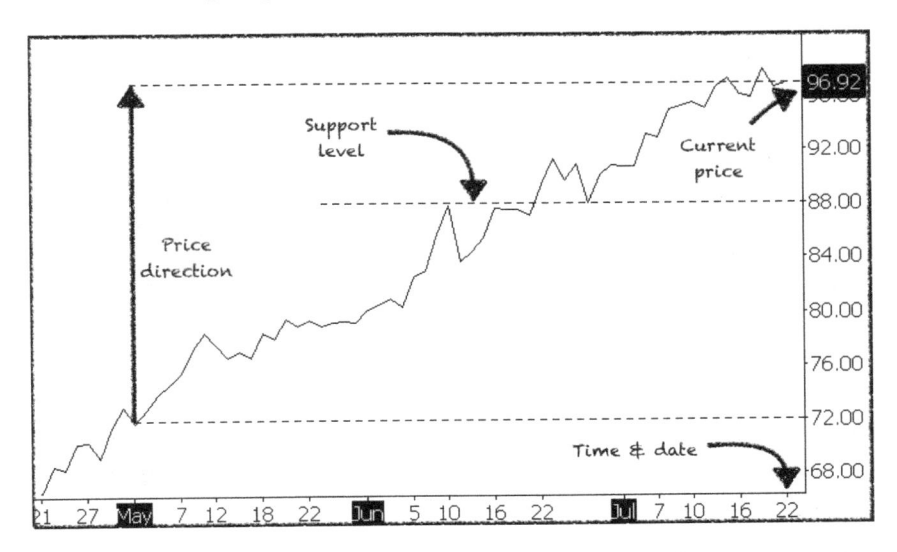

Figure 4.1: Basic line graph showing time on x-axis and price on y-axis.

The markets are a lot like dating. You have your up-trends where everything is new and exciting and you're raking in the dough. Then you have your down-trends where things are getting stale and you're just trying to break even and be only friends. And, finally, you have your sideways movement where you're just kind of treading water, not really going anywhere. Of course, the goal is to find that up-trend and ride it all the way to the bank. But the reality is, most of us are just trying to avoid the down-trend and stay afloat. So, whether you're in a bull market or a bear market, just remember, it's all just a matter of perspective.

Candlestick Charts. For the more astute trader, I recommend using candlestick charts rather than bar charts or other tools. Candlestick charts provide the most detailed information about price action in any given moment. You can see how prices are moving up or down, and they also offer a clear view of support levels. This is incredibly useful for day traders who need to make quick decisions about when to enter the market. Candlestick charts are also popular because they provide information about trend and momentum. The length of the candlestick bodies can give you an idea of which way the market is moving, while the size of the tails can provide information about volatility. In short, candlestick charts are the best way to get a complete picture of what is happening in the market.

Candlestick charts are often seen as being more detailed and complex than other types of charts, but this isn't necessarily a bad thing. In fact, for traders who are just starting, the extra information can be helpful in getting a better understanding of what's going on in the market. However, too much information can also be overwhelming, and this is where combining a candlestick chart with a line graph can be beneficial. By seeing both the big picture and the details, you can gain greater clarity on your analyses. Figure 4.2 shows an example of how this can be done. Later chapters will describe how to use a moving average, which is a type of line graph, to identify trends.

Volume Bars. As shown in Figure 4.2, are an indicator that is often used by traders to understand how many shares have been traded on a given stock. The overall sentiment is represented by the volume of people buying or selling in a given moment. They can help you spot trends more effectively than other indicators like support and resistance levels because they provide a live representation of the number of transactions. For example, if the volume bars are green and rising, it indicates that more people are aggressively buying (demanding) than selling, and the price is likely to rise. If the volume bars are red and rising, it indicates that more people are aggressively selling (supplying) than buying, and the price is likely to fall. However, it is important to remember that volume is just one of many factors that can affect price movements, so it should not be used in isolation.

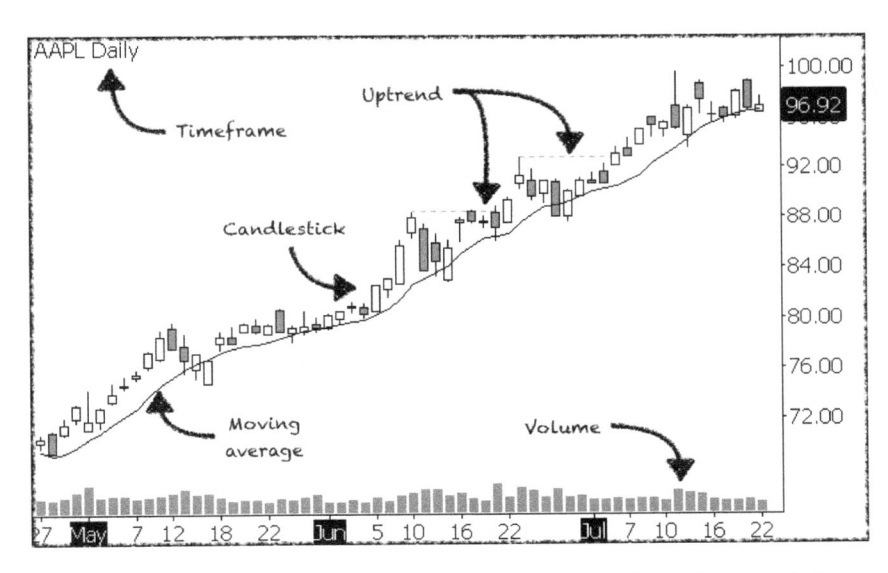

Figure 4.2: A basic candlestick chart displaying volume bars and time frame.

Time Frames. If you've ever looked at a stock chart, you know that they come in all different shapes and sizes. One thing that can complicate matters is that there are different time frames for charts. A daily chart specifies data for days, with one candlestick representing one day. But you can also find charts that cover shorter periods, like hours or even minutes. As a result, you can have conflicting trends for a particular stock when considered using different time frames. It's quite usual to find a stock in a primary downtrend on a larger time frame (say, the weekly chart) while that same stock is in a short-term or intermediate uptrend in a much lower time frame. So, what does all this mean? Essentially, it means that you need to be careful when interpreting charts. Just because a stock looks like it's in a downtrend on one time frame doesn't necessarily mean it will continue to decline. And vice versa—just because a stock looks like it's in an uptrend on one time frame doesn't mean it will continue to rise. The key is to look at multiple time frames and get a sense of the overall trend before making any decisions.

Throughout my trading experience, I have discovered that a lot of beginners just lock themselves in on a chart, analyzing and drawing trend lines without looking at the bigger picture. I have also found traders who trade the primary trend without zooming in to capture the finer details in an ideal short-term time frame. So which time frame is best for you? To answer this question, let's first look at what a "time frame" is; simply put, it's the amount of time that elapses between the opening and closing of a trading period. For example, if you're a day trader, you might choose to set a time frame of one hour, while a swing trader might hold a trade for several days or even weeks. So, what's the best time frame for you? The answer, of course, is "it depends." If you're looking to capture bigger moves in the market, you'll need to hold your trades for longer periods of time. However, if you're more interested in shorter-term profits, then you'll need to be more active and attentive to your trades. Ultimately, the best time frame for you will be the one that aligns with your trading goals.

As any experienced trader knows, time frames are everything as regards to making money in the markets. The general rule of thumb is that the greater the time frame, the more accurate the signal. That's why many traders focus on the weekly or monthly charts to identify the primary trend before zooming in to lesser time frames to find entry and exit points. Of course, lower time frames can be useful, too—but they can also be full of false signals and noise. That's why it's important to identify the primary trend first, then use your preferred time frame to identify the intermediate trend, and finally use the lowest time frame possible to identify the short-term trend. Choose your time frames wisely and you'll be well on your way to success!

TRADING BREAKING NEWS

Stock market news can seem like a never-ending stream of noise. But for experienced traders, this information is essential to making profitable investments. Stock market news covers a wide range of topics, from the latest trading activity to upcoming IPO's and hot investment opportunities. By staying up-to-date on this information, traders can make good investments that can lead to big profits. Of course, not all stock market news is created equal. Some sources are more reliable than others, and it takes experience to determine which sources are worth your attention. But, for those who know how to sift through the noise, stock market news can be a powerful tool for making money in the markets.

Bloomberg Terminal is a financial service that provides real-time data and analytics. It's often been referred to as the "most expensive service" because of its monthly subscription fee. But for those in the know, it's an essential tool for monitoring what's happening in markets, political debates and more. While the subscription fee is certainly steep, it's a small price to pay for such a valuable service. And for the average investor, investing in this terminal is not ideal. With so many other options available, there's no need to break the bank on this one.

If you're looking for an alternative to traditional news streaming services, CNBC is a great option. This all-business news network offers 24-hour coverage of the stock market, global and regional market movements, and more. Over 100 million Americans tune in each day to watch programs like "Squawk Box," "Mad Money," and "Power Lunch." And with a focus on diverse perspectives, CNBC is a great platform for hearing multiple viewpoints on the same issue. You might just find that it's exactly what you've been missing.

There's no need to spend hours glued to the television or poring over the newspaper for the latest news when you can just as easily stream it online for free (or for a very affordable price). Benzinga is one such service—it's a financial media company with an international presence, and its goal is to deliver the most relevant news and analysis in the shortest possible time frame. So, whether you're a trader of any instrument or level of experience, you're bound to find valuable insights and commentary on Benzinga that will broaden your perspective on markets. Plus, its professional show content is designed to educate investors as well as entertain them—and it also reports on financial deals such as mergers and acquisitions for startups, life sciences companies in biotech/pharma, venture capital firms, and private equity firms. In other words, if it's happening in the world of finance, chances are you'll hear about it first on Benzinga.

Yahoo Finance is the best way to follow breaking news and the markets. No other site offers the same combination of live updates, charts, and insightful analysis. The news section covers everything from business and politics to lifestyle and health, so you can always stay up-to-date on the latest developments. And to understanding finance, Yahoo Finance is in a league of its own. Its homepage makes it easy to track important data points like stock prices and leading equity indices. So, whether you're a casual observer or a serious investor, Yahoo Finance is the perfect place to get your financial fix.

Finviz is a company that provides financial reports, free stock market data, live market quotes, and important news updates on companies around the globe. It includes charts of stocks, ETFs, mutual funds, indexes, actively traded currencies/commodities, and indices. Users are able to customize their view by selecting from dozens of visualization styles and always have access to expert commentary that helps them see the institutional significance. It's important to be able to compare your investments with other markets, so it makes sense to check out Finviz for breaking news from around the world. Financial information can also be found on this site.

Many people think that they don't need to get professional financial advice before making investment decisions. After all, there's a ton of information available online, and it's easy to find "experts" who are more than happy to share their opinions. However, the fact is that most people don't have the time or expertise to properly research every investment decision, and even the best investors make mistakes. Getting professional financial advice can help you avoid costly errors and make better investment choices. In addition, a good financial advisor can provide valuable insights into the market and help you develop a comprehensive financial plan. So, if you're thinking about making any major investment decisions, be sure to get professional advice first. It could save you a lot of money in the long run.

TRADE IDEAS WITH STOCK SCREENING

If you're like most people, when you go to the store, you probably don't just pick up the first thing you see on the shelf. You probably look at a few different items, compare them, and then choose the one that's right for you. The same is true for buying stocks. Just because a stock is trading at a certain price doesn't mean it's a good deal. That's where stock screeners enter the picture. A stock screener is a tool that allows you to filter stocks by various criteria, such as price, market capitalization, and sector. This helps you narrow the universe of stocks to find the ones that are most likely to meet your investment goals. So, next time you're looking for stocks, be sure to give a stock screener a try.

As any trader knows, stock screening is an essential tool for finding profitable trades. And while most stock screens only allow you to filter for basic items like company size or share price, the best stock screens offer much more advanced features. For example, you can use a good stock screener to filter for stocks with high average volume over the past week, insider buying, or selling activity, or earnings announcements due within a set time window. Other useful attributes to look for include market capitalization, price-to-earnings ratio, and other fiscal numbers. Plus, a good stock screener will also give you alerts when there is movement in your favorite stocks without you having to watch them all the time.

Typically, using a stock screener is a simple process: just enter an industry symbol, select the parameters you want to use to screen stocks based on fundamentals and/or technicals, and view the list of stocks that meet those criteria. They're great for finding well-known, high-liquidity stocks. And if you want to get really specific, you can customize the screens to include trading volume, average price per share, and technical secondary indicators like MACD.

Sectors are a group of stocks that are part of the same industry. For example, energy, financial services, and healthcare are all sectors. So, when you're looking at stocks, it's important to keep sectors in mind. In the business world, energy is often referred to as the lifeblood of commerce. It refers mainly to the sector that includes mining operations, oil refining, and exploration companies, and it plays a crucial role in supporting industries like construction and agriculture. Consumer durables (also known as C&D) and construction materials (CM) are two examples of industries that rely heavily on energy inputs. Lockheed Martin, and BAE Systems, large defense contractors, are two examples of industrial companies that depends on energy to power operations. The fact is, energy is essential to almost all aspects of modern life, and the companies that produce it play a vital role in keeping the world economy humming.

Healthcare, Information Technology, Financial Services, Utilities, REITs, Consumer Discretionary, and Basic Materials are all important sectors of the American economy. Each one serves a different purpose and plays a vital role in the overall health of the economy. However, there is one sector that is often overlooked: the service sector. The service sector includes businesses that provide services rather than goods. This includes everything from banks and stock brokerages to companies that provide healthcare and insurance. While the service sector may not be as glamorous as some of the other sectors, it is an essential part of the American economy. Without the service sector, the other sectors would not be able to function.

There are four different categories of market capitalization: mega-cap, large-cap, mid-cap, and small-cap. Mega-caps are the largest companies, with a total market capitalization of over $200 billion. Large-caps are less than that but still have a market cap of over $10 billion. Mid-caps have a market cap of between 2 and $10 billion, and small-caps have a market cap of under $250 million to $2 billion. Small caps are considered riskier because they tend to be more affected by economic conditions. However, they also have the potential for higher returns.

There's more to consider than just the numbers. One important factor is the share float, or how many common shares are available for investors to trade at any given time. A lower share float can lead to greater volatility, as there is less volume being traded. Conversely, a high share float is beneficial for trading because of the liquidity of a stock. This means that there are more shares available on the market, allowing buyers and sellers to quickly and easily find one another. Additionally, a higher share float makes it easier for traders to enter and exit positions in a given stock with minimal impact on its price. So, when you're considering your next investment, be sure to take the share float into account.

There are a few key terms that every trader should know. One of these is "average volume." Simply put, average volume is the number of trades that your shares will undergo during a given trading period. This information can be useful in a number of ways. For one, it can give you an idea of how active the market is for your particular security. If the average volume is low, it may be indicative of a lack of interest from buyers and sellers. On the other hand, a high average volume could mean that there is brisk trade activity and that it is in high demand. In either case, it pays to keep an eye on the average volume for your stocks and shares.

In conclusion, the most important thing, though, is to not over-complicate things, especially when you are just beginning. I recommend that you do not go any further than this for now and continue on where we will cover the basics. So, what have we learned? And that's just the beginning! There's a whole world of stock selection out there waiting to be explored. So, get out there and start screening!

POWER OF TECHNICAL INDICATORS

Technical indicators are like weathermen. They're usually wrong one-third of the time, but we still trust them implicitly. These indicators are used in stock trading to predict future prices. They help us understand how traders behave, and this understanding can generate price trends that recur over time frames longer than day-to-day. The problem is that few people know what technical indicators actually mean. We blindly follow them without truly understanding the complicated math that goes into them. In general, they help forecast where markets may go by analyzing past data or some other analysis. But as we all know, forecasting is an imperfect science at best. So, the next time you're tempted to trust a technical indicator, remember that it's just a guess. And, like all guesses, it might be wrong.

There are two main schools of thought. There are the emotional traders who make trades based on their gut feelings, and then there are the technical traders who rely on data and analysis to make better trades. While both approaches have their merits, it's important to remember that emotion will always play a role in stock trading. After all, human beings are not robots, and we cannot help but be influenced by our feelings. That's why technical indicators are so important. They provide a way to take emotion out of the equation and focus on the facts. By considering all of the different technical indicators, investors can make better trades that are less likely to be influenced by emotions.

As any seasoned investor or trader knows, technical analysis is a complicated topic consisting of several important quantitative indicators. The five most important technical indicators to know are moving-averages, commodity-channel-index, relative-strength-index, average-true-range, and moving-average-convergence-divergence. While this may sound like a mouthful, each indicator provides valuable insights that can help you. Moving averages help to smooth out price data and identify trends, while the commodity-channel-index can be used to spot potential reversals. The relative-strength-index is a popular momentum indicator, and the average-true-range can be used to measure volatility. Finally, the moving-average-convergence-divergence indicator can be used to identify changing trends. While there is no magic formula for success, familiarizing yourself with these important indicators can give you a leg up on the competition.

Moving Average. MAs are the simplest type of moving indicator. Put simply, a MA is the average price over a given time period. This book has a full chapter dedicated to MAs, but here I only present a summary. Modern traders see this simple method as one of the most important tools in their trading arsenal because it can eliminate some of the inherent variability that comes with trading and give them a more accurate picture of what is going on with price at any given time. For example, if you're looking at the MA for a stock over the course of a year, you're essentially seeing the average price of that stock over 12 months. This can be extremely helpful in seeing whether the stock is trending up or down overall. If the MA is consistently moving up, then it's likely that the stock is in an upward trend; if it's moving down, then the stock is likely in a downward trend. Of course, like all things in trading, nothing is ever 100% certain, but MAs are generally seen as reliable indicators. So, if you're ever feeling lost in all the numbers and charts, just take a step back and look at the MAs—they'll give you a good idea of what's taking place.

Meta (FB) is one popular stock, and, as Figure 4.3 shows, there are four popular moving averages associated with it. Later in this book, we'll explore in detail how exponential moving averages (EMA) and simple moving averages (SMA) work, including when to use the different periods. For now, SMAs are the most basic way to get an indicator of market prices. They track the drift of price through its history. Once again, a MA is one simple way to smooth out fluctuations in prices, which makes it easier for analysts to see current and historical trends. You can think of a MA as a "smoother" version of a raw data set; it creates an average reading using several points rather than just one point from the beginning or end. By analyzing Figure 4.3, we can see that the 50-day SMA is currently above the 200-day SMA. This means that the shorter-term trend is up. However, both

MAs are rising, which could mean that the long-term trend is also up. As always, it is important to use multiple indicators in conjunction with one another when determining the direction of price.

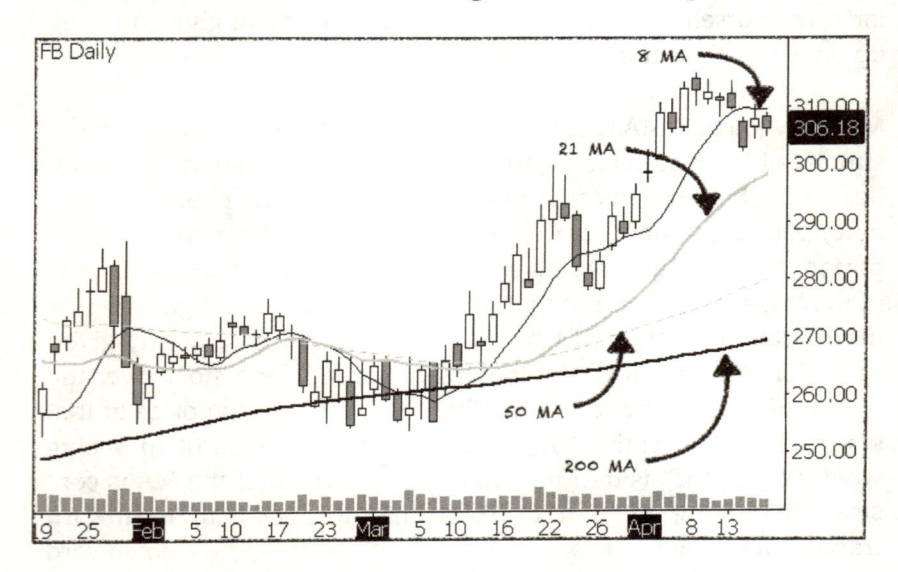

Figure 4.3: The four popular moving averages on a single chart.

Commodity Channel Index. The CCI is a popular tool among traders, and for good reason. It was invented by Donald Lambert in the 1980s and quickly gained popularity due to its simple rule-based approach. The CCI is a measure of volatility that takes into account both prices and standard deviations from past price changes. Its key feature is that it can provide a clear buy or sell signal—buy when the CCI is over -100, sell when the CCI is under 100. While the CCI can be useful as a general guide, there is no single indicator that is perfect. As with all trading tools, it's important to use the CCI in conjunction with other information sources before making any trades.

This indicator can be used to act as an early warning system, although it may signal minor shifts too late to avoid major losses. Once the current trend starts reversing, it reliably signals drastic moves when conditions are right. Shown in Figure 4.4 is a depiction of the CCI at "overbought" and "oversold." As you can see, the CCI can be a useful tool for identifying potential turning points in the market.

However, it is important to remember that the CCI is not infallible, and there will always be some degree of uncertainty when using any technical indicator.

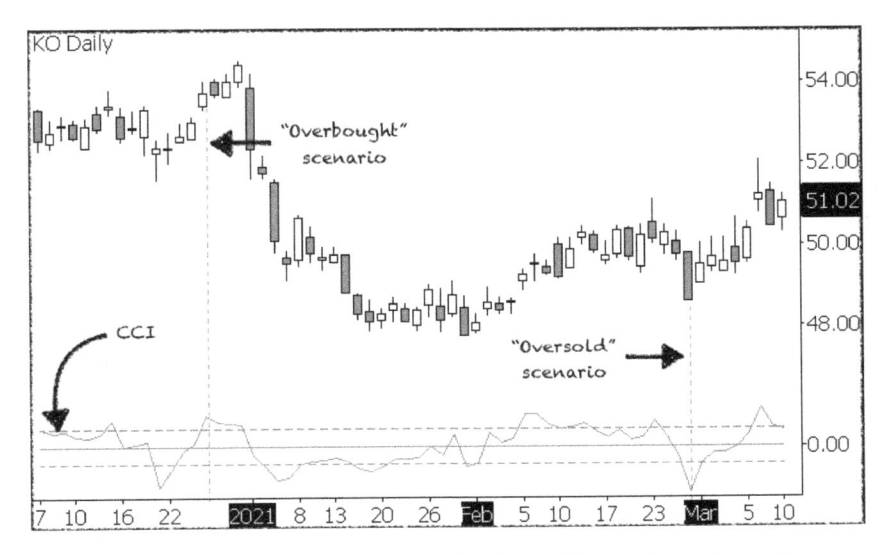

Figure 4.4: The commodity channel index with overbought and over-sold scenarios

Relative Strength Index. If you're trying to get a handle on where the market is heading, the RSI is also a popular indicator to watch. The RSI is a leading indicator that can accurately forecast the movement of price before it happens. It's an oscillating momentum indicator that points to stocks that are overbought or oversold. It's also commonly used in conjunction with other indicators when trying to determine if a trend may be beginning or ending. So, if you're looking for a way to get ahead of the market, keep an eye on the RSI.

The Average True Range. The ATR is an indicator that calculates the distance between a high and a low over time. It is the simplest and least-complex indicator to measure volatility and momentum, making it a popular choice among traders. The ATR can be used to predict how far price can move, providing an edge in trading. While the

ATR is a useful tool, it is not without its limitations. The most important thing to remember when using it is that it is a lagging indicator, meaning it will only tell you what has happened in the past, not what will happen in the future. As such, it should be used in conjunction with other indicators to get the most accurate picture of market conditions.

Moving Average Convergence Divergence. MACD is a technical indicator that shows the relationship between two moving averages, typically a slower and faster one. The bars represent the difference between the readings on two different exponential moving averages (EMA). Should this gap diminish, and the fast EMA crosses above the slow, it could be interpreted as sentiment in favor of increased value for the underlying asset. Conversely, if this gap widens, market sentiment would not support any further upward trend in price movement. As depicted in Figure 4.5, MACD is used in conjunction with other indicators, such as volume and average true range, to confirm short-term stock price moves up or down before they actually occur by identifying overbought or oversold areas on any given time-period-unit chart.

Traders rely on MACD because it's considered one of the best momentum indicators available. MACD is calculated by subtracting the 26-period EMA from the 12-period EMA. A 9-day EMA of MACD, called the "signal line," is then plotted on top. When MACD falls below its signal line, it's a bearish sign indicating that prices may start to decline. Conversely, when MACD rises above its signal line, it's a bullish sign indicating that prices could start to increase. MACD histograms are used by some traders to predict short-term turning points more accurately than conventional MACD settings. They do this by plotting vertical bars that correspond to the distance between MACD and its signal line at any given point in time. A histogram that's rising indicates that MACD is increasing faster than its signal line, which is seen as a bullish sign. A histogram that's falling indicates that MACD is decreasing faster than its signal line, which is seen as a bearish sign.

The most common settings for MACD are the default settings of 12-26 days. These settings were established by Gerald Appel, who believed they were optimal for forecasting market turnarounds 3-9 days in advance. Many traders use smaller values, such as 5-13 or 6-12, to make MACD more sensitive and responsive to short-term changes in prices. Others use longer values, such as 17-26 or 25-37, to make MACD less sensitive and better suited for spotting long-term trends. There's no correct setting for MACD because different settings work better in different market conditions. You'll need to experiment with different settings until you find the ones that work best for you. MACD can be an extremely useful tool for picking winning stocks. By understanding how MACD works and what each of its components represents, you can know when to buy and sell stocks. Remember, however, that no indicator is perfect and there will always be false signals. Using MACD in conjunction with other technical indicators and tools is essential.

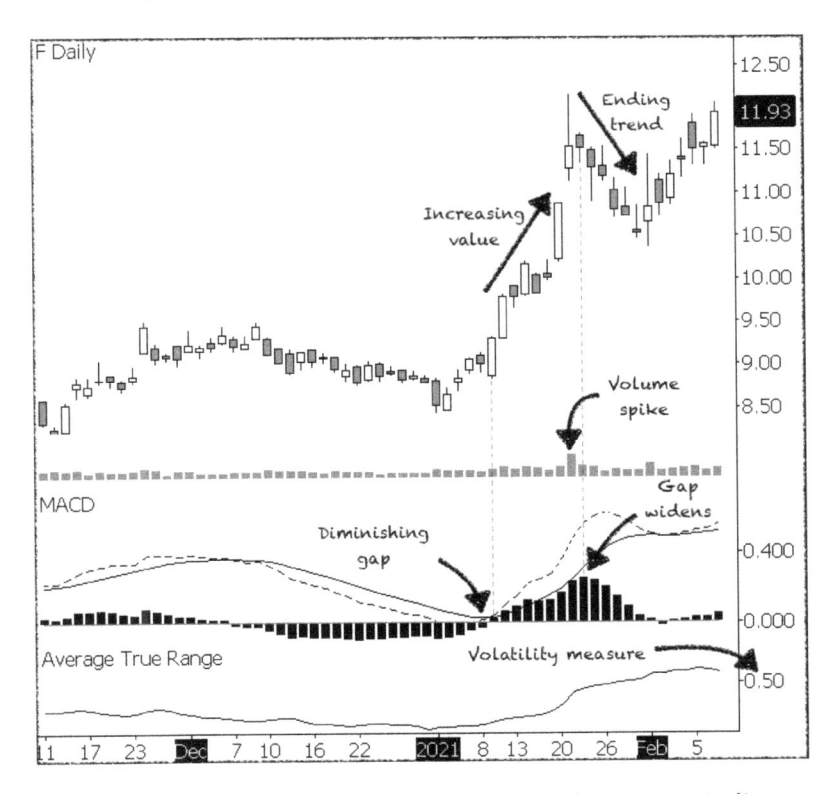

Figure 4.5: The moving average convergence divergence indicator.

There are so many indicators and acronyms flying around, it's enough to make your head spin. But don't worry, you don't need to understand all of these indicators to be a successful trader. In fact, many experienced traders will say that indicator-based trading is a complete waste of time. Instead, they focus on things like price action and market momentum. So, if you're just starting, don't get too hung up on the indicators.

GETTING MOST OUT OF EXECUTION PLATFORM

Imagine you want to buy a new car. You find the perfect one and you go to the dealership to make your offer. The dealership offers you a price (the "ask"), and you counter with your bid. If both parties agree on a price, then the transaction occurs, and you drive off in your new car. The same process occurs in the stock market, but instead of cars, traders are buying and selling stocks. Execution platforms are the proverbial dealership, providing an opportunity for traders to buy and sell stocks. This is where the stock market begins, as trades take place on these platforms. They allow people to create electronic orders for their stocks, and they trade with other traders, brokers, and exchanges. In the professional trading world, an execution platform is known as an electronic communications network (ECN). So next time you're watching the stock ticker on CNBC, remember that it all starts with a simple trade on an execution platform. When a buyer wants to purchase shares, he or she bids the price. When a seller wants to sell shares, he or she offers a price (which is the "ask"). In the end, the bid and ask are matched, which then leads to the transaction.

ECN means that orders can be submitted and executed by electronic input with a computer-based broker instead of routing through an exchange floor. In other words, ECN is a financial trading platform for stocks and other equities that matches buy and sell orders electronically without people on either side of the transaction. The advantage of ECN order execution is that it's faster and more efficient than traditional methods, but the downside is that trades are usually not guaranteed executions, meaning that you might not get your desired purchase price. Nonetheless, ECN remains a popular choice for many traders looking to get the best possible price for their trades.

ECN offers Level I data as a way to most likely guarantee executions. What is Level I data? It's a standardized quote feed that shows the bid, ask, and last executed price (See Figure 4.6). Level I data provides programmatic access to real-time trade activity, including price quotes for every US equity symbol traded on the major US stock exchanges: NYSE, NASDAQ, and AMEX. To put it differently, there is a significant amount of information that traders must have to gain an edge. ECN's Level I data is reliable and accurate, making it a valuable resource for any trader looking to stay ahead of the competition.

Figure 4.6: Level I data feed showing the bid, ask, and last executed price.

The idea behind market depth is that traders will execute their trades at the best available price rather than executing a trade based on "current" prices. Market depth data is the list of "asks" (supply) and "bids" (demand) at different price levels. This service dates back to when firms would list desired quantities of shares for sale by listing shares below the asking price and offers above the bidding price. Now, this information is known as Level II. To access Level II (real-time quotes from the electronic order book), you need to have a direct market access broker, which can be costly. Level II Data shows for what big traders are going for at any given time, giving traders an edge about their trades. In other words, it's a tool that can help you buy low and sell high at the right time (See Figure 4.7).

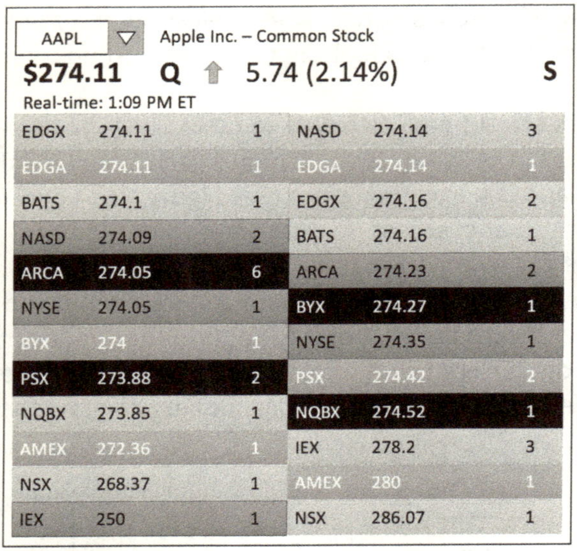

AAPL ▽	Apple Inc. – Common Stock					
$274.11	**Q** ⬆ **5.74 (2.14%)**					**S**
Real-time: 1:09 PM ET						
EDGX	274.11	1	NASD	274.14	3
EDGA	274.11	1	EDGA	274.14	1
BATS	274.1	1	EDGX	274.16	2
NASD	274.09	2	BATS	274.16	1
ARCA	274.05	6	ARCA	274.23	2
NYSE	274.05	1	BYX	274.27	1
BYX	274	1	NYSE	274.35	1
PSX	273.88	2	PSX	274.42	2
NQBX	273.85	1	NQBX	274.52	1
AMEX	272.36	1	IEX	278.2	3
NSX	268.37	1	AMEX	280	1
IEX	250	1	NSX	286.07	1

Figure 4.7: Level II market depth showing individual bids and asks at various prices.

Time and sales is a market term for the display of last-trade prices and volume information on stock exchanges (See Figure 4.8). It represents everything that is currently going on in the market.

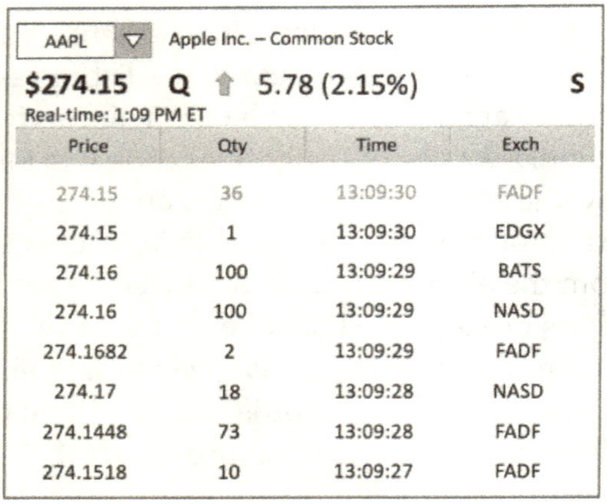

AAPL ▽	Apple Inc. – Common Stock		
$274.15	**Q** ⬆ **5.78 (2.15%)**		**S**
Real-time: 1:09 PM ET			
Price	Qty	Time	Exch
274.15	36	13:09:30	FADF
274.15	1	13:09:30	EDGX
274.16	100	13:09:29	BATS
274.16	100	13:09:29	NASD
274.1682	2	13:09:29	FADF
274.17	18	13:09:28	NASD
274.1448	73	13:09:28	FADF
274.1518	10	13:09:27	FADF

Figure 4.8: Time and sales

We understand that with trading, the spread is a big deal. The spread refers to the price difference between the bid and ask prices. When you use a market order, you are buying at the current ask price or selling at the current bid price. Market orders always fill at these prices and are the quickest way to trade. The lowest spreads guarantee fast and efficient filling of your order at the best possible price without any slippage. Bidding can be automated with a limit order or done manually by a human trader. With limit orders, traders can specify how much they are willing to pay, and the order will be filled if it can meet that price. There are other order types that we will go over in the next chapter. For now, just remember that traders are always looking for the best price possible.

5 Trade Execution

Chapter Overview

- » Understanding order executions.

- » Executing advanced order types.

Tale of Navinder Sarao "Flash Crash"

On May 6, 2010, US stocks suffered their worst one-day percentage drop since the 1987 crash. The Dow Jones Industrial Average plunged 998.5 points, or 9.2%. It was dubbed the "Flash Crash" and it sent shockwaves through the financial markets. What caused the Flash Crash? When it comes to stock manipulation, few people have made as big of an impact as Navinder Sarao. By some estimates, Sarao is responsible for single-handedly causing the 2010 "flash crash" that briefly wiped out $1 trillion in market value. During the crash, he allegedly used a technique called "spoofing" to manipulate the market and make millions of dollars in profits. Spoofing involves placing fake orders in the market as a means to trick other traders into thinking that there is more demand (or less supply) for a particular stock than there really is. This can lead to artificially inflated prices and, eventually, a crash. Not bad for a guy who was trading from his parents' house in suburban London at the time. Some people believe that manipulation is the key to success in the stock market, while others believe that it's a major factor that can lead to disaster.

Sarao is a self-made, self-taught London-based stock market trader who heavily influenced the markets through his development across the financial markets. He has since shown interest in developing financial patterns and interpreting financial data. His focus on the stock market placed him in the limelight as one of the typical leaders and influencers in the stock market. His story is an inspiring one of a man who carved out his own success in a complicated and ever-changing field.

On the morning of May 6, 2010, Sarao placed a large number of "buy" orders for futures contracts on the Chicago Mercantile Exchange (CMEX). These orders were designed to drive down the price of the contracts and create a "sell-off" in the market. As prices began to fall, other computer-driven trading programs began to sell off their positions, exacerbating the decline. Of course, he didn't do it all on his own. He had help from a sophisticated computer program that he had developed to exploit gaps in the market. But his exploits didn't come without consequences. In 2015, he was indicted by the US Department of Justice for his role in the flash crash.

He now faces hundreds of millions of dollars in fines and up to 380 years in prison. Despite his legal troubles, Sarao remains a legend in the world of stock manipulation. And his story is a reminder that there are always people looking to exploit any weakness in the system. It also underscored the importance of liquidity in the markets. When there are few buyers willing to step in and buy from sellers, prices can plunge quickly.

So, what's the truth? Well, it turns out that manipulation is actually very common in the stock market. Some people are born with a silver spoon in their mouth. Others, like Sarao, are born with a computer algorithm in their hand. He used his talents to develop a program that would allow him to manipulate the stock market to his benefit. As a result, he was able to make huge profits while trading with some of the top US companies. So, while manipulation can certainly be profitable in the short-term, it can also be extremely dangerous. Those who engage in manipulation are playing with fire and it's only a matter of time before they get burned. But while his actions may have had the legitimacy of financial intelligence, they also went against the existing goals of the stock market. As a result, Sarao's activities ultimately led to his arrest.

The events of the Flash Crash have led to a number of reforms in the markets. The US Securities and Exchange Commission (SEC) and the Commodity Futures Trading Commission (CFTC) jointly implemented rules designed to limit the ability of traders to place large orders that could manipulate the market. In addition, exchanges now have mechanisms in place to halt trading if prices fall too quickly. The Flash Crash highlighted some of the risks associated with computer-driven trading. The recent case of Navinder Singh Sarao has shone a light on the shadowy world of stock market manipulation. What's fascinating about Sarao's story is that it highlights the role of intelligence in stock market manipulation. Most of Sarao's success came from exploiting gaps in technology; he was able to make consistent profits by taking advantage of these loopholes. But as the law catches up with these types of fraudsters, it's becoming harder and harder for them to make a living. Sarao case is just one example of how the intelligence community is increasingly playing a role in the world of finance.

INTRODUCTION TO TRADE EXECUTION

It's not always about strategy. It's all about execution, and much like Mortal Kombat, there are no second chances if you mess up in the round. If you go into the game without knowing your character's combos, your chances of success are remote indeed, as your opponent unleashes on you with all the agility of a freight train from Hell barreling down on your helpless character. You'll get slaughtered—your character will be overwhelmed by sheer numbers of hits and brute force within seconds, just before one of those brutal "finishing" moves. After torrential blast-fire emerges from semi-solid ground to knock your character out, they perform yet another disembodied skull finishing move.

I love to play video games and my favorite is Mortal Kombat. I played it with my childhood friend, Carlos, and he was better than me because he knew the combos. Carlos would do his combo, then if I didn't block or "combo break," he would continue the combo until he won with a finishing move. One day, after school, I would practice by memorizing all the combos and combining them with strategy—like knowing when to attack and when not to attack a way to reduce the chance for him attacking me back. The next time we played, I executed all the combos and strategies so well that he had no way of beating me.

Understanding trade execution is essential for anyone who wishes to understand how the stock market works, because executing trades is what drives the prices of shares up and down. With every trade, there are buyers and sellers in competition for a limited quantity of stock. For price stability, we need to have interested buyers along with willing sellers at all times. The term trade execution refers to the process by which a trade on an exchange is carried out. A trader has two ways of executing a trade, either through what are called "limit orders" or "market orders." With market orders, traders simply buy at the prevailing ask price, or sell at the prevailing bid price of a stock and expect it to be filled at the current market price. Alternatively, traders can place limit orders in which they specify the maximum price they are willing to pay for stocks, or a minimal price at which a trader is willing to sell a stock. The buyer's order also specifies how many shares he wants to buy or sell, as well as any specific request related to the timing of the transaction like day-only, after hours or before hours trading.

The more competition there is among buyers for a stock, the higher the asking price will be that the seller accepts—conversely, if there's too much supply with no demand at something low enough to sell at today's price, then that causes pressure on prices that could eventually force a liquidation. The difference between tactics and execution arguably lies in the ability to stick with one's plan through thick and thin. This chapter will help you understand these different order types and how you can use them to your advantage. We are going to discuss all it takes for you to grasp the concept of buying and selling stocks from your broker. There are three order types that a trader can place with his or her broker: market, limit, and stop loss. At the end of the chapter, you should be able to: understand the various types of market orders, understand how to use limit orders and stop orders, and understand when to use each order type.

MARKET ORDERS

If you want to buy quickly, consider a market order, also known as a "marketable order." With this order type, you simply specify how many shares you want to purchase, and your order will execute at the current market price, whether that's at the high, low, or anywhere in-between. The best part is that you don't have to worry about where the price is being traded because you just want the shares now. However, keep in mind that market orders are executed during regular market hours. So, if you're looking to make a quick and easy trade, then a marketable order is the way to go.

 Market orders are used to purchase shares at the current market rate, and are typically used when buying on short notice. In other words, you immediately re-

ceive your shares by filling out your order. For example, if a trader wants to buy Intel shares (or any other highly liquid stock), and they want them now, they can submit a marketable order. With one click of their mouse, they are immediately filled by their broker.

With market orders, there are benefits and drawbacks to consider. On the plus side, they can be filled quickly, which is great if you need to get in or out of a trade fast. And because they're given priority over other orders, you're more likely to get the shares you want. On the downside, they don't always guarantee the best prices. We will later explain the reasoning for this scenario later in this section. And, if you're looking for the absolute best deal, you might be better off with a limit order. But if speed is of the essence, marketable orders are definitely better.

 I'm sure we've all been there before. We see a stock that's skyrocketing and we think to ourselves, "This is my chance to make some serious money!" So, we jump in without thinking and place a market order. And then...we watch in horror as the stock price plummets moments later. It's a painful lesson to learn, but it's one that every investor needs to understand. Market orders are not a guarantee that you will get the best price for a stock. In fact, you might not even get the price you were expecting. That's because market orders are fulfilled promptly at the available prices, which can fluctuate rapidly in a volatile market. If you're new to trading, it's important to take your time and learn how the markets work before jumping in with both feet. Otherwise, you might end up making some costly mistakes.

Let's examine a market order to get a better understanding of how they work. Figure 5.1 is a daily chart of Microsoft where I placed a market order after the market closed, with the expectation that it would be executed tomorrow at around today's closing price of $205. Unfortunately, as soon as the market opened, Microsoft stock's price gapped from $205 to an astonishing $210. As a result of this large gap, the market order was executed at a price that was five dollars higher than expected. This is just one example of the risks involved with placing market orders: they can be filled at undesirable prices if there are unexpected changes in the stock's price during the time between when you place your order and its execution. To avoid situations like this one, consider placing your orders during market hours when you can better monitor stock prices.

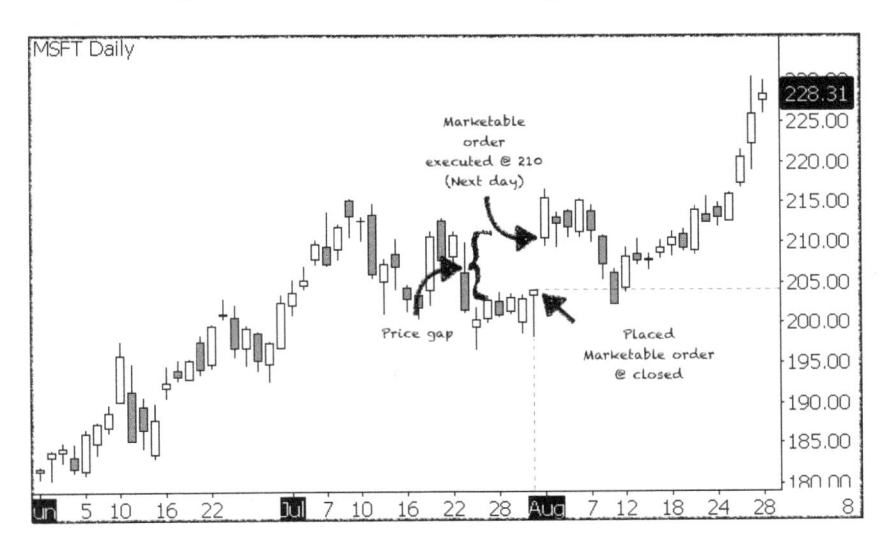

Figure 5.1: Placing market order after the market closed can result into bad order execution.

There are a few things you should know as a counterbalance to avoid getting hurt. For example, if you're trading low-liquid stocks, you need to be careful with market orders. This is because the order might not be filled quickly enough, or it might not be filled at all. You're essentially buying at the high price (ask) and selling at the low (bid) price, and this could be problematic for you if the price and bid-ask spread are quickly changing. If the bid-ask spread widens, you could get your order filled at a price that does not benefit you. So, next time you're considering trading low-liquid stocks, be sure to watch the bid-ask spread or use limit orders instead of market orders.

In conclusion, you may use a market order to buy or sell at the current price. First, market orders are typically used when you want to get in or out of a position quickly, and don't care about the specific price. Second, this type of order can be risky because it may not be executed if there's no liquidity available for that particular stock at that time. Lastly, if you're looking for more control over your trades, consider using limit orders instead. Limit orders allow you to specify the exact price at which you want your trade executed, while still guaranteeing execution as long as there are enough trading shares available. You'll also have peace-of-mind knowing your trade only be executed if the market meets your price. So, whether you're a risk taker or cautious trader, there's an order type that's right for your trading preference.

LIMIT ORDERS

So, you want to trade, but you don't want to spend all day glued to a screen, monitoring prices. You want to set it and forget it. Well, my friend, you need a limit order. Limit orders are the type of orders that have a maximum or minimum price at which stocks can be purchased or sold. They're like the hands-off investor's or trader's best friend. Plus, they eliminate the worry of your trade being executed at an undesired price by protecting your trade against slippage. So, go ahead and set those limit orders—then sit back and relax knowing your trades be executed at your desired price when the market trades at that price.

As any trader knows, timing is everything. If you buy too early, you might miss out on profits; but if you buy too late, you could end up taking a loss. That's why limit orders are such a valuable tool. By setting a limit order, you can automatically take profit when the price reaches your target level. And since limit orders can be placed for a quick in-and-out trade, you don't have to worry about missing your opportunity. As shown in Figure 5.2, Apple currently trades at $104 per share and you think it will trade even higher next month. One approach would be to submit a sell limit order for $130 per share. The advantage of this strategy is that you can easily set your desired exit and also your entry price.

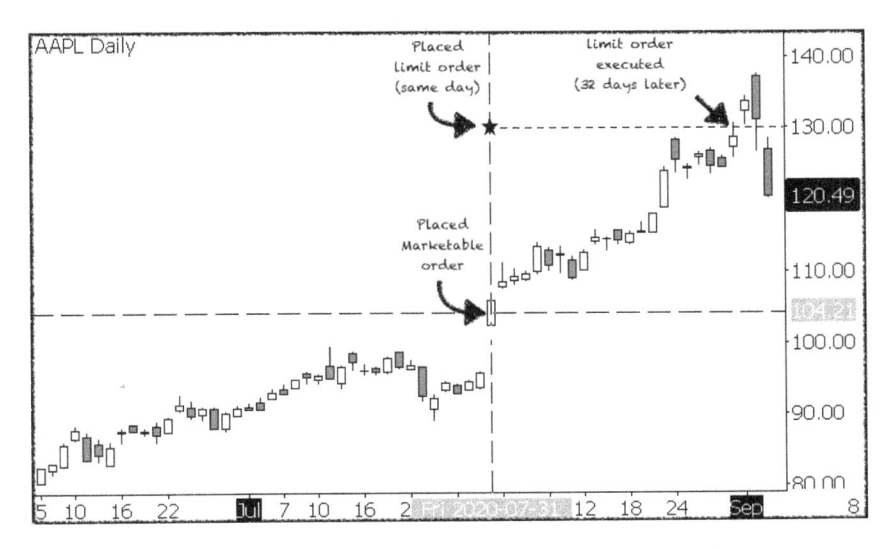

Figure 5.2: Using limit order to take profit when price reaches your target.

Have you ever placed a limit order only to see it partially filled? It can be frustrating, especially if the stock price is trading around your limit price. But don't worry, you're not alone. This happens to traders all the time. Limit orders are a great tool for traders looking to take profits, but they can be tricky to use when entering or exiting a stock that's trading far away from the limit order price. In these cases, brokers only fill your order partially, even if it trades around the same price. This can be frustrating for traders who are trying to exit a position quickly or enter a new one. However, limit orders can still be useful in these situations. If you're willing to wait for the price to reach your limit, you can use a limit order to lock in a profit or loss. Just be sure to watch the stock closely so you don't miss your chance.

Figure 5.3 shows Facebook stock chart starting at the beginning of 2021. On January 26, I placed a limit order at $265 for Facebook stock, which closed that day at $282. However, at the moment, Facebook is trading at a price that exceeds my limit price and my broker isn't executing the order as a result. Three days after placing our order, Facebook went from $282 to $265 per share, so my order was executed and I now hold shares of Facebook. Next, I decide to take profit as the price increases using a simple market order sixty days later.

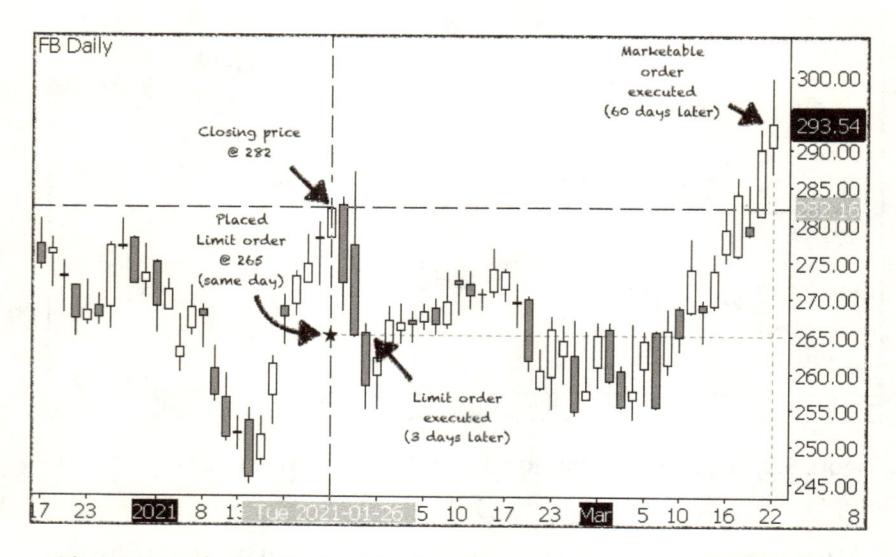

Figure 5.3: Placing limit order in advanced to execute in the future when price reaches limit price.

For the stock market, prices always fluctuate, but there are particular times when the prices drop more than usual. This sudden drop is called a dip and is often followed by a price rebound. A lot of investors take this opportunity to buy stocks at a lower price in the hopes that they will rise again. This strategy is called buying the dip and it's not guaranteed to work all the time, but it's worth a shot. I'll be explaining this strategy in more detail later in the book, so stay tuned!

Depending on the market, there are a couple of different ways limit orders can be disadvantageous. There's nothing quite as frustrating as watching a stock price steadily rise and then not being able to sell at that price because your limit order wasn't reached. A limit order is an order type to purchase or sell shares of stock at a specified price (the "limit") or better; when the current market price matches the "limit" price, the broker executes the trade. A buy limit order only executes at the given limit price or lower, while a sell limit order only executes at the given limit price or higher. The particular disadvantage of this strategy is that if the stock never reaches your price (perhaps because of a news event), then your request will never be met and no trade occurs. As shown in Figure 5.4, let's say you place a sell limit order at $56, and then the price trades below at $50, never reaching that point—this means the order will never be executed.

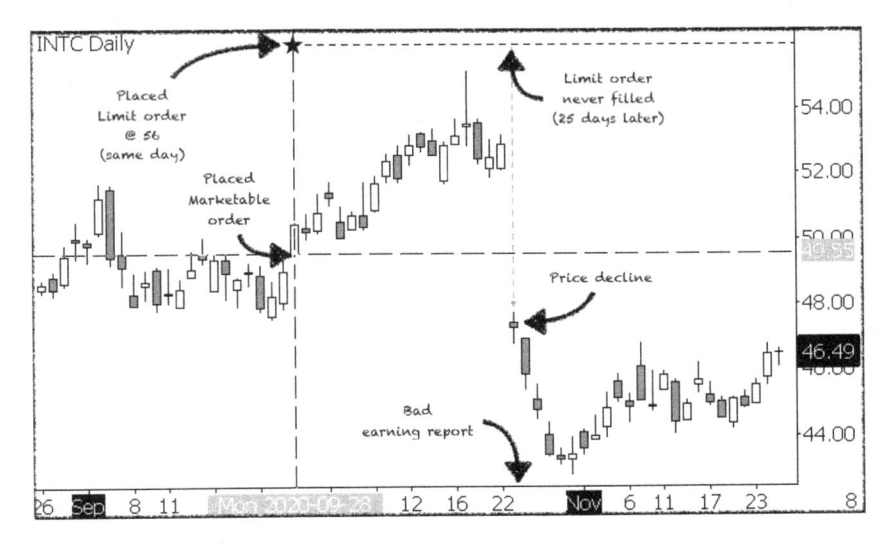

Figure 5.4: Placing limit order in advanced but target price is not reached.

In conclusion, use limit orders when you want to buy or sell a certain amount of stock at a desired price or better. The market is volatile and there are many other factors that affect the price. On the other hand, stop orders allow traders to exit or enter a stock automatically. This type of trade allows me certainty by constraining my loss and not leaving myself vulnerable due to external factors, like news events etc. Let's discuss more about stop orders in the next section.

STOP ORDER

You've been watching a stock for a while and you think it's about to crash, but what if the price keeps going up? The next day, the stock plummets and you get nothing but red on your screen. It is all so sudden; one day the stock is performing well, and then suddenly you're down on the trade. If only there was a way to set an automatic order at a certain price level so that your broker would sell your stocks automatically once they reach that point. The stop-loss order type is a great way to mitigate risk. By setting a stop-loss order, you can rest assured knowing that your position will be closed automatically once the stock price reaches your predetermined level. This way, you can limit your losses and avoid the emotional anguish of seeing your investment plummet. So, what exactly is a stop-loss order? It's an order to buy or sell a share in the future at a certain price. You can also use a stop order to enter a trade by setting it to your desired entry price. When the order is triggered, it will act as a market order and the transaction will be executed at the next available opportunity.

Stop-loss orders are one of the best ways to protect your trades from a sudden shift in the market that causes open trades to move in a negative manner. But many people don't use them as much as they should because they don't know how stop-loss orders work or what they do. I will explain everything you need to know about stop orders, including how to use them and when it's appropriate to use them. You'll also learn more about the different types of stop orders that are available.

There are three main types of stop orders: stop-loss, stop-limit, and trailing stop orders. Stop-loss orders are placed at a specific price below the current market price in the case of a sell order, or above the market price in the case of a buy order. A stop-limit order is an order type that combines the features of a stop order and a limit order. A stop-limit order will be filled at the limit price or better, but only after the stop price has been reached. Trailing stop orders are placed at a certain percentage of the current profit amount of the trade or dollar amount from the current price. The trailing stop order adjusts automatically as price moves in your favor, so you can lock in profits and limit your losses.

Stop-Market Order. They are an excellent way to automatically sell when price reaches your stop price—but they can also lead to losses if you're not careful. In fact, stop-market orders are often triggered at prices that don't make sense, which is why they're not very popular with traders. Some say this is a sign of an amateur, but it's really just the opposite. For example, in Figure 5.5 of a daily chart of Pfizer, I placed a stop-loss order at $32—below the current market price of $33. Then, an unexpected news story caused Pfizer's value to drop and my stop loss was triggered—even though there was no real change in demand for or supply. So, if you're planning to use stop-market orders, be sure to set your target exit price carefully. Otherwise, you may find yourself selling at a loss. This means I'll end up selling at a lower-than-expected price just because of bad timing on my part.

There's no surefire way to know how much a stock will plummet. But, at the very least, you can put in a stop-loss order to protect your portfolio in case of any sudden drop. I learned this lesson the hard way when I purchased shares of Pfizer after it showed signs of strength. Unfortunately, the stock then plummeted on bad news. If I had put in a stop-loss order, I would have been protected from further losses. So, if you're worried about a stock taking a nosedive, consider using a stop-loss order to help mitigate your losses.

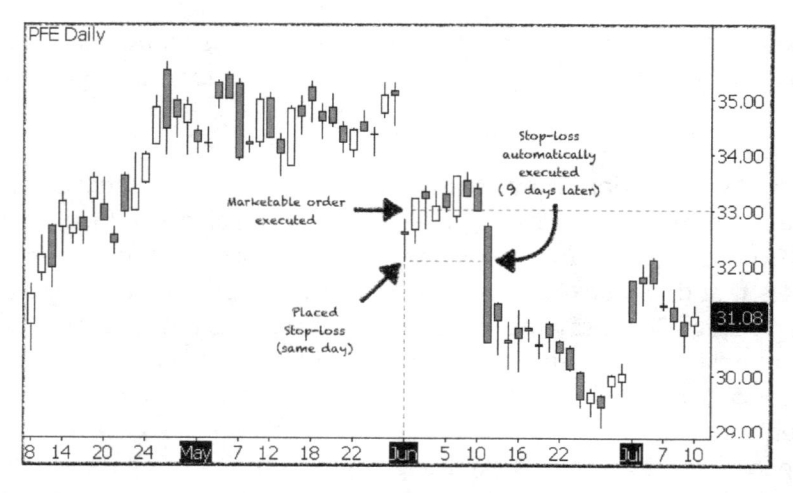

Figure 5.5: Placing a preventive stop loss order to exit the trade.

Stop orders can be used to trade a breakout strategy. As any savvy trader knows, stop orders are a vital tool in the market arsenal. And as anyone who's watched Netflix knows, it can be a volatile stock. So, when I saw the two come together in Figure 5.6, I knew I had to take advantage of the opportunity. I placed a stop-market order with a trigger at $440 to buy, and sure enough, the price pulled back and hit my order. The stop-order entry strategy worked like a charm, and I was able to take advantage of the breakout. But if Netflix's price never reaches $440, I'll be protected from downside potential. So, it's a win-win!

Stop-Limit Order. The problem with stop-market orders is that they can be triggered by momentum fluctuations, and you may not get the best possible price for your trade, as shown in Figure 5.7 of Facebook. The solution is to use stop-limit orders instead of stop-market orders. A lot of brokerage firms offer this feature as part of their online trading platforms, but if yours doesn't, then you should consider switching to brokers who do offer them because they're very useful tools for managing risk in volatile markets like today's stock market climate.

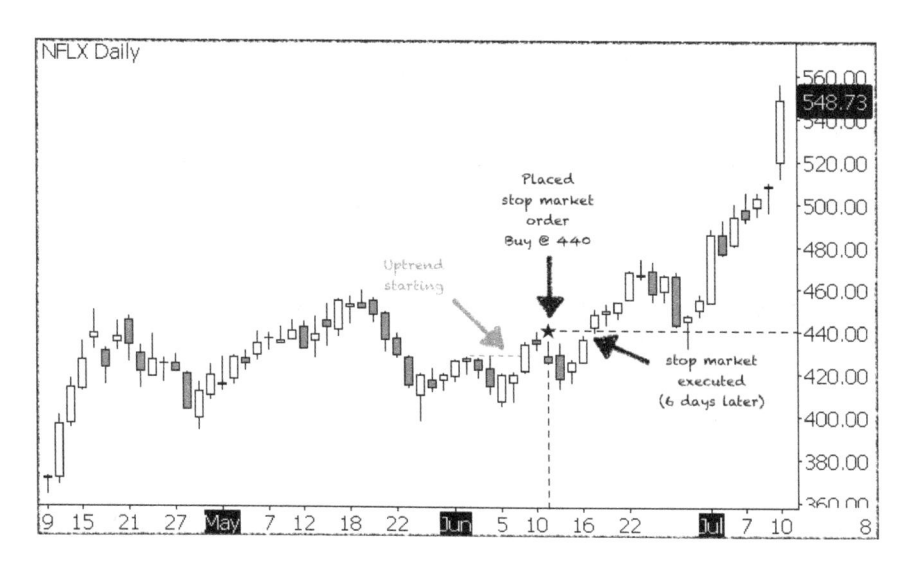

Figure 5.6: Placing a stop order in advanced to enter in a position when price is reached.

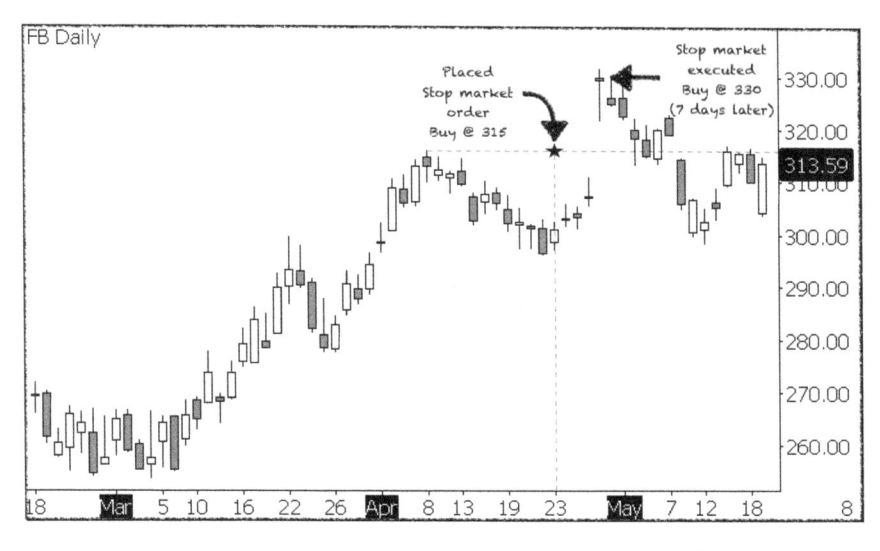

Figure 5.7: Placing a stop order in advanced but order executes at a higher price.

With stop-limit orders, you have more control over your trades. You can specify a maximum limit fill price, which guarantees that your order be filled at that price or better if the limit price is reached. However, there is still some risk involved because if stock prices move too fast or gaps past your specified limit price, then your order may be skipped entirely. So, next time you find yourself in a similar situation, remember to set a stop-loss order to protect yourself from potential losses.

Ultimately, there are several things you need to consider before placing a stop loss, including your risk tolerance, time horizon, and trading strategy. You also need to decide whether you want a standard stop-loss order or stop-limit order. If you're not sure how to use stop orders, talk to your broker for help. In summary, there are a variety of different strategies that you can employ. One such strategy is the use of stop losses. As stated before, stop losses are typically used when traders believe that the price is about to take a dip. If you're looking to protect yourself from the potential downside, then a stop-market order may be the right move. And, they are also a type of order that enable traders to dictate when they want their trade executed. All in all, stop losses can be a useful tool in your stock-trading arsenal—just be sure to use them wisely.

TRAILING STOP ORDERS

As any trader knows, one of the hardest things to do is to put a stop-loss order in place that won't get triggered by normal market volatility. That's why I rely on trailing stops to take advantage of short-term price fluctuations, but still have protection against large drops. A trailing stop is an advanced trading strategy designed to limit losses and lock in gains as price stair-steps up or down. This way, I don't have to be glued to the computer all day, monitoring every single move of my trades, but I can instead spend more time with friends and family. Sure, it's not a perfect system, but it's the best way I've found to strike the balance between managing my positions and enjoying my life outside of the market.

Trailing stop orders are a common tool used by traders to help limit their losses on a trade. This is different from a typical stop-loss order, which has a fixed stop price that doesn't move as the market fluctuates. With a trailing stop, your stop price follows behind the price movement, only activating when it reaches your predetermined criteria.

A trailing stop is a mechanism that provides traders with the opportunity to protect their positions without having to constantly monitor them. Essentially, a trailing stop order is an order to buy or sell once it reaches a certain price. The key difference between a trailing stop order and a regular stop order is that the former allows the trader to set a trailing stop, which adjusts automatically as the price moves. For example, if you want my stock to maintain a loss at 20 points down, I could set my trailing stop at 20. If that price goes down 20 points the trade will cut off so that the profits are locked in. This type of order can be helpful in volatile markets, where prices can move rapidly and unpredictably. However, it's important to note that trailing stop orders are not guaranteed to limit your losses, as they will only be executed if price falls below the predetermined level, as shown in Figure 5.8.

Trailing stop orders are designed to protect your investments by automatically selling your shares if the market starts to turn against you. While this may seem like a good idea, there are actually some downsides to using this type of order. First, trailing stop orders can actually lead to you missing out on some big market swings. If you're not willing to take the risk of losing money, then you might want to avoid using this type of order. Additionally, you also have to be careful about setting your trailing stop too close to the current trading price. If the market starts to rebound quickly, you could find yourself getting stopped out at a loss. Overall, the decision of whether or not to use a trailing stop order is up to you. Just be sure that you understand the potential risks and rewards before using them.

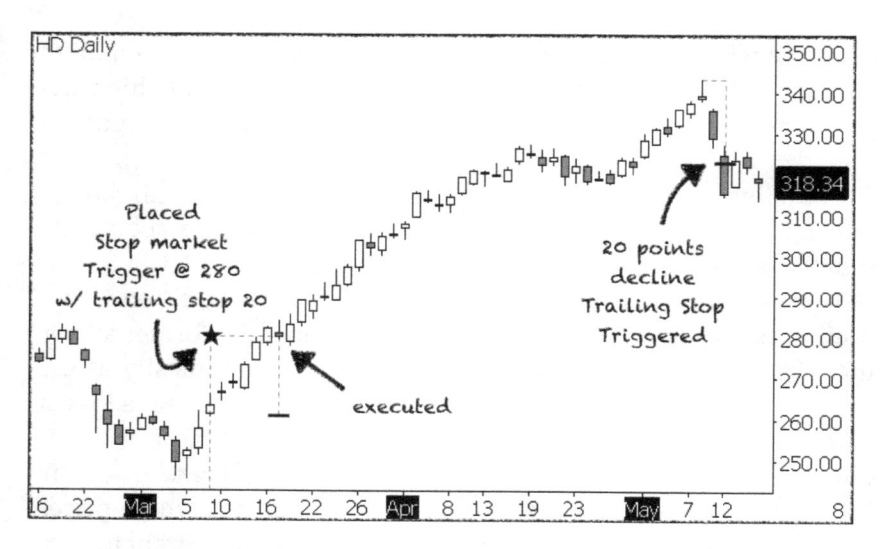

Figure 5.8: Attaching a trailing stop order to an existing position.

In summary, trailing stops are a superb way to protect your trades from sudden market swings. By keeping a close eye on your positions and using trailing stops, you can minimize your risk while still maintaining a good chance of making a profit. By using a trailing stop, you can make sure that your trade is protected while still minimizing your risk.

ONE CANCELS THE OTHER

I'm a big fan of the one-cancels-the-other (OCO) order type. It helped me out of some sticky situations and into some profitable ones. Essentially, it allows me to place three orders at once. One is to buy, and the other two are sell orders for when my stop-loss price or target price is reached. The idea behind it is to get into trades without having to constantly monitor my positions, while also guaranteeing an exit point for if it goes wrong or if the profit target is reached. This is the best way to trade because it allows me to automate my trades.

Plus, this strategy has a higher success rate than regular buy-sell orders, which means fewer headaches. So, if you're looking for a foolproof way to trade, the OCO order is the way to go, I believe.

An OCO or bracket order is an order type that combines a limit order to buy and a stop-loss order to sell, or vise-versa. Stop-range orders are also called OCO. The idea behind this combination is that it allows the trader to enter a trade at or near the market price while setting up their exit point before entering the trade. These types of orders will automatically cancel all other orders when one particular trade reaches its predetermined target or exit price. Therefore, these orders allow traders to set an exit point without having to place separate orders themselves.

By placing your order as OCO, you are essentially opening a buy and sell position on the same stock. For a long position, the stop loss is set below the entry price and the target price is set above the entry price; while for a short position, the stop loss is set above the market price and the target price is below the market price. When one trade is executed at your desired price, the other trade will be automatically cancelled when the target or exit is hit.

For instance, shown in Figure 5.9, I placed an OCO stop-market buy order at $280 while setting my stop-loss limit price at $250 in case things don't go as planned. A few days later, when it hit that price, two sell orders were placed for my target price of $250 and for my profit target price of $310. The stock price must stay above the stop loss or below the target price, but once the target price is hit, the stop loss order is cancelled. By placing my order as OCO, I am essentially creating a fence around the current price.

If you're interested in automating your trades, I would recommend using OCO. The problem with one cancelling the other is that it can be hard to find brokerages that support this feature. Not only do you need access to this feature in your account, but you also need technical knowledge of how to set up these automated trades. As any savvy trader knows, it's important to have an execution strategy in place before placing any trades. That's why I always use an OCO. By setting a stop-loss limit price and a target price, I'm essentially creating a fence around the current price. That way, if the stock price starts to rise, I know that I'll still be able to make a profit. And if the stock price starts to drop, I can rest assured that my losses will be limited. So, using an OCO is a great way to protect your investments and ensure that you always come out ahead.

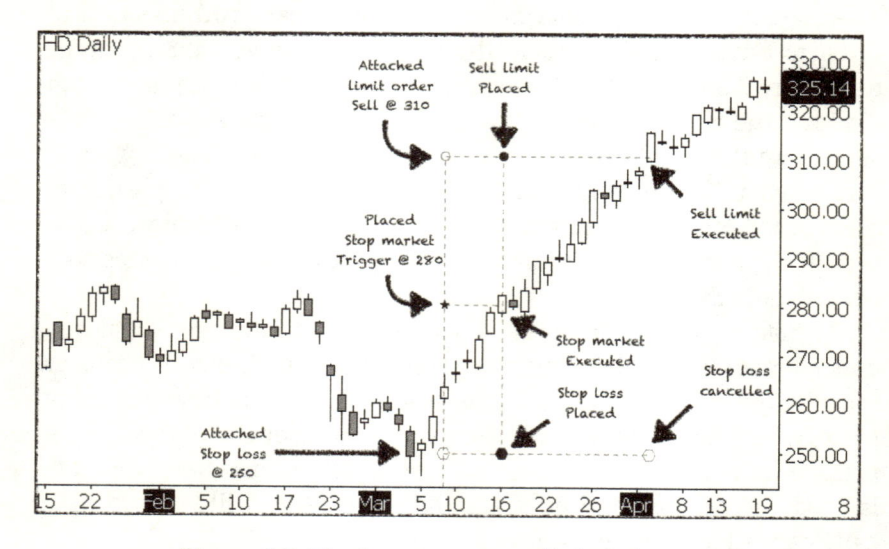

Figure 5.9: Placing a one cancels the other order.

6   Market Instruments

Chapter Overview

- » What are options and futures contracts?
- » What are exchange-traded funds?
- » Foreign and crypto currencies.

Tale of the Aristotle and Thales

A history of a Greek philosopher? In high school? Sounds like my worst nightmare. I'm sure most people would rather forget about history class, but I do remember one interesting fact. I was a high school student who was learning about Greek philosophy and agriculture. One day, my teacher asked me to write a story about someone who learned an important lesson. I decided to write about Aristotle, who was always known to have been a wise man. Aristotle was known to be a very famous philosopher, and he also wrote about many things, including agriculture. Aristotle believed that farming was an important occupation. Also, he thought that it was the best option for meeting a household's needs. After all, you need land, animals, and equipment to farm successfully. And let's not forget that farming supplies food for urban populations, too. So, the next time you're at the grocery store, take a moment to think about the farmers who made your meal possible. Without them, we would all be in big trouble.

Aristotle relates a story about how a fellow Greek philosopher, Thales, profited handsomely from an option-type agreement around the 6th century B.C. According to the story, one year ahead, Thales forecast the next olive harvest would be an excellent one. As a poor philosopher, he did not have many financial resources at hand. But he used what he had to place a deposit on the local olive presses. As nobody knew for certain whether the harvest would be good or bad, Thales secured the rights to the presses at a relatively low rate. When the harvest proved to be bountiful, and so demand for the presses was high, Thales charged a high price for their use and reaped a considerable profit. This story is often cited as an early example of the application of options-type thinking to business. It is also worth noting that Thales was using an option to hedge his risk. He was not gambling on the outcome of the olive harvest, but rather hedging against the possibility of a poor harvest. This type of use of options would become increasingly common as the options market developed.

Options were first used by farmers in Ancient Greece as a way to hedge against volatile crop prices. In the late 1960s, weather changes resulted in increased volatility in agricultural prices, which led to bust years for the Chicago Board of Trade. The board was looking for an approach that would provide more stable annual performance. Executives began exploring ways to augment their future offerings in agriculture, with an initial focus on single-stock futures. In 1969, the idea of options was born. This was furthered enhanced by the existence of small over-the-counter stock options markets. It was later agreed that stock options would be the solution going forward. This led to the regulatory approvals, research processes, product development, and personnel recruitment needed to get options trading off the ground. Until the debut and development of Chicago Board Options Exchange (CBOE), options prices were obtained from newspapers and word-of-mouth.

While this story may be apocryphal, it does illustrate the basic idea behind options contracts. An option is a type of derivative security that gives its holder the right, but not the obligation, to buy or sell an underlying asset at a specified price within a certain time period. Options are traded on exchanges or over-the-counter and are used by hedgers to protect against price fluctuations in the underlying asset, by speculators who hope to profit from movements prices and by arbitrageurs who seek to exploit price discrepancies between different markets. Today, options are traded on a variety of different assets, including stocks, bonds, commodities, and currencies.

STOCK OPTIONS

Worried about stock market volatility? The stock market is volatile, and it's hard to know when the right time to buy or sell stocks. Volatility in the stock market can cause a lot of anxiety for investors. You may feel like you're constantly guessing whether you should buy or sell stocks, and if you make the wrong decision, you could lose a lot of money. Options contracts are a vehicle to protect your portfolio from stock market swings. You can lock in a price for a set number of lots of 100 shares, regardless of whether the market goes up or down. This gives you peace of mind and protects your investments. They are a contract that gives the investor the right, but not the obligation, to buy or sell stock options at a set price before or on a specific date. However, they can be complex and confusing, so it's important to consult with an expert before entering into any options contracts.

There are two types of options: puts and calls. A call option is like a "Get Out of Jail Free" card in Monopoly. You have the right, but not the obligation, to buy the stock at a later date for a predetermined price. If the stock price goes up, you can exercise your call option and buy the stock for less than it's worth on the open market. If the stock price goes down, you can just let your call option expire worthless and move on with your life. So, call options are basically like insurance contracts that protect you from losses if a stock price goes down. Put options are like the opposite of call options. They give you the right to sell a stock at a later date for a predetermined price. So, if a stock price goes down, you can exercise your put option and sell the stock for more than it's worth on the market. And if the stock price goes up, you can just let your put option expire worthless.

Hedge yourself against potential losses by purchasing put options. By using this method, you can avoid having to sell your portfolio during a market downturn, which would result in losses and potentially high tax costs. As any savvy investor knows, a hedge can be a powerful tool for mitigating risk. When the value of an investment portfolio decreases, a hedge can appreciate in value, offsetting some or all of the unrealized losses. This is especially useful for investors who are fixed on high-risk investments. By purchasing put options, they can protect themselves against potential market downturns. Put options give investors the option to sell when prices hit above the strike price. While hedging a portfolio may come with some drawbacks—such as transaction costs, and premium fees—it can still be a useful tool for managing risk in a volatile market.

Options can also be a great way to earn profits and reduce risk, but there are also some potential downsides to consider. One of the main advantages of options is that their financial commitment is lower. This can be beneficial for investors who want to leverage their money and potentially make a higher return on investment. However, it's important to remember that options also come with a certain amount of risk. While the potential returns are great, there is also the potential for loss. They also provide greater flexibility, which can be a pro or a con depending on the investor's position. And finally, while options can be used to hedge an investment and potentially earn some extra income, they can also be complex and challenging to trade.

Investors need to be aware of the many dangers that come with this type of financial instrument. However, once they are understood, options can be a great way to hedge or earn income. Options have their own rules and jargon that investors need to comprehend. Investors who do not have trade experience should avoid them and take time to understand them. The entire amount of premium is at risk, and unfavorable price movements can quickly work against the investor. All of these factors make them a high-risk investment, and one that should be approached with caution. So, before deciding to trade options, be sure to weigh the pros and cons carefully.

FUTURES

Worried about the future of the stock market? Futures contracts are one of the most common ways to hedge against just that. They offer a way for investors to speculate on the market and protect themselves from potential losses. By trading futures, you agree to buy or sell an asset at a set price in the future. This allows you to take advantage of price changes without having to worry about being locked in at a bad price. And because they're traded on popular exchanges, you can get in and out of them quickly and easily. But don't forget, they aren't without risk. That's why it's important to understand what you're doing before you start trading them. If you're not comfortable with the risks, then they might not be for you.

Futures can be defined as financial derivatives in which a party agrees with another party to sell or buy an asset at a future date for a set price. Financial instruments like bonds and stocks, as well as physical commodities, are traded using futures. Futures have conditions, prices, and expirations that are known from the start and cannot be subjected to change. The prices agreed upon when a future is being established must be paid for that asset, regardless of the market changes during the expiration of the agreement. They can be useful to investors for speculating on market directions and hedging against losses.

For example, let's say you are an investor who is bullish on the S&P 500 index. You could buy a future contract that allows you to purchase the index at a set price on a future date. If the index rises before that date, you will profit from the difference between the price you agreed to pay and the higher market price. On the other hand, if the market falls, you will still be obligated to purchase the index at the original price, resulting in a loss. They can be risky investments, but they can also offer opportunity for those who are willing to take on the risk. Types of futures contracts:

Financial Futures. Financial futures contracts refer to agreements where the exchange commodity is traded. These contracts are used to speculate on the future price movements of various assets, including stocks, bonds, commodities, and currencies.

Currency Futures. Currency futures refers to contracts that guarantee the future exchange rate of two currencies. These contracts are often used by investors and businesses to protect themselves from fluctuations in currency values.

Energy Futures. Energy futures refers to futures contracts for selling and buying one of the fuel sources. It allows energy developers and buyers to trade energy commodities to better manage risks. The contracts are binding, meaning that both parties have to agree to the conditions set forth in the contract. The common types of energy futures include natural gas, electricity, and crude oil. It is a hedging tool that helps protect against price swings in the energy market.

Metal Futures. A precious and industrial metal futures contract is a legal agreement. It involves the delivery of metals. It's a way to hedge against price movements in the metals market, such as silver and gold. The metal futures have a long-standing history, as they attract everyone. The widespread popularity of the metal contracts results from their usefulness in protecting buyers and sellers from volatility and price risks, as well as in allowing investors to pursue various opportunities.

Grain Futures. Grains future refers to a legally binding agreement. This agreement legally binds the seller to deliver a certain quantity of grain to the buyer at a specified price and time in the future. They provide a lucrative and risky approach to speculating the grain harvest. In these contracts, the grains are sold before they are harvested. The seller agrees to deliver a certain quantity and type of grain to the grain buyer, who will, in turn, pay a specified price for the grains. Common grain futures include corn, oats, soybeans, rice, and wheat, among others.

Livestock Futures. The prices in the livestock exchange are determined by demand and supply. The level of demand for a particular type of livestock affects the price that buyers are willing to pay. The quantity of livestock that is available for sale also plays a role in setting prices. When there is a large supply of a certain animal, sellers may have to lower their asking prices as a means to attract buyers.

Hedging and speculating are two important aspects of futures contract trading. Hedging is all about minimizing the risks associated with price changes in the underlying asset, while speculation is about trying to profit from those same price changes. Both activities are essential for a well-functioning futures market. Speculation increases market liquidity, which in turn makes it easier and cheaper for investors to buy and sell their contracts. Hedging is a technique used to eliminate risk from an investment. When investors are unsure about whether or when the value of their investments will change, they can use hedging strategies that take both gains and losses into account so as not to have any surprises during portfolio management time frames. Investors use derivatives to balance the losses and gains of the assets. Hedging aims to reduce the price volatility of an asset by taking an offsetting position that is different from what investors believe. In short, both hedging and speculating are necessary for a healthy futures market. Trading futures can be a great way to make money, but it's important to understand the concepts of leverage, margin, short selling, tax benefit, and diversification.

Leverage and margin. In the world of futures trading, leverage and margin are two key concepts that every trader needs to understand. Leverage refers to the ability to control a large position with a relatively small amount of capital. Margin, on the other hand, is the amount of money that is required to open a position in a futures contract. Exchanges set the margin rates based on the stability of the markets and also the risks associated with changes in prices. Margin requirements are designed to ensure that investors can meet their obligations in their trading account.

Short selling. Investors who trade in futures benefit from short selling because it allows them to take advantage of downward price movements. Short selling can be a risky proposition, but when done correctly, short selling can be a very profitable venture for investors.

Tax benefit. Taxation is a necessary evil—there's no getting around it. But, if you're going to be subject to the government's greedy hands, you might as well do everything in your power to minimize the amount it takes from you. And one way to do that is by investing in futures. Sure, stocks have their own tax benefits. But with futures, the tax advantages are even more significant. For instance, capital gains are taxed at a lower rate for futures investors—which means you get to keep more of your hard-earned profits. In other words, if you're looking to keep as much of your money as possible come tax time, investing in futures is the way to go.

The wash sale rule can be a bit of an obstacle with respect to taxing equities, but did you know that it doesn't apply to investors in the futures market? They are exempt from the wash sale rule. The rule prevents the investors from making claims on a loss that they repurchased similar to stock after taking a loss from the purchase. This rule is a great obstacle in taxing the equities. However, the rule does not apply to the investors in the futures market. Futures offer a much lower tax rate than other investment vehicles–60% is taxed using the minimum rate, while 40% is taxed using the maximum rate. This makes them a great place to invest your money.

Diversification. Investing in the futures market can be a daunting task. It's hard to know where to start, and even harder to make money if you're not an expert. With the stock market being so unpredictable lately, many people are looking for other ways to invest their money and protect themselves from risk. Diversification is key. By investing in them, investors can spread their risk across multiple markets, making it less likely that they will lose all their money if one sector crashes. Investors in futures can also speculate on different sectors in an economy, such as foreign currencies, commodities, energy, bonds, and agriculture, among others. The ability of traders to broadly diversify using a single class of asset is unmatched if compared with stocks. Futures investors can trade many markets at once to diversify their portfolios and hedge the equity index exposure risks.

Most people think of futures trading as something only Wall Street traders do, but that's not the case. Futures contracts are available for all sorts of products, including commodities, stocks, indexes, and currencies. Trading futures provides unique benefits to investors, which equities and FOREX stocks do not. Although they also come with risks, investing in them is a great way of increasing your success rate and adding diversification. Some major reasons for trading in them include: you can trade with no worry of pattern-day trading rules, lower transaction costs, low minimum deposit requirements, extended market hours, and high leverage that could lead to greater profits. Although trading futures do have some disadvantages, such as complex terms and conditions attached to the contract, trading them still offers more advantages than disadvantages. All in all, trading futures is a great way to invest your money.

EXCHANGE TRADED FUND

You want to invest in a particular market or sector, but don't want the hassle of tracking and pricing individual stocks. It can be tough to keep up with the ever-changing stock price, and even tougher to track each one of them correctly. If you make a mistake, not only do you lose money on that investment, but it could also have a ripple effect throughout your portfolio. Exchange-traded funds (ETF)s are extremely popular among investors for their ease and simplicity. Unlike equities, which require an investor to purchase multiple stocks as a way to achieve diversification across different markets with just one investment grade security (or lack thereof), ETFs offer easy access into various asset classes without having too many worries about maintaining accurate prices on individual stocks. This makes them perfect if you're looking not only for long term portfolio stability, but also accessibility!

Bond ETF. Did you know that there's more than one kind of bond ETF? That's right—They come in all shapes and sizes. From government Bond ETFs to corporate Bond ETFs, there's an ETF out there for everyone. And further, they are a great way to get exposure to bond markets without having to take on the risks of investing in individual bonds. They offer the benefits of monthly dividends, annual capital gains, and no maturity date. They are also available in the secondary market, transparent in the pricing, and liquid to enhance their trading on the floor. The liquidity of the ETF bonds enhances their ability to emulate the index, as well as being trader friendly. So, whether you're looking for income or just want to diversify your portfolio, they are worth considering.

Stock ETF. They are a type of security that can be bought and sold on a stock exchange. They are similar to mutual funds in that they hold a basket of securities, but they trade like stocks. They can track multiple companies in various industries, sectors, or the whole index of equities. They offer investors exposure to a variety of equities and the potential benefits of diversification, without the high fees associated with traditional mutual funds. ETF shares are bought and sold throughout the day, with prices fluctuating as a result of supply and demand. While they provide investors with a cost-effective way to diversify their portfolios, they also carry specific risks associated with the companies represented in the baskets of companies.

Industry/Sector ETF. They are pooled vehicles of investment that specifically target a certain industry or sector. For example, an Industry/Sector ETF focused on the energy sector would invest in stocks related to energy companies. They have become popular among investors because they can be used for speculation and hedging. The stocks in these funds are highly liquid, which minimizes tracking errors from the index. They provide investors with a way to invest in a particular industry without having to pick individual stocks.

Commodity ETF. They are exchange-traded funds that invest in various physical commodities, such as natural resources, precious metals, and agricultural products. They focus on either investment in the future contracts of commodities or a single commodity that is held in physical storage. They track the changes in the price of specific commodities like gold and oil. The ETFs contain derivatives contracts that emulate the underlying commodity prices. They are popular because they offer investors exposure to commodities without the need for storing or transporting the physical goods. They are also relatively liquid, meaning that they can be easily bought and sold on stock exchanges. They are a great way for investors to get exposure to raw materials and commodities without having to directly purchase the commodity itself. They give investors exposure to various physical goods, such as agricultural products, precious metals, and energy resources. These ETFs can provide portfolio diversification and risk reduction. In most cases, the price correlation of commodities with equities is low and therefore many investors use commodities in their portfolio as a form of diversification and also hedging risks.

Currency ETF. They allow traders to trade a group FOREX markets through a managed fund without necessarily placing individual trades. They can be useful in speculating on the FOREX market, hedging against currency fluctuations, or simply diversifying one's portfolio. They track the relative value of currency or a basket of currencies. The investment vehicle in the currency ETFs provides exposure to currency or foreign exchange markets and the changes in the exchange rates of one currency or a pair of currencies. They are useful for traders who want to get involved in the FOREX market but don't necessarily want to place individual trades. They provide exposure to a basket of currencies or a single country's currency, and they are passively managed. They are traded on exchanges just like corporate stock shares, and they can be useful for hedging against currency fluctuations or for speculating on the FOREX market.

Inverse ETF and Leverage ETF. Inverse ETFs are exchange-traded funds that are used to profit from the decline in the value of a benchmark underlying index. They permit investors to make money when there is a decline in the underlying index or market, without selling anything short. Investing in inverse ETFs is comparable to holding a short position while seeking to purchase them later at a lower price.Most inverse ETFs use the daily futures contract to produce returns. They are marketed as an approach to profiting from the investors or hedging the investor's exposure to markets that are moving downward. Leveraged ETFs, on the other hand, seek to provide multiple index performance or the benchmark return by utilizing financial derivatives and debt instruments. In general, a 2x leveraged ETF will aim to provide twice the return of the benchmark index on a daily basis, while a 2x inverse ETF will aim to provide the opposite of twice the benchmark index return on a daily basis. In simple terms, an inverse ETF seeks to profit from market decline, while a leveraged ETF seeks to profit from market movement regardless of direction.

FOREIGN CURRENCY

When you travel to a foreign country, you have to exchange your currency for the local currency. The same is true for businesses that operate in multiple countries. They have to buy and sell foreign currencies to conduct business in those countries. The foreign exchange market is where these transactions take place. It's a global, decentralized market where currencies are traded. FOREX determines the exchange rate for foreign currencies. FOREX comprises all aspects of exchanging currencies, selling, and buying at current or determined prices. The foreign exchange market is huge. It's estimated that over $5 trillion worth of currencies are traded each day. That's more than any other financial market. The foreign exchange market is open 24 hours a day, six days a week. It's also one of the most volatile markets. Currency values can fluctuate rapidly due to political and economic events. If you're thinking of investing in the foreign exchange market, you need to be aware of the risks involved. But with careful planning and research, you could make a lot of money trading foreign currencies.

The foreign exchange market is among the more exciting and dynamic markets in the world. It is also one of the most accessible, with a variety of account types that allow investors of all levels of experience to participate. When traders first enter the FOREX market, they are typically unaware of the different types of accounts that are available to them. In this section, we will discuss the most common account types and provide an overview of each. One type of account that has become increasingly popular in recent years is the micro-FOREX account. As the name suggests, a micro-FOREX account allows retailers and beginners to participate in the foreign exchange trade using small trading sizes. These investors seek to have exposure in FOREX trading but fear risking a larger amount of money. The account presents 1,000 units which are equivalent to 1% of the standard lot size of 100,000. This makes it an ideal way for novice investors to dip their toes in the water without risking too much capital. So, whether you're a beginner or a seasoned pro, a micro-FOREX account might be the right choice for you.

This is ideal for beginner investors who want to get their feet wet in the currency market without putting too much money at risk. So, if an investor deposited $1,000 into a mini account, they would be able to trade a total of 10,000 units of currency in their trade terminals. This account type also limits potential losses and lowers the risks associated with FOREX trading. So, if you're new to the game or just want to play it safe, a mini-FOREX account might be right for you.

Traders can set up a FOREX account in as little as 1-3 days and start trading with as little as $50. Plus, trading can be done entirely online, where traders can access news, market pricing, tools, price charts, and FOREX strategies via online trade policies. Another big advantage of FOREX trading is the access to leverage and other resources for investment purposes. Leverage allows traders to trade with more money than they actually have in their account, which can lead to bigger profits (or bigger losses). But either way, it's an advantage that gives FOREX traders an edge over other kinds of assets. For those looking to invest, FOREX may be the way to go.

But what if you're not a currency trader? What if you're just a regular person who wants to know what the world's major currencies are? Well, fortunately for you, I've compiled a list of the world's major currencies and their nicknames. So, whether you're a currency trader or not, hopefully this will help you. The most commonly traded currencies in the world are known as the majors. The major pairs are: EUR/USD, GBP/USD, USD/JPY, USD/CHF, AUD/USD, NZD/USD and USD/CAD. These pairs are traded the most because they are the most liquid (they have the greatest volume of trades). These include the US dollar (USD), Euro (EUR), Pound sterling (GBP), Japanese yen (JPY), Canadian dollar (CAD), Swiss France (CHF), Australian dollar (AUD) and New Zealand Dollar (NZD).

The USD is also known as the greenback due to its green color. The EUR is nicknamed the single currency because it is used by 19 of the 28 European Union countries. The GBP is often referred to as the Cable because it was historically used to transmit telegraph messages between Britain and America. The JPY is sometimes called the Ninja because it is associated with ninjas and samurai. The CAD is sometimes called the Loonie because it has a loon on one side of the coin. The CNH is also known as the RMB or yuan. The AUD is nicknamed the Aussie due to its association with Australia. The SEK is sometimes called the Crown because it has a crown on its currency symbol. The NZD is nicknamed the Kiwi due to its association with New Zealand.

In the case of currency exchange, the spread is the difference between the quoted buy and sell price. The width of the spread, also known as the bid-ask spread, depends on the currencies involved. The world's major pairs of currencies typically have the tightest spreads since they're the most heavily traded. For example, the spread for EUR/USD is usually just a few pips. On the other hand, exotic pairs like USD/SEK or USD/TRY usually have wider spreads since they're not as heavily traded. So, if you're looking to trade currency pairs with tight spreads, stick to the majors. Leverage in FOREX refers to the ratio of a broker's credit size to traders' funds. FOREX leverage size is more than the amount of capital invested. Leverage in FOREX implies that an investor has a small amount of capital but controls a larger amount in the foreign account.

The FOREX market is the largest and most liquid financial market in the world. This liquidity makes it an ideal market for traders who want to take on more risk to potentially make larger profits. However, with greater rewards come greater risks. Trading in the FOREX market can be volatile, and it is important to remember that you can lose money as well as make money. Before trading in the FOREX market, it is important to understand the risks involved and to have a solid trading plan in place. Also with FOREX trading, accessibility is one of the major pros. This is because FOREX has the potential to give traders a faster return on their investment. FOREX has deep liquidity, which increases the potential for fast returns. Other pros of FOREX include its short selling, technical strategy, liquidity, automation, and fewer commissions and sales. FOREX could be the right market for you. Just be aware of the volatility.

CRYPTOCURRENCY

Cryptocurrencies are a new and untested technology, and there is a lot of risk associated with investing in them. However, the potential rewards for those who invest early could be huge. They are still in their early stages, so there is a lot of opportunity for growth. If you're willing to take the risk, now is the time to invest in cryptocurrencies. They are any type of digital currency that exists virtually or digitally and secures the transaction using cryptography. They do not have a regulating authority or a central issuing authority, but use a decentralized system for issuing new units and recording transactions. The currency uses encryption algorithms to ensure that cryptocurrency functions as both a virtual accounting system and a currency. They are rumored to be often used by criminals or those seeking to avoid government regulation, but they can also be used by legitimate businesses or individuals. While the concept of cryptocurrency is still relatively new, it has the potential to revolutionize the way we conduct transactions and store value. Only time will tell whether cryptocurrencies will become a mainstream form of currency or remain a niche product.

What's blockchain? You've probably heard about Bitcoin and other cryptocurrencies, but you're not sure how they work or why they're so important. Cryptocurrencies, such as Bitcoin, are made possible by blockchain technology. Blockchain is a distributed database that stores information in a digital format. This information can be accessed by computer network nodes. In a cryptocurrency system, blockchain is used to maintain a decentralized transaction record. This record is secure and cannot be changed or removed. Blockchain technology guarantees security and fidelity on recording data. It also generates trust without involving a third party. As a result, blockchain allows digital information to be recorded and distributed without being changed or removed.

There are two main types of cryptocurrencies. Proof-of-Work (PoW) and Proof-of-Stake (PoS). It can be hard to keep up with all the new cryptocurrency lingo. What do PoW and PoS mean? In short, POW refers to the competition between miners in solving cryptographic algorithms or equations, as well as validating transactions, to earn blockchain rewards. PoS, on the other hand, refers to the random implementation of chosen validators to ensure that there is a reliable transaction that compensates them with cryptocurrency. So, there you have it! The next time you hear someone talking about PoW or PoS, you'll know exactly to what they're referring.

Mining cryptocurrency and staking cryptocurrency can be profitable if you have a powerful computer that is capable of solving complex mathematical problems, or patience necessary to receive rewards. Cryptocurrency mining is a process of solving complex puzzles to secure the network and prevent network hijacks. The first cryptocurrency, Bitcoin, was created in 2009 by an anonymous individual or group of individuals known as Satoshi Nakamoto. Cryptocurrency staking is a process of validating transactions and achieving consensus with other nodes in the decentralized system. They are digital or virtual tokens that use cryptography to secure their transactions and to control the creation of new units. They are decentralized, which means they are not (yet) subject to government or financial-institution control. They are often traded on decentralized exchanges and can also be used to purchase goods and services.

Crypto exchanges. Crypto exchanges are platforms where traders can buy, sell, and trade cryptocurrencies. There are a variety of different crypto exchanges, and each one has its own set of features and benefits. Crypto exchanges are businesses that permit customers to trade digital and cryptocurrencies for other assets. The online marketplace allows users to sell, buy, and trade cryptocurrencies. The current types of cryptocurrencies include hybrid exchanges, centralized exchanges, and decentralized exchanges. Crypto exchange platforms have been known to be somewhat difficult to use for first-time buyers of cryptocurrency. This is due to the fact that these exchanges require the user to set up a "wallet" prior to trading. A wallet is needed to hold onto your cryptocurrency until you are ready to sell it or use it. Crypto exchange platforms also tend to be less intuitive than traditional stock exchanges. However, they are slowly becoming more user-friendly with each passing year. Crypto exchanges are an essential part of the cryptocurrency ecosystem and will likely continue to grow in popularity as more people become interested in Bitcoin, Ethereum, and other digital assets.

It is important to weigh the pros and cons of cryptocurrencies before making a decision about investing in them. With crypto, personal information is not disclosed during transactions and the payments are completely encrypted. They also allow for a secure and instantaneous transfer. The transfer can easily be done without consulting anyone. The trade is also self-managed and self-regulated, where the miners keep updated and accurate records, thus preserving the integrity of the cryptocurrency. In today's environment, we need all the help we can get to keeping our personal information safe. They offer us that help with their private and secure transactions.

While cryptocurrencies may have some advantages, there are also several disadvantages to consider. For example, the value of cryptocurrencies can be volatile and fluctuate rapidly. This means that investors could suddenly lose a significant amount of money if the value of their coins decreases. Additionally, they are not backed by any government or Central Bank, which could make them less stable than other investment options. Finally, it is important to remember that they are still a relatively new technology, and they have not yet been widely adopted. This means that there could be unforeseen risks associated with investing in cryptocurrencies.

PART III

MODERN PRICE ACTION

Munehisa Homma was a Japanese rice trader who is considered the father of candlesticks and chart patterns. Unlike most other parts of the world, Japan has utilized these tools for centuries, dating back to 300 years ago when traders analyzed past market behavior to use it as a basis for predicting future trends. Specifically, it can be credited to Homma, who made the first attempt at using past price changes before his time to predict future trends within markets.

Did he succeed? And I said yes! In the 1980s and 1990s, a few traders in the Western world decided to study Homma's methods of candlestick analysis, which had been popular among Japanese analysts. Steve Nison was one such analyst from America who wrote two bestsellers explaining Homma's system, of which one was "Beyond Candlesticks: New Japanese Charting Techniques Revealed and Strategies for Profiting from Japanese Candlestick Charts."

I know you might be wondering what the correlation might be between stock trading and Japanese's candlesticks. This fascinating technique is not just a relic from history, but it's also still actively used by traders today. In this section, I'll explore how Japanese candlestick patterns can help you understand stock market basics and why they're so important for both beginners and experts alike.

When you're looking to invest in a company, it's important to pay attention to not only the information that is available about the stock, but also the technicals. Technical indicators are popular among traders, who use them to analyze trends and make predictions. There are three main indicators I seek: price movement (the direction and degree), volume over time (how often people buy and sell), and MAs, which tell us where we should expect prices to go next.

Let's get to the point. I need a simpler way of analyzing stocks and making decisions about them so that I can cut down on the time spent figuring out what my preferred entries are without sacrificing accuracy. That said, being able to simplify things doesn't mean it'll be less effective; in fact, you might say it has more potential for success.

Market indicators, price action, and trend analysis are just a few of the analytical methods I may utilize to identify a certain pattern. However, it should not be too complicated to read the trend. We can simplify trends by defining them using the three general directions: going up, going down, or going sideways. A lot of traders add multiple layers of interpretation when identifying the trend, but it doesn't necessarily mean they get better results. For novices who want an easy way into trading stocks without having any prior knowledge about technical analysis or even investing at all, for that matter, this is the chapter for you. For now, we will focus our attention on mastering how to correctly interpret basic price trends.

Our discussion includes examples of scenarios so that you can visualize the use of the tool and can better decide on when the best entry and exit points are. We will learn about what a trend is, how it influences decision making, and what each trend line says about the market. By the end of this section, you should be able to read price action and trend lines.

7 Technical Analysis

Tale of Robert Edwards and John Magee

The stock market is a complex and ever-changing environment, and it's tough to stay ahead of the curve without access to the latest information and analysis. If you want to be successful in the stock market, you need to understand the work of Robert Edwards and John Magee. Even if you are familiar with their work, it can be hard to keep up with all the latest research and developments. That's where Robert Edwards' and John Magee's principles enter.

Edwards and Magee are two of the most important figures in the world of stock market analysis. Their research and writings have influenced the way that traders and investors approach the market, and their contributions have had a profound impact on the development of the industry. Edwards is often referred to as the pioneer of trend analysis, and his work on patterns and indicators has been hugely influential. Magee, meanwhile, is considered to be the father of technical analysis, and his insights into market behavior have shaped the way that many traders operate. Together, these two men have changed the way that the stock market is understood and analyzed, and their work continues to influence the strategies of traders around the world.

John Magee graduated from Pomfret Academic in Connecticut and Massachusetts Institute of Technology, which shaped his career. From the passion generated from his father, Magee focused efforts on market analysis to determine the trends and patterns across the stock investments. In 1942, John Magee joined Robert Edwards to refine the research on the stock investments. These two stock experts developed their interests in stocks because of the possibilities they saw. The determination of the best procedures and insights for managing the respective market concepts remained their main goal. Most of the insights came from models and strategies to figure out what people need in the market. This helped them understand what was happening with price. Edwards' and Magee's concepts eventually led to what is now known as "Technical Analysis."

Their book, "Technical Analysis of Stock Trends," was published in 1948 and laid the foundation for much of the analysis that exists today. The book was ahead of its time in many ways, offering insights into the changing nature of the stock market and the rules that govern it. One of the key concepts in the book is the determination of trends, which Edwards developed into a highly effective tool for predicting market movements. The book remains an essential guide for anyone interested in stock market analysis and is a testament to the vision and expertise of its authors.

John Magee is best known for his work that laid the groundwork for modern charting techniques. However, Magee also wrote several other books on finance and investing. These include "The General Semantics of Wall Street" and "Wall Street, Main Street & You." Both of these books were motivated by Magee's continued research on the stock markets and the application of newer ideas in meeting the stock requirements for success. The developments across the books focused on how the study of the various and respective trends could influence the study of the stock markets and their influence on the decisions that the investors should make. As a result, Magee's later books offer a deep insight into his thinking on financial markets and investing.

The two authors were responsible for combining their cognitive insights to meet the stock trader's needs. As a result, Magee and Edwards initiated the development of newer versions of the "Technical Analysis of Stock Trends." These versions tried to incorporate technology and use of modern working environments to ascertain the application of the stock theories and models that work for the modern world. The two authors were actively involved in developing and creating stock inputs based on trend analysis, pattern development, and technical analysis until they passed away. Consequently, many critiques argue on the personal application of the concepts Magee and Edwards initiated. Nevertheless, there is no denying that these two men had a profound impact on the world of technical analysis.

This book provides traders with everything they need to know about the technical analysis patterns from these two legends of the industry. I bring you concise, easy-to-read summaries of their latest analysis techniques, so that you can stay informed. This tale is significant because the technical analysis observation made by Magee and Edwards were based on studying the crowd-trading behavior. For instance, in the stock market, we are trading against other people who are taking money from your pocket to put into their pockets, similar to the game of chess, where your opponent is trying to capture your pieces. To get an edge, you have to study the other person's moves by identifying and recognizing behavior patterns. In this chapter, we will study chart behavior patterns that represent behaviors that we can exploit to profit from them. So, stay tuned and keep reading to learn how to beat the market by understanding trading behavior!

INTRODUCTION TO TECHNICAL ANALYSIS

Chess is a board game in which players are given pieces and the goal is to capture the other player's king. Also, chess is a game in which the player has pieces with different moves and relies on strategy. It is believed that chess has been around since as early as the sixth century, but it gained in popularity 500 years ago. There are pieces resembling those of modern chess dating from the 10th century. The Indian game of Chaturanga is something that looks very similar to the modern-day chess board, which is similar in purpose to our current-day game of chess. This suggests that India is an ancient breeding ground for this strategic board game.

Learning to play chess was one of the first memories I had with my dad. It all started when he taught me how to play at the age of five. He bought me a chess set and we would play intense matches together, but he always came out on top. Since my dad was often at work, he rarely had time to play with me in his busy schedule. So, he got me the computer version of chess, but I could never beat the computer, no matter what I tried.

One day, when I was playing chess against the computer for the millionth time, my dad walked in. He asked me if I was winning. I told him that the computer always beat me every time because it knew what to do with each move better than I did. He told me that you will improve as time goes on and to never be discouraged. The next day, my dad came home with a book that had the title "Bobby Fisher Teaches Chess."

Bobby Fischer was an American-Hungarian chess grandmaster. He became famous both for his genius at playing chess as well as for being the World Chess Champion from 1972–1975. Grandmaster Bobby Fischer has published this easy-to-understand, no-nonsense, practical, and progressive chess instruction book. My father let me borrow it because he knew it was something I really wanted to do well and, more than anything else, beat him.

I read it every day after school, for long hours on end. I eventually became better than the computer at playing chess. After playing against the computer for two weeks, I had managed to win more often than not. When I felt that playing against the computer was not challenging enough anymore, I needed someone who could push me even more. My dad. So, one lucky night when my dad was home, I challenged him to a game of chess. I was still apprehensive, but at the midway point of the game, he looked at me as if his world had been turned upside down. I was so much better. "Checkmate," I finally won my first game against my dad.

There are many similarities between chess and the stock market. In both cases, you're playing a game against another person with the goal of winning. They're both games with objectives and rules that are played. However, the two differ in some ways, including that in chess it doesn't matter who goes first; however, in the stock market, it's determined by an auction or dice roll. You can also see these differences—while people take turns moving pieces on a chess board to make them capture one another and get closer toward winning (knowing how to jump forward or back), stock traders try to buy low and sell high for a quick profit.

Trading is like chess, you're trying to predict the movements of your opponent and make decisions based on what happens in front of you, so it's important to analyze risk before making a move that puts yourself or other pieces at an advantage/disadvantage. Both chess and the stock markets involve choosing one move from many possible moves, some more complex than others. More risky moves have high reward ratios, while less risky moves have lower reward ratios. The best players will find the best balance for their level of expertise while risking as little as possible, knowing that higher returns could be obtained by taking on more risk. Players who don't know what they're doing aren't going to make it very far, no matter how brilliant they might be.

This chapter will teach you all about using technical trading strategies for your own benefit. It explains what they are, how they work, when you should use them, and much more. With this information at your disposal, there should be no reason why you can't be successful.

WHAT ARE CANDLESTICKS

Technical analysis is a method of predicting future price movements based on past market data, using charts and graphs to help make decisions about when to buy or sell. In this section, we will briefly discuss the basics of price action and how they can be used in conjunction with one another. Then we will look at many examples so that you can see how it works in real life. By the end of this section, you should have a good understanding of technical analysis and how it can be used to improve your trading results.

The candlestick is a rectangle figure with wicks that show the opening, closing, and high/low price. The different shapes on this chart show us important elements, such as if it was an up or down period. There are a couple of factors to bear in mind while interpreting a candlestick chart. First and foremost, the candlestick has three components: The real body, which is bound by the trade period of the open and close price; the upper shadow, which represents the high price; and the lower shadow, which denotes the low price. There are occasional situations in which a candlestick has no upper or lower shadow, or neither. In these cases, the high and/or the low of the real body are the high and/or low of the period. The real body is white or green when the closed is higher than the open, and black or red when the open is greater than the close. Importantly, the color of the real body can give you clues about market sentiment: A black (or red) real body typically indicates that bears are in control, while a white (or green) real body suggests that bulls are in control. In addition, candlesticks can be classified based on their shape. For instance, a doji is a candle with a small real body and long shadows, indicating indecision in the market, while a long red candle may signal that bears are about to take control. As you can see, candlesticks provide valuable information about market sentiment and momentum (See Figure 7.1).

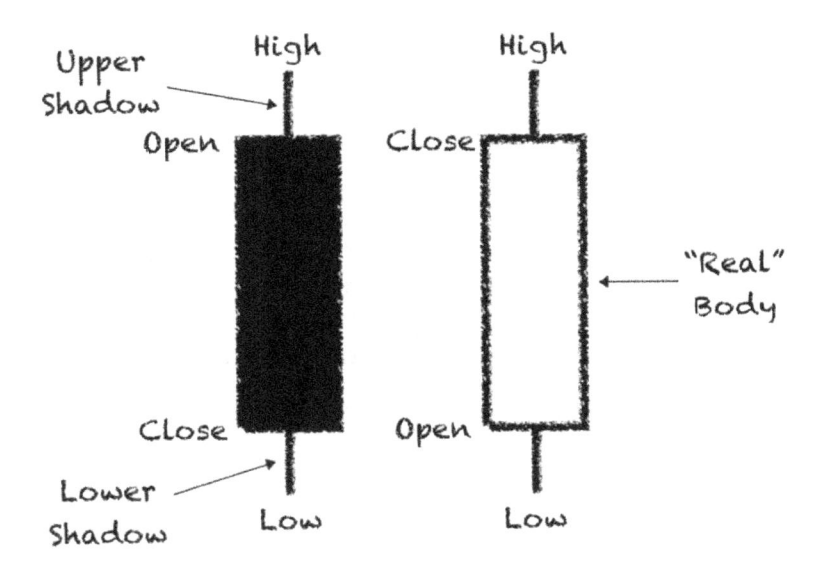

Figure 7.1: Candlestick's opening, closing, high, and low price.

To reiterate this point, candlesticks are a type of Japanese chart that helps you visualize the highs and lows for a given period of time. This makes it easier to see when the market is trending up or down. With candlesticks, you can easily identify buy and sell opportunities. The length of the upper shadow indicates how strong the buyers were at the peak of the trading period, while the length of the lower shadow indicates how strong the sellers were at the low point. By understanding the meaning of the different elements of the candlestick, you'll be able to better predict future price movements.

READING CHARTS

Trading is a stressful profession. Finding the best entry and exit points involves time and effort. However, there are so many methods out there that it's easy to become overwhelmed by all of the possibilities. How can you know which ones will be crowned champions? For instance, candlestick charting enables me to detect patterns in a visual manner, making it easier than ever to comprehend what's going on with price direction.

In technical analysis, there are three types of candlesticks: Doji (or tight-range), Marubozu (or wide-range), and everything else in-between (or narrow-range) (See Figure 7.2). When a market is trending, it is easy to trade. In contrast, when a market is in a range, it can be difficult to determine which side of the range will win and to figure out which type of bar on which to enter. Also, we need an objective way to measure the power of each side in order for us to make trades with consistency. The market is either trending or not. When the market is not moving, it trades in a range.

On a (daily) per-bar basis, it is either a wide-range, narrow-range, or tight-range bar, as discussed earlier. Either the bulls or bears have complete control of the bar, partial control, or equal control.

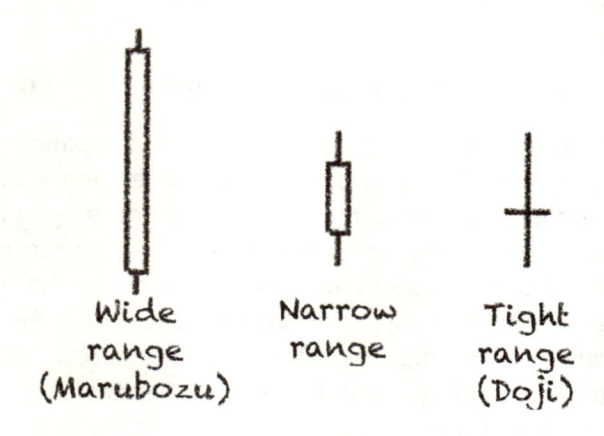

Wide range (Marubozu)   Narrow range   Tight range (Doji)

Figure 7.2: The three types of candlesticks

Range. The narrow range bar is a sign of little price movement during the session. These bars can be found on the charts and are used to spot consolidation. Price consolidation is common just before price breaks out into a trend. Using the term "range" is unfamiliar to most traders, so all range bars will be referred as either bullish/bearish bars or indecision bars. The bullish/bearish or indecision bar is a very useful signal. It tells us whether the market is trending, ranging, or not moving at all. This helps us know when we should be buying and selling stocks. If the body on the chart is thin or nonexistent, the candle is an indecision bar, and neither the bulls nor the bears dominated the bar, and the bar is merely a one-bar tight trading range. For example, a market begins at one price, trades higher or lower during the day, but ends at roughly the same price as when it opened, producing a crosshair on a gun sight.

Body. Larger bodies, in general, indicate more power. A series of strong momentum bars shows a strong trend and, more simply, momentum. However, an unusually large body after a long move or a breakout suggests the presence of an exhaustion bar, which I will discuss later in this chapter. If the bar has a body, it means that the close trended away from the open and that it is a momentum bar. Obviously, if the bar is too wide and the body is too tiny, there may be little or no control. Furthermore, there may be mostly sideways movement within the bar, and further information about the size of the shadows is needed to determine the directional bias.

Shadow. The long upper/lower shadow implies that buyers/sellers were unable to force the price to close significantly in either direction. A modern term for the word "shadow" is tail, which is widely accepted by most traders; a bar that has little to no body, with the tails (high and low) indicating the amount of price volatility that happened during the session. The longer the tails, the more volatile the condition. Understanding tails is fundamental in understanding the high or low price to which a stock rose or fell. The upper tail is also called the topping tail, while the lower tail is called the bottoming tail. The highest point of the upper tail signifies the high price for the stock for that time frame, while the lowest point signifies the lowest price for that time frame, and the difference between the high price and the low price represents the trading range. One of the most essential parts of trading using Japanese candlesticks is forecasting price direction, which predicts the direction or price. It can tell whether there is more fear or greed at work, and it can forecast where the price will go from here. Often, the length of the tail becomes important during analysis.

Bar-in-formation. To get a better understanding of what is happening inside the bar price action, let's dissect it further by looking at each element that makes up a candlestick. Price action can also be determined by analyzing patterns that form on the candlesticks themselves. These patterns will give you clues about future market direction. Bar-in-formation indicate periods of indecision (or trend) and help you understand potential market reversals as well as continuations.

To further help you understand how to read candlesticks effectively, I will use Figure 7.3 as a guide for explaining the concept. The price of the stock opens at $5, rallies until it gets to a low price of $4.50, rises to a high price of $10.50, before closing at $10. The trading range is therefore $10 - $5 = $5. You may be wondering how the price movement was decided. The candle representation next to its intra-day chart aids in determining stock behavior for this time frame. It clearly indicates that the price rose consistently from the starting price to the high price before increasing rapidly and steadily to the high point, then dropping slightly at the close. So far, I've concentrated our conversation on candlesticks with bodies, as you can see from the graphics I've given below.

Not all candlesticks are created equal. Some candlesticks, like the ones known as indecision candlesticks, don't even have bodies. These types of candlesticks simply show the data for a trading period during which the opening and closing prices were the same. In other words, they indicate that traders couldn't make up their minds about where the price was going. Indecision candlesticks usually foreshadow a reversal in trends, as you'll learn more about in this chapter. For example, let's say the price of a stock opens at $10, falls to $5, rises to $15, and then falls back to $10 before the end of the trading period. This would create an indecision candlestick (See Figure 7.4). So, if you see one of these on a chart, it's probably a good idea to be ready for some changes in direction.

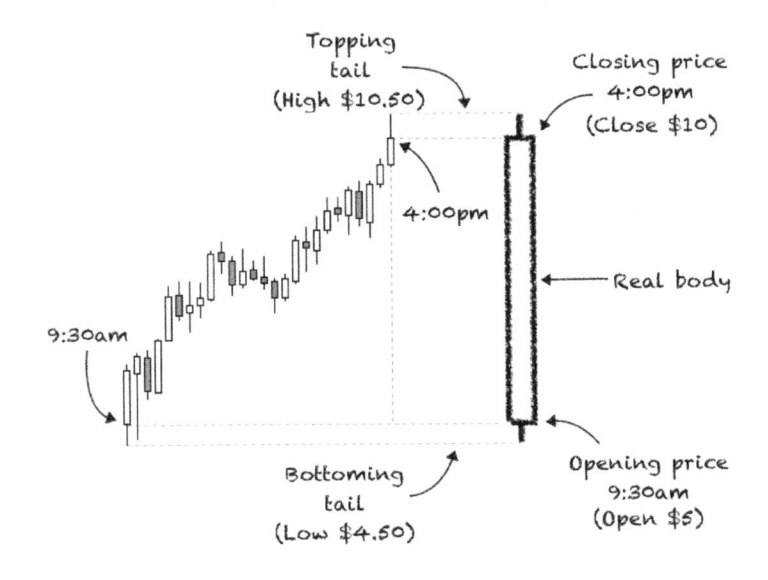

Figure 7.3: Wide range candle represented by its intra-day chart.

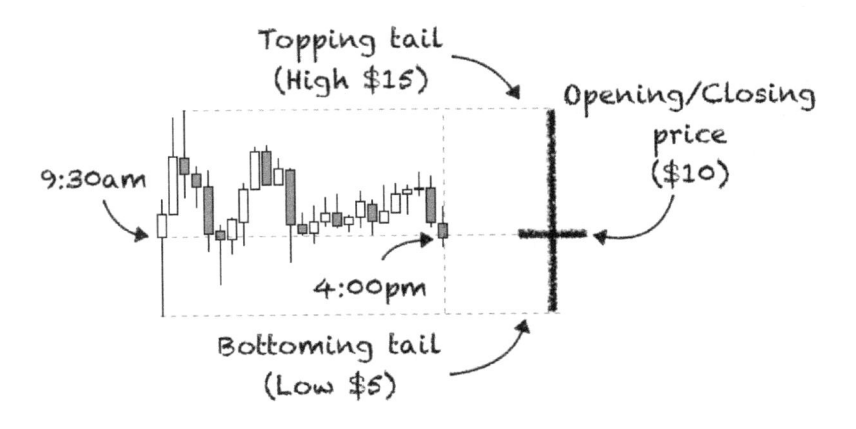

Figure 7.4: Tight range candle represented by its intra-day chart.

In conclusion, candlestick analysis is a great tool for every trader, but it has one significant flaw—it does not reveal from where the price has come from or where it is likely to go next. Aside from what you've learned thus far, the many candlestick types and their significance are important concepts to understand. When you grasp these concepts, you will be one step closer to being a better stock trader. To truly benefit from candlestick analysis, you must understand the basics of what each candlestick type means. However, the true value of candlesticks lies in their ability to give traders a glimpse into the future direction of the market. While no tool is perfect, candlesticks come pretty close. With a little practice, you'll be able to use them to your advantage.

CONSOLIDATION PATTERN

The consolidation pattern is one of the more powerful patterns in all of technical analysis, and knowing how to trade them is a must-have skill. They happen so often that developing the skills to identify and trade them will pay off in your trading. Consolidation patterns are simple concepts that can be applied across any time frame. Once you've learned what they look like, they are simple to spot on your charts. You'll learn about how they work and why they're so critical for you to master. If you're ready to take the next step in mastering this powerful price movement, this is exactly where you need to start.

This section will give you everything that I know about consolidations, and I show it all through examples of real-world trades that I have taken myself. Next, I will explain how to identify consolidation zones, and when it's appropriate to trade them. We will also look at some examples of how these types of patterns can play out so that you can get a better understanding on how they work. If you understand what consolidation zones are and why they occur, then you should be able to use them as an effective tool for your own trading strategy. With that being said, let's dive right into our first definition.

Consolidation patterns are very important because they can help us enter into the start of a potential move. They also help identify potential areas where we might see price reverse in the opposite direction. A consolidation zone forms when price moves sideways, but then fails to make any further progress before reversing direction and moving back toward the opposite side of the trend channel from which it came. This is precisely what I mean by "consolidation," when prices merely trend sideways without making any significant progress in one direction (up or down). The key word here is "significant" because there is little movement whatsoever during this period of time. The key to identifying these areas correctly is by using the following technique for clustering candles.

We must have at least two adjacent narrow-range-bars opposing each other for a pattern to be considered a consolidation pattern. As illustrated in Figure 7.5, nearly similar candles trading in opposite directions must be trading within range of one another. Take the highest and lowest candle extremes and draw a line to the right. Candles that closed within this range can be grouped together. Repeat for each additional candle until the next candle no longer can be combined. This approach should give you a consistent method of finding areas of consolidation.

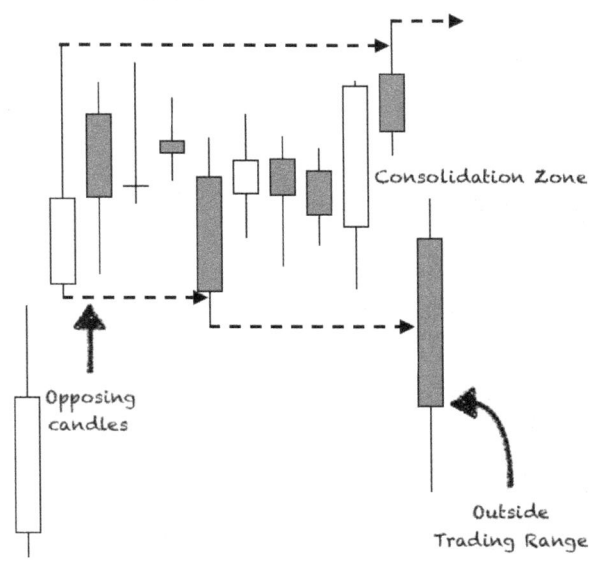

Figure 7.5: Grouping candles to find the consolidation zone.

Consolidation zone strategy. They are often described as a trading range. When the price of a stock is confined to a tight range for an extended period of time, this is referred to as a consolidation zone. Consolidation zones are periods when the market has difficulties reaching a consensus on the next price move. They usually occur after a big move from either direction, and it may be identified by flat trading activity with few, if any, gains or losses. As a result, traders will take more risk-averse positions until this uncertainty is resolved by a breakout above resistance or a collapse below support levels.

Another approach is sandwiching alternating bullish and bearish candle together. Take the alternating candle technique, for example G-R-G or R-G-G-R, draw a box around the maximum and minimal openings or closures, measure their midpoints, and draw a line from the midpoint to the right as shown in Figure 7.6.

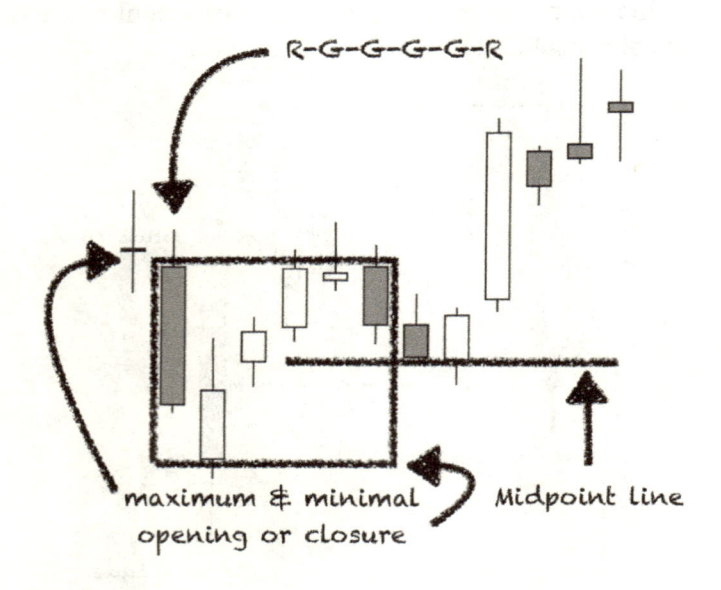

Figure 7.6: Sandwiching candles to find support and resistance.

Breakout strategy. There are specific formations that occur at the end of trends, which signal an impending reversal or continuation of the trend. If the price action goes up, then consolidates, and then breaks out again in the same direction, this is called a bullish breakout (See Figure 7.7). If the price action goes down, then consolidates, and then breaks down again in the same direction, this is called a bearish breakdown (See Figure 7.8). If the price action goes up or down, consolidates, and then breaks out again but in the opposite direction (i.e., if it broke out downward after going up) (See Figure 7.9), this would be called a breakout reversal.

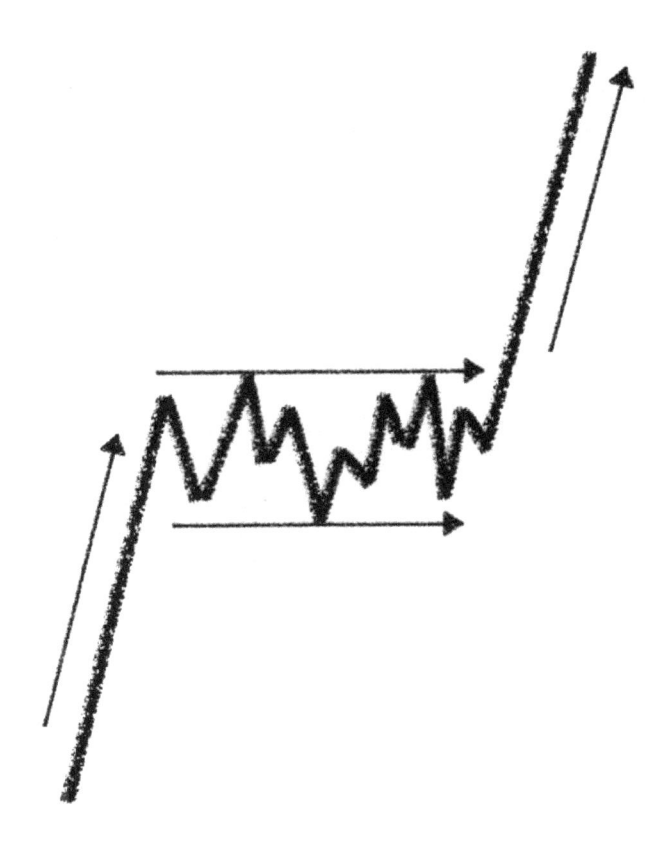

Figure 7.7: Bullish breakout after consolidation

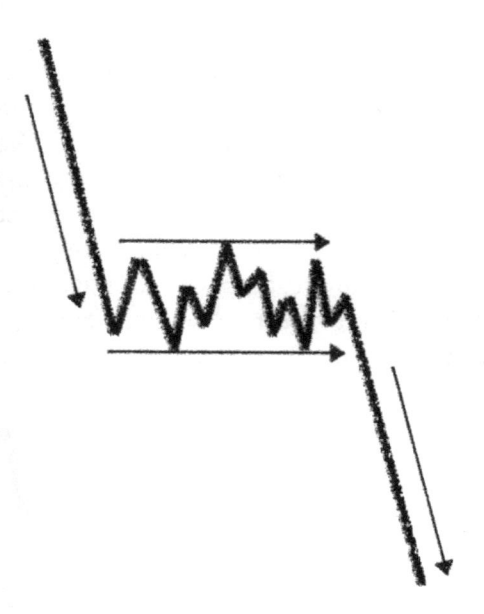

Figure 7.8: Bearish breakout after consolidation.

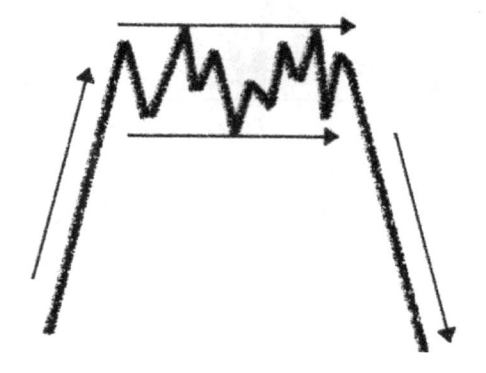

Figure 7.9: Reversal breakout after consolidation

Perhaps the best way to trade breakouts is by using orders placed just outside the consolidation areas on either side of them (for example, going long above bullish breakouts or shorting below bearish breakouts). The key to effectively trading consolidation breakouts is to wait for the confirmation rather than entering prematurely with anticipation of the breakout. As any trader knows, breakouts are a frequent occurrence in the market. They happen when prices break through an area of resistance, which becomes a price support level, or vice versa. Many traders are aware of support and resistance, but many don't know how to correctly identify them. An alternative approach for identifying possible support and resistance levels is to use consolidation zones. To begin, utilize candle clustering to locate consolidation zones. Draw a box around the extreme opening and closing prices. Then, from the center of the box, draw a horizontal line to the right. This box denotes a probable location of high supply of resistance or support maintained by demand. By using this method, traders can more accurately identify potential areas of support and resistance. The horizontal line shows levels of support or resistance that are projected to the right.

Retest Strategy. In fact, most traders tend not to notice the breakouts and let them pass. They then lose out on big profits when these consolidation patterns result in a large move that happens shortly after. Although you can find an entry at the breakout, let's now consider entries at the retest-confirmation. The retest-confirmation approach helps you find good entry points, which is extremely useful. Price either breaks out or returns to the beginning of the consolidation and "retests" the consolidation boundaries. This gives us an opportunity to enter at a better price than we would have if we had entered on the breakout alone.

You can see from Figure 7.10 that price retested resistance at 500 before gapping below the next day. Just as gravity always pulls objects toward the center of the Earth, prices always seem to end up retesting support and resistance levels before continuing in their original direction. This creates an excellent opportunity for those who were looking for a better entry point. Price action will either form a pin bar or reversal pattern after retesting support or resistance. If you are not familiar with these patterns, I have an entire section explaining what they are. However, even if you don't understand the patterns, you can still benefit from this strategy by simply waiting for price to retest a support or resistance level before entering your trade.

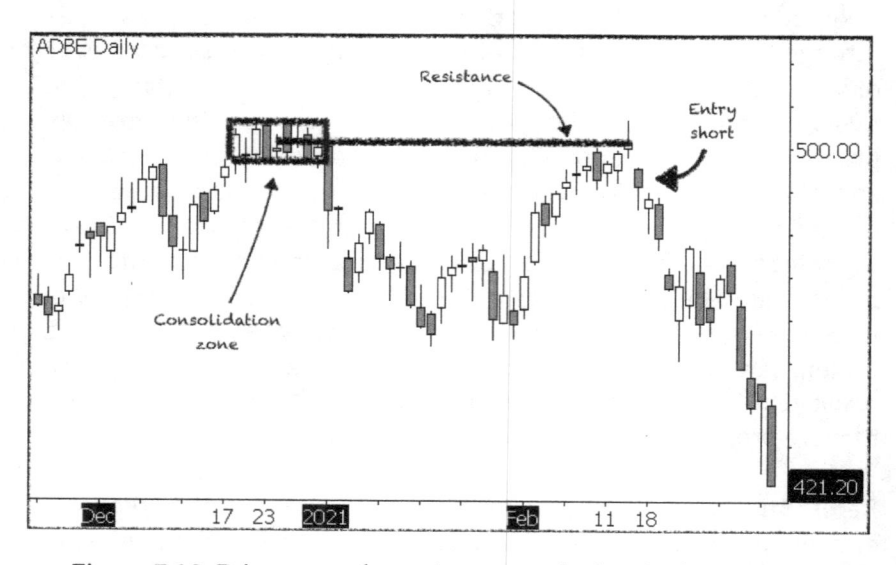

Figure 7.10: Price retest the resistance at the level of consolidation.

See Figure 7.11 for an example where price retest support nears 330 before continuing upward. This strategy creates an excellent opportunity for those who were looking for a better entry point. Price action will either form a pin bar or reversal pattern after retesting support or resistance. Essentially, what you're looking for is a sharp movement in price followed by a period of consolidation. This signals that the market is undecided and is likely to move in the direction of the initial move. So, in the case of our example, you would want to buy when price retests support near 330.

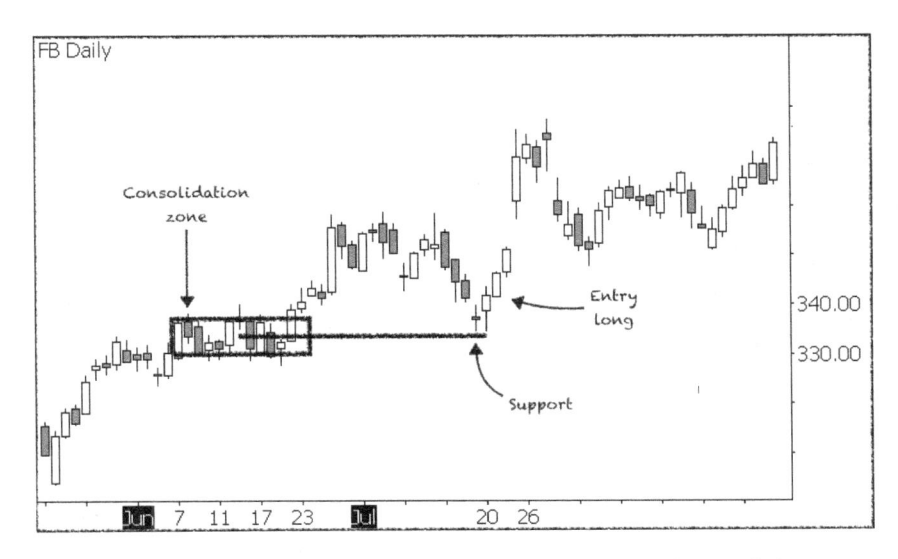

Figure 7.11: Price rebound off support at the level of consolidation.

Consolidation periods are like a holding pattern for stocks. Everyone is just kind of hanging out, waiting to see what will happen next. And during these periods, stocks can make some of their biggest moves. That's because they're necessary for identifying accumulation and distribution zones, which is where the "larger players" utilize them to enter their larger positions. Breakouts are one of the most powerful tools in a trader's arsenal. They can be used for both short-term and long-term trading, with many traders using them as part of their daily routine. But if you don't know how to properly use breakouts, they won't help you. That's because breakouts usually occur during consolidation periods, and if you don't know how to identify those periods, you'll miss the opportunity to make money. So, if you want to be a successful trader, learn how to properly use breakouts and consolidations periods. It'll help you make a lot more money in the long run.

MOMENTUM PATTERN

Traders usually have a hard time identifying the exact entry and exit points, especially with candlestick patterns. It is important that you know how to spot these patterns with regard to making the right trades. For an easy-to-spot pattern that will help you identify the trend, a "rapid" movement in price is known as the Momentum Pattern. In this section, I will teach you step-by-step how to identify momentum, and what it means when it appears on your stock chart.

For me, I need to know when the market is trending and when it's not. Using momentum is a great way to identify a change in trend or confirmation of current trend. When candlesticks are wide with little-to-no tails or shadows, this is called a wide-range bar. This means that the opening or closing price is near the low or high price. If the wide-range bar is followed by several bars moving rapidly in that direction, these are called Momentum Bars. Momentum can show up as a single bar or series of white or green bars when bullish, and red or black bars when bearish (See Figure 7.12). This pattern can be seen in all time frames and are very easy to trade because they have clear signals.

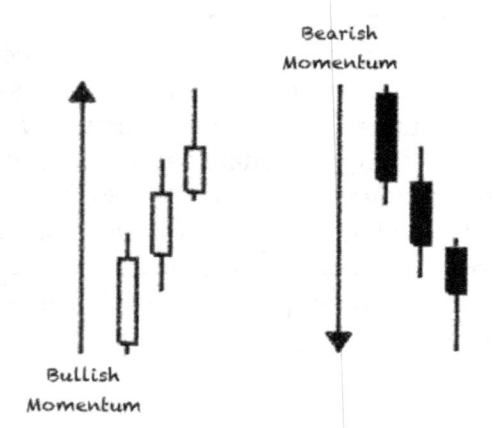

Figure 7.12: Consecutive candles in the same direction shoes momentum.

What is the market thinking? The wide range bar candlestick pattern can be used to get an idea of what the future direction of a stock price will be. Buying and selling stocks is like two teams playing tug-of-war, each fighting for control. Sometimes one team dominates so much that it is able to force its opponent to give way. As a result, the spike in price gives us valuable insight into the market sentiment by telling us there is more buyer/seller pressure in one direction than the other, and there are little fluctuations. Let's call the two types of wide-range-bars what they are and give them different names: bullish and bearish bars.

In a bullish bar, the open price is near the low and the close price is near the high. This bar shows how many buyers were willing to pay higher prices for a stock on the given day. When this bar appears after an uptrend, it indicates that traders are still bullish about the stock and will buy it at any price. But the moment a wide range bar appears in a downtrend, it typically means that sentiment has changed, and the market is now bullish. A trader should look for buying opportunities because we might see bullish patterns over the next few days. The first bullish bar to break the high of the last bar in the downtrend is known as a "bullish" Surge Bar.

In a bearish bar, the open price is near the high and the close price is near the low. A bearish bar is a candlestick pattern that shows the market's downward momentum. The bearish bar indicates that sellers are in control of the market and will continue to drive prices lower. If a bearish candlestick appears in an upward trend, the bearish bar is a reversal pattern that forms after an uptrend. It indicates the sentiment of the market has changed from bullish to bearish. The first bearish momentum bar to break the low of the last bar in the uptrend is also known as a "bearish" Surge Bar (See Figure 7.13).

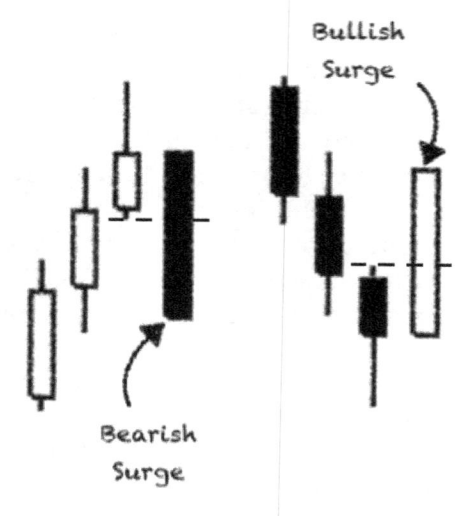

Bullish Surge

Bearish Surge

Figure 7.13: Surge in the opposite direction of trend indicating change in the trend.

In the case of bar trading, I tend to enter into the first formation of a bar with the expectation that the price will continue to move in that direction. For example, look at Figure 7.14, it's a daily chart of Adobe that depicts a bullish bar followed by a bullish move. Even though the price dips momentarily, it continues to be bullish after that. So, in this case, I would have made money by being bullish on Adobe.

One signal alone is not enough to justify a trade. Knowing supply and demand zones solves this problem by showing me exactly what happened before the trend started, as well as why it started. With these two pieces of information I can finally make smart trades based on these predictable patterns. So, stay tuned as we explore the basics of supply and demand zones. We'll also look at how these two types of zones work together to create an effective trading strategy that will help you.

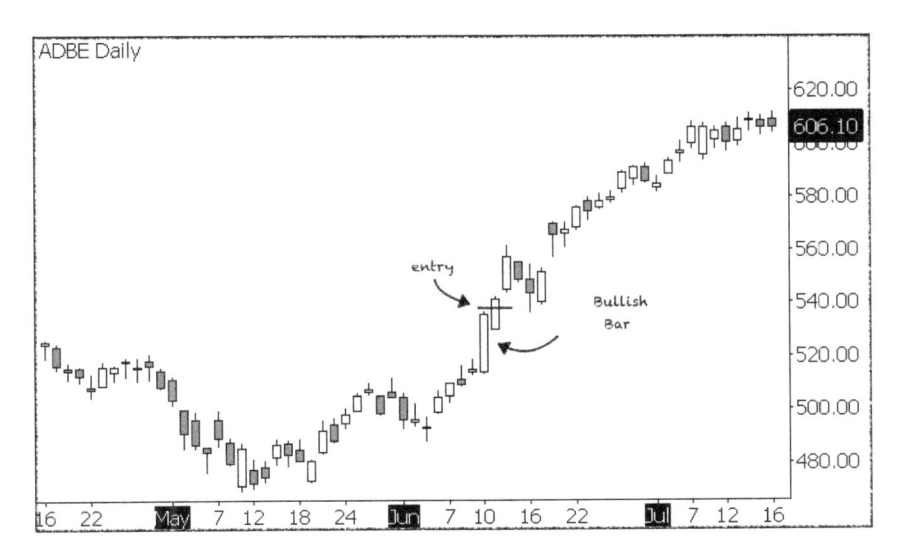

Figure 7.14: Daily chart of Adobe with a bullish momentum bar.

Finding supply and demand. If you want to trade with the supply and demand, it is important to identify them first. For a trader, supply-and-demand zones are a powerful tool. Finding them can be hard, especially when you're new to them. They are areas on the chart where price has moved a lot in either direction. They can help you identify areas of selling and buying, which is the backbone of the market. The best way to find supply-and-demand zones is by looking for momentum bars. You should look for successive large candles with quick movement in price, as well as establishing where this big move started from a zone of support or resistance. Let's call these candles the Breakout Bars, which are made up of two variants: a surge breaking above resistance, Breakout Bar, or a surge breaking below support, Breakdown Bar.

Breakout Bar, or Breakaway Bar. A Breakout Bar is an important candle where the range of the bar breaks and closes into a "new" confirmed trend. To be a valid Breakout Bar, it should completely cross above or below the previous resistance or support. A Breakout Bar generally signals the start of a trend and has good potential to cause substantial movement in the direction. This type of candle is used in technical analysis when assessing whether to enter a trade or not. Since it doesn't matter in which direction you are trading, these candles will always have some significance because they can be used to confirm supply-and-demand levels.

A price chart of Tesla Motors after it had reached all-time highs before declining into a downward trend is shown in Figure 7.15. After a bounce, a pivot is formed, and TSLA stays in a trading range until its breakaway (Breakout) bar succeeds in breaking through the pivot price. The demand zone that is created by the range on this Breakout Bar acts like a trampoline, where price appears to bounce out. After establishing the Breakout Bar, price frequently trades in the direction of the subsequent Breakout Bar. The numerous trading possibilities that this pattern creates are evident.

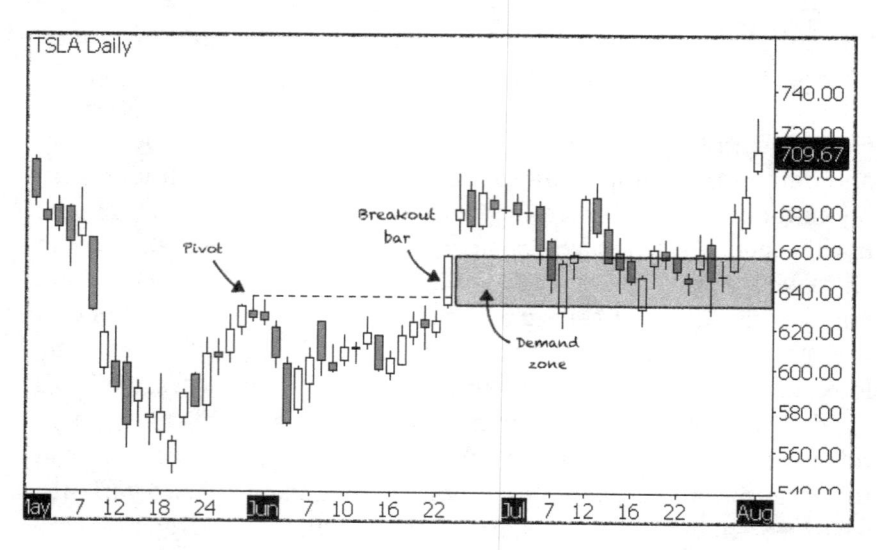

Figure 7.15: Daily chart of Tesla depicting the demand zone of the breakout bar.

Follow-through Bar. We want to make sure that our trades are as profitable as possible. We also don't want to miss out on any opportunities because we missed a signal and entered too early or too late. The follow-through bar is an important pattern to recognize and can help us make better trades. It is the bar that extends far outside the range of the prior bar of any of the varieties of wide-range bar types, the bar that followed in the same direction as the previous bar, as its name implies (See Figure 7.16). You must be able to spot these bars because any entry into the closing may be considered a late entry and more confirmation is required. This bar is also important since a failure might result in price pulling back or reversing.

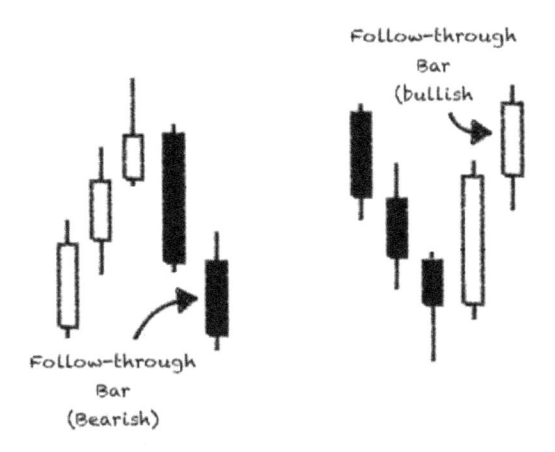

Figure 7.16: Follow-through bar may be considered a late entry.

Momentum Bars Entry Strategy. The momentum bars pattern is a signal that shows strength in the market. It's impossible to determine exactly when price will break out. However, it's easier to forecast a potential continuation after a Breakout Bar because this is the bar that has more power than a normal bar. This is also true with all other types of momentum patterns. When the Breakout Bar is followed through twice by wide-range bars, it's an indication that the price will likely continue even after a retracement. The Momentum Bars are drawn by an arrow indicating the trend's direction and a middle line marking the retracement area, as seen in Figure 7.17.

Using Momentum Bars as a signal for entering into supply and demand: supply and demand zones are not as obvious as support or resistance lines, but using them can be very effective. For example, if I know the areas where buyers and sellers meet, I just place my orders there. But remember that trading around supply and demand zones requires patience, so I always place my limit orders before-hand. In this case, a "speculative" demand zone is created by a Breakout Bar on the Adobe price chart. Instead of taking a position near the top of the Breakout Bar as I did in the previous example, I wait for the Momentum Bars pattern to develop. On a down day, I utilize limit orders placed within the demand zone to anticipate a price pullback and continuation of the trend.

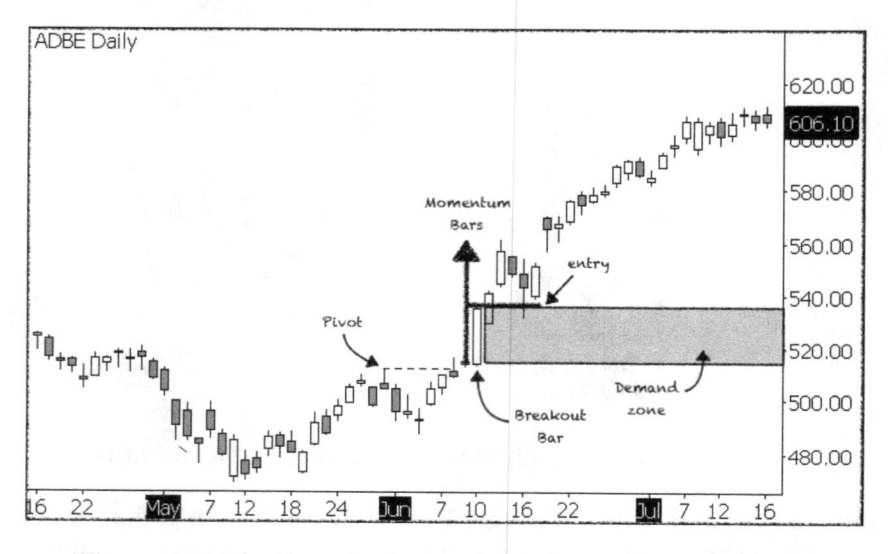

Figure 7.17: Placing order inside the demand zone to enter into a position on a pull back.

As with all candlestick charting patterns, there is no guarantee that they will produce profitable results every time they form. Alt-hough it is important to see what technical analysis is indicating, you also need to be aware of the patterns of which they are part. It is often not too difficult to trade Momentum pattern because one side is gen-erally in control, Bulls or Bears. Take time to study this pattern until you mastered it.

REVERSAL PATTERN

Reversal patterns are a great way for traders to identify potential turning points in the market. In this section, I will go over some of the most common reversal patterns and provide examples on how they can be traded. We will also discuss what makes each pattern unique and when it is best used. A reversal is a pattern that occurs at the end of a trend, and it can be either bullish or bearish. To be a valid reversal pattern, the market needs to have been in an uptrend or downtrend before it forms.

Let's say a bearish reversal pattern occurs at the end of an uptrend, which shows that traders are starting to panic and sell shares. This usually occurs near resistance levels that are previous areas of interest where traders will attempt to sell. On the other hand, a bullish reversal pattern occurs at the end of a downtrend that shows that traders are starting to get nervous and begin to buy back shares to cover their short. In both cases, reversals usually occur near price levels that are previous areas where people will attempt to exit or enter their trades. In fact, the better way to identify a reversal pattern is by looking for a bounce near resistance in an uptrend, or a bounce near support in a downtrend, as shown in Figure 7.18.

Ultimately, there are many different ways that traders use reversal patterns, but there are two main types of trading strategies that utilize them: Pinocchio (also known as the Pin Bar) and engulfing. Both strategies have their merits, depending on your risk tolerance, strategy, and personality as a trader. So, it is important to understand which strategy fits you best before committing capital toward any one specific type of setup. Now let's get started!

 When trading reverses, traders will often look for price action confirmation in the form of candlesticks, such as the bearish or bullish engulfing pattern.

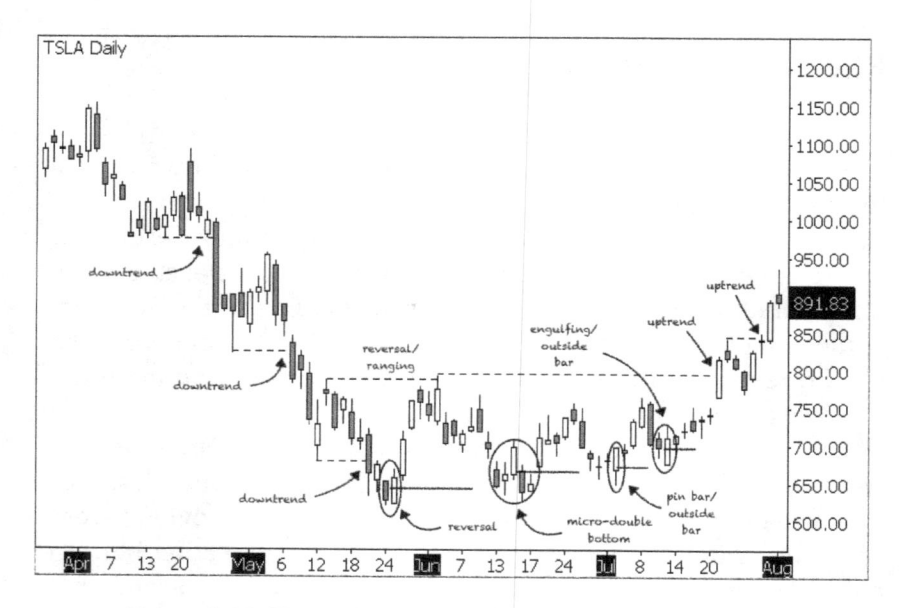

Figure 7.18: Use resistance to identify reversal patterns.

Engulfing Pattern. As mentioned earlier, reversal patterns usually take two or more days to form. Also taking into consideration the relationship between the candlestick bodies for both days, the tails are not consequential to the formation of this pattern. As shown in Figure 7.19, the bullish engulfing pattern occurs when the body of a white (or green) candlesticks completely covers the body of one or more black (or red) candles. The bearish engulfing pattern occurs whenever there is a bearish candle (red or black) that completely engulfs (or covers) the body of one or more white (or green) candles.

Bullish Engulfing. When the bullish engulfing pattern occurs, there is a transition from the bearish to the bullish trend. When this pattern appears at the bottom of a downtrend, this pattern provides the strongest signal and indicates an increase in buying pressure. If large enough, this pattern frequently causes a reversal of an existing trend as more buyers enter the market, driving prices even higher. The large bullish candle indicates that buyers are aggressively entering the market, providing the initial bias for further upward momentum.

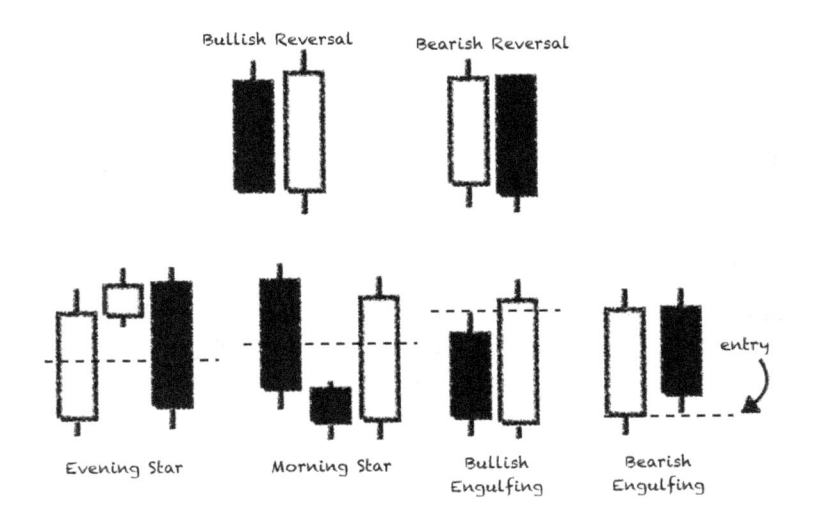

Figure 7.19: Various types of engulfing patterns.

Bearish Engulfing. The bearish engulfing pattern is the inverse of the bullish pattern. When it appears at the top of an uptrend, it provides the strongest signal and indicates an increase in selling pressure. The bearish engulfing pattern frequently signals a reversal of an existing trend as more sellers enter the market, driving prices even lower. The pattern also consists of two candles, with the second or more candles engulfing the previous green candle's "body." When the bearish pattern appears, price action must show a clear uptrend. The large bearish candle indicates that sellers are aggressively entering the market, providing the initial bias for further downward momentum.

I will then use indicators, levels of support and resistance, and subsequent price action that occurs after the engulfing pattern to confirm whether or not the trend is indeed turning around. Engulfing patterns help traders spot reversals, indicate a strengthening trend, and can also provide an exit signal.

The engulfing candle is a candlestick pattern that can be used for trading reversals, continuation, and exits. It's important to remember that the engulfing candle is just one piece of the puzzle and that it should not be used as a standalone indicator. The best way to trade is by using a combination of indicators in conjunction with support and resistance levels, or using other trading indicators, such as RSI, CCI, or a stochastic for trade confirmation. By doing this, traders can increase their chances of success and avoid getting caught up in false signals.

Outside Bar. Trading outside bars can be exceptionally difficult in comparison to their counterparts because it is difficult to anticipate which direction the price will go, and they commonly do not follow the market trend. Most traders are unaware of the existence of trading an outside bar and regularly lose money by buying or selling at the wrong time. This bar has a higher high than the previous bar and a lower low than the previous bar. The prior bar takes up the majority of the previous bar. Because the new outside bar is larger than the previous bar, it indicates that both bulls or bears had dominance at some point during that time period, with one being slightly more dominant because the close of this bar extends out more than the previous day. This would almost certainly result in a reversal over the next few bars. The outside bar is related to the engulfing signal because it indicates weakness in a trend which should be taken as a warning to avoid entry in the wrong direction at this point. Figure 7.20 shows the outside bar pattern.

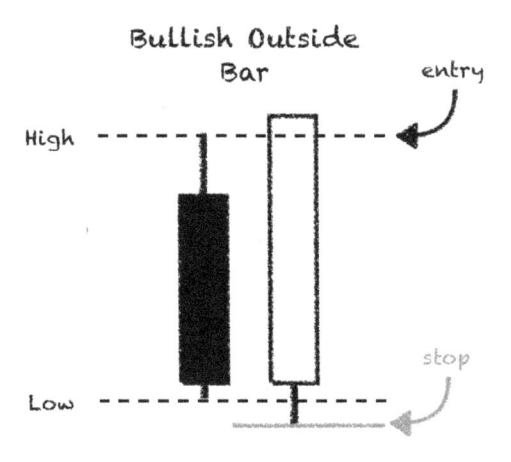

Figure 7.20: Outside bar.

Pin Bar or Rejection. Pin bars are a popular reversal pattern, but many traders don't know about them. Most traders don't know how to identify them in real time, and when they do spot one, it's too late. A Pin Bar is either a bullish/bearish reversal pattern that occurs at the end of a trend. It usually happens near support or resistance levels that were previous areas of interest. When these patterns form, it means that traders are starting to get nervous.

The upper tail represents selling pressure while the bottoming tail represents buying pressure. In Figure 7.21, you see the structure of a pin bar and its variations. The candle's distinctive structural features include a long tail, a compact body, and a short tail on the opposite side. The long tail of a pin bar should be at least two-thirds of the total candle length.

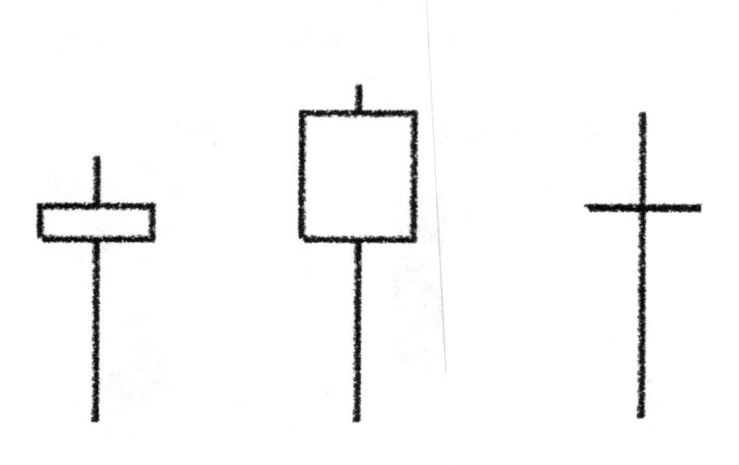

Figure 7.21: Various types of pin bars.

A tail of a pin bar is a rejection zone where major market players have responded at a certain level. The tail has previously been part of the body of the candle before it closes into a pin bar. In other words, before it closed, the pin bar candle had displayed a significant amount of activity in the direction of the trend. As a result, this may suggest that the trend will continue, which is the contrary idea. The enlarged tail is then seen as a large candle wick. Typically, "The bigger the nose (wick), the larger the lie."

This is where the name "Pinocchio" originated. As a result, the greater the tail on the pin bar, the more powerful the reversal pressure is anticipated to be. When a trader spots a pin bar, they can anticipate that the price movement that brought the price up will continue into the next candle. Traders may attempt to go long in the indicated setup, anticipating price will rebound from the pin bar's low values and rise. It's important to remember that not all Pin Bar opportunities are "tradable," (See Figure 7.22).

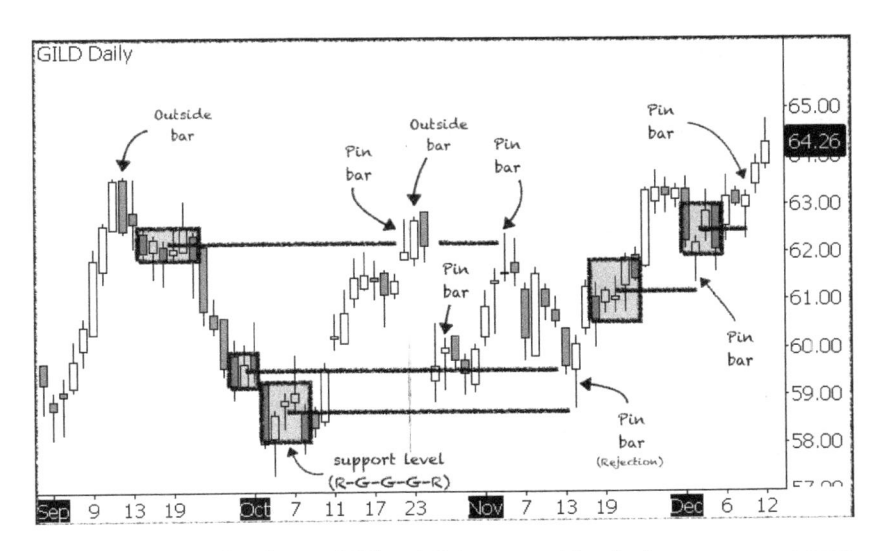

Figure 7.22: Daily chart of Gilead Sciences with pin bars near support
and resistance.

Pin bars are inherently inconsistent with present price movement. Take a look at what's going on in GILD to see where the pin bar forms with respect to the support and resistance levels. A common rejection of the support/resistance level is also seen. At the time the candle was forming, it looked like a breakout and a continuation to the downside. But once the candle was complete, all premature sellers were trapped, and the price traded significantly higher. Rejection bars usually have long wicks, penetrating a previous low or high. This shows that the market is rejecting the current price and is likely to move in the opposite direction. It's also possible for a candle to be engulfed by expanding this pattern, as evidenced by the following rejection pattern.

Tweezer Bars or micro-double bottom. This pattern is not as easy to spot as some others, but once you learn how to identify it, you will understand why this reversal pattern works so well. The bearish tweezer is a reversal formation that occurs when the market fails to make a higher high. On the other side, the bullish tweezer is a reversal pattern where the market has failed to make a lower low. It can be used as an early warning of a possible trend change, and it can also be used for confirmation with another indicator. It can signal the end and the beginning of a new trend. Generally, it is two candles occurring after a strong trend (See Figure 7.23).

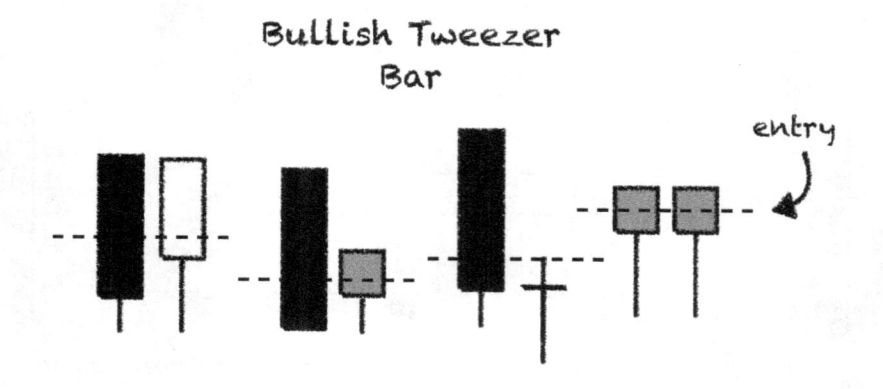

Figure 7.23: Various tweezer bars.

For this pattern to work best, the first candle must open near its high or low and the second candle must open at the close of the previous candle. This ensures that there are no gaps between the two candles. If there is a significant gap between these two candles, then it's likely not a tweezers formation and should be ignored. When identifying tweezers, look at the previous price action before spotting this pattern as a way to have more conformation in your trade entry point. Shown in Figure 7.24.

The Tweezers Pattern occurs after a strong trend and signals the start of a trend. Many traders miss the Tweezers Pattern because they are looking for a longer-term signal. This pattern is so powerful that it can confirm trend reversals within hours after being formed. A tweezers trading strategy requires two pin bars. Identifying this price action tells us that there has been a change in momentum because the candles have closed at or near their highs. This pattern shows us that participants have been able to push price twice, but they were unable to hold it there for very long. The other traders then stepped in and took price back in the opposite direction.

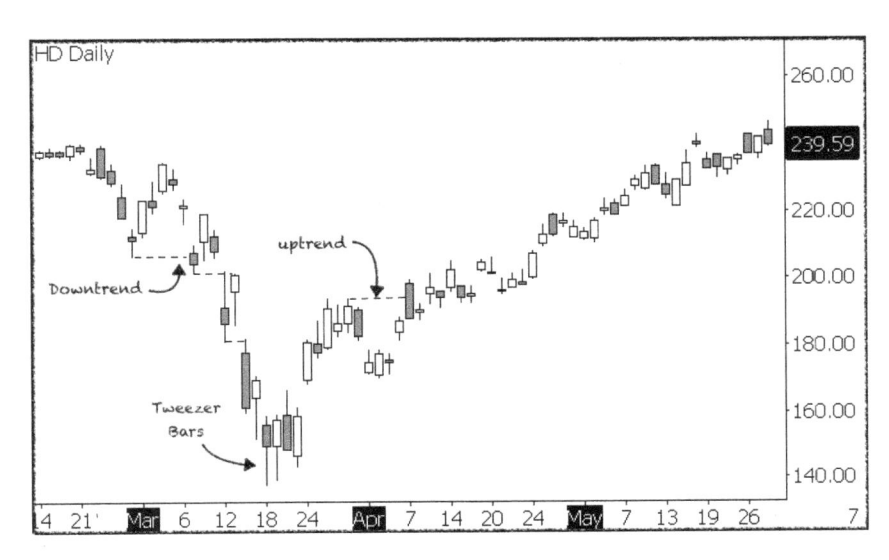

Figure 7.24: Daily chart of Home Depot with a tweezer pattern near the lows.

Exhaustion Bar. An exhaustion candle is an important indicator of a reversal of a trend. It is a candlestick pattern that typically forms at the end of an extended move, and it signals that the market is running out of steam (See Figure 7.25). An exhaustion candle is usually followed by a period of consolidation or a reversal. Exhaustion candles are not to be used as a primary signal to enter a trade. Instead, they are best used in conjunction with other indicators to confirm an end of a trend.

First, we need the exhaustion candle to be in the right place in your charts. This means that the candle should be at a key level of support or resistance. Second, we need to see some other confirmation that the trend is indeed exhausted. Finally, we need to see some follow-through after the exhaustion candle has formed.

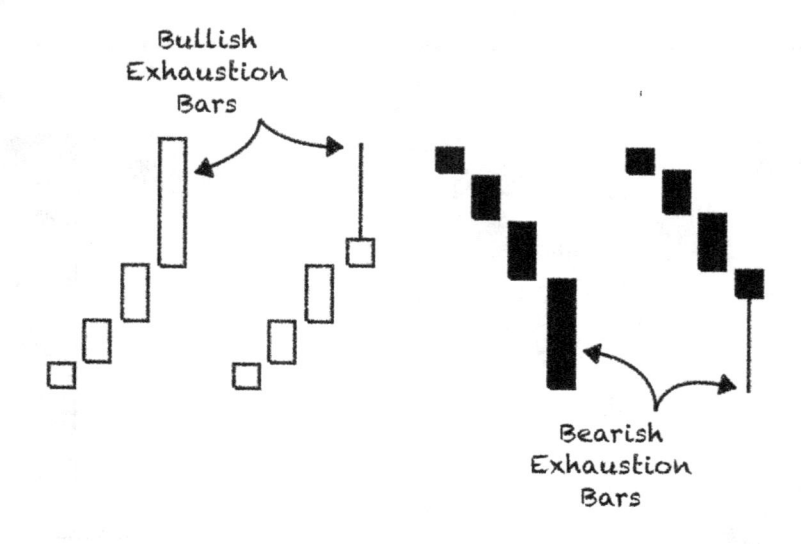

Figure 7.25: Various exhaustion candle patterns

If you spot an exhaustion candle on a chart, pay attention to the price action that follows. If the market starts to consolidate or reverse after the candle forms, this could be an indication that the trend is indeed coming to an end. However, if the market continues to move in the same direction after the exhaustion candle forms, this is not a good sign, and you should be cautious. An important thing to remember is that not all exhaustion candles are created equal. Some can be very small and insignificant, while others can be very large and powerful. It is important to use your discretion when trading exhaustion candles. If you see a small candle at the end of a long trend, it is probably not worth taking the trade.

Identifying reversals should be no longer a mystery—they allow the trader to enter a trade at the optimal level and ride the trend to completion. The engulfing candle is just one tool that traders can use to identify reversals. Trend continuation—Traders can use the reversal pattern to support the continuation of an existing trend as a way to identify a pullback. For example, spotting a bearish engulfing pattern during a downtrend gives traders more confidence that the trend will continue. Also, spotting a bullish reversal pattern during an uptrend gives traders more confidence that the trend will continue. Exit strategy—If the trader has a position in an existing trend that is about to end, the pattern can be used as a signal to exit the trade. For example, if the trader is in a long position and spots a bearish engulfing pattern, it could be an indication that the trend is about to end, and they should exit the trade.

RETRACEMENT PATTERN

I'm a trend trader, but the problem is that it's not always easy to see when the trend will continue or reverse. For instance, the market is trending up; however, I don't know how long the trend will last. When a pullback occurs in an uptrend, it can be hard to tell whether or not if the pullback is enough information to speculate if trend will continue. As a result, I use the Retracement Pattern as my guide to me help identify price direction. The Retracement Pattern is a trend continuation pattern that occurs during an uptrend or downtrend. Looking for Inside or Pullback Bars followed by a Continuation bar is one way to identify this pattern. The Inside Bar is among the more reliable patterns in technical analysis. They are common type of price-action bar that occurs in an uptrend or downtrend, but it's not the same as just an indecision, Doji or a spinning top.

The Inside Bar is used as a continuation signal, and they're easy to spot. The Pullback Bars are made up of a set of opposed bars with a specific configuration. The Continuation Bar is the bar that ignites from the Inside or Pullback Bar pattern to continue the trend. Retracement Pattern is a common chart pattern that can be used to trade the market. The problem with this pattern is that it can look very similar to other patterns and it's easy to get confused. It's also hard for new traders to understand how this pattern works in relation to price action without a clear guide. In this section, I will explain what an Inside Bar and continuation bar pattern is and how they work in relation to price action. I will then show some examples of real trades that were traded using this method. Then I'll go through how to spot the pull-back bars in detail and give examples.

These two patterns can be used together as part of your trading strategy to spot a start of a trend continuation.

Inside Bar. The market is either trending or not. When it is trending, it usually starts with either a Surge Bar or breakaway bar igniting from a base pattern. The next bar is normally thin or nonexistent, and neither the bulls nor the bears dominated this bar. If there is a body, it means that the close trended away from the open and that the bar has a narrow trend. The entire pattern consists of two (or more) bars, with the bar to the left engulfing the bar to the right. The bar on the right is referred to as an Inside bar since it seems to be "inside" the bar to the left. Inside bar is a small, brief pause that can goes against the trend and is unable to match the bar that is before it (See Figure 7.26).

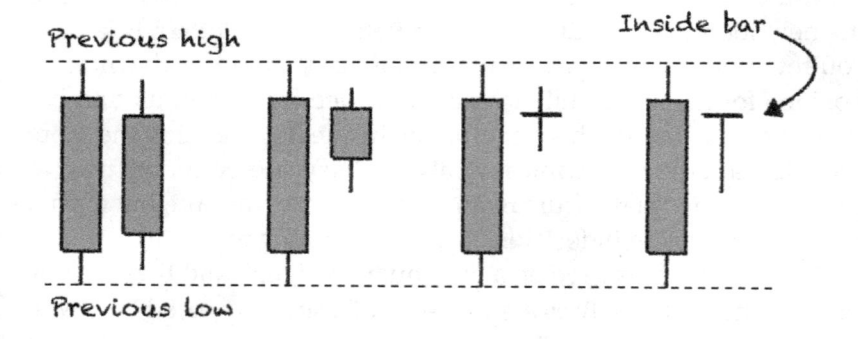

Figure 7.26: Various types of inside bar patterns.

The Inside Bar pattern is very similar to the Consolidation Bar pattern. However, there are a few differences. Although both patterns have some similarities, the Inside Bar has one major difference from the Consolidation Bar pattern that makes it unique and more effective than its counterpart. The Inside Bar is distinguished by the bar that precedes it, which must be a Breakout or a powerful Surge Bar. The inside bar also closes and opens within the parent bar's range. If either the open or close are outside but near the parent's bar range, it can be still classified as an Inside Bar; but use with discretion.

It might seem strange that an Inside Bar is a strong indicator of a trend continuation, but the reason is simple. When a stock has been moving in one direction for a while, it will run into some support or resistance. With the relentless force of the trend, price will eventually break through and continue on, making the Inside Bar indicator an excellent form of contrarian trading. This pattern indicates indecision by buyers and sellers that typically leads to continuation of the prior trend direction. This lack of clarity about which way prices will move after an indecisive period can make traders uncomfortable, so they typically wait for confirmation before entering trades. Inside Bars are usually small and don't have much volume behind them, so they may be hard to spot if you aren't looking for them specifically. However, traders who are able to identify Inside Bars as they form have a huge advantage over those who cannot spot them until after they continue.

Using Inside Bars as a signal for continuation. Inside Bars are a very powerful momentum play that can be traded in either direction. In order for an Inside Bar trade setup to work well, there needs to be some sort of direction present in the market first. Finding the right price to enter a trade can be difficult, especially when you're new. When using this setup, you have two choices: buying into strength (buying high) or selling into weakness (selling low). A buy signal occurs when the price breaks the high/low of the previous bar; however, these signals are defined differently by traders. The traditional (or conservative) entry for a Continuation Bar signal is to put a buy or sell stop order (or stop-limit) at the highs or lows of the previous bars (usually the parent bar) so your entry order is filled when the price breakouts into newer high or low prices (See Figure 7.27).

The aggressive method is to place a stop order one tick beyond the high or low of the inside bar, depending on whether you're going long or short. A buy or sell stop at the high or low of the parent bars is the best entry for an Inside Bar signal, so your entry order is filled when the price breaks out into new price territory. Traders often use

Inside Bars as an entry signal because they are easy to spot and offer solid risk/reward ratios. It should be determined by how aggressive your approach is—if you don't want to take less risk, go for something more aggressive, like an Inside Bar. If you want to take more risk, go with the parent bar strategy. The choice is up to you. I believe in the conservative approach, the best way is to place a stop order just beyond the parent bar so you're targeting an entry on the break of the high or low of parent bar, in the direction of the trend.

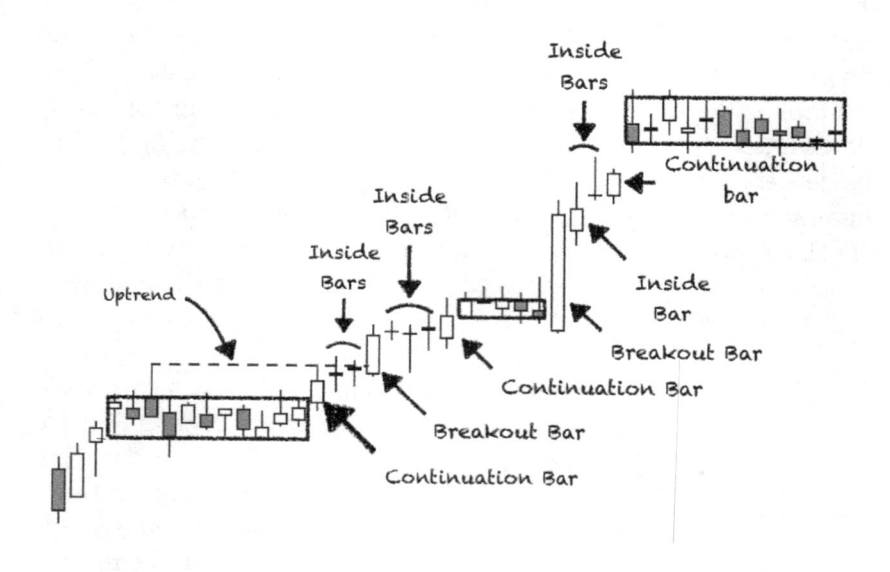

Figure 7.27: Continuation bar signaling a continuation of the trend.

Pullback Bars. A pullback can be observed. Pullback Bars are simply candlestick patterns that indicate when the price has reached a point on either side of its current position, indicating that there may be some consolidation pattern before continuing with the trend. Pullback Bar indicates that there was some sort of retracement within the larger trend, possibly suggesting where future support and resistance levels might be found. You should use Pullback Bars to help you determine when to enter a trade, exit a trade, or avoid trades altogether based on price movements that have already occurred.

This is especially true when understanding retracement in an uptrend or downtrend.

The stock's lowering peaks and troughs can indicate a retracement in an uptrend, and a temporary pause or downtrend can be observed. As a result, there are lower highs and lower lows in price changes. As an uptrend is about to begin, it may be wise to employ a strategy of entering before the price resumes its uptrend. Retracement in a downtrend is the same: a downtrend can be observed when the peaks and troughs are rising. Prices might be observed as higher highs and higher lows in that uptrend. This indicates that it is time to sell before a downtrend develops (See Figure 7.28).

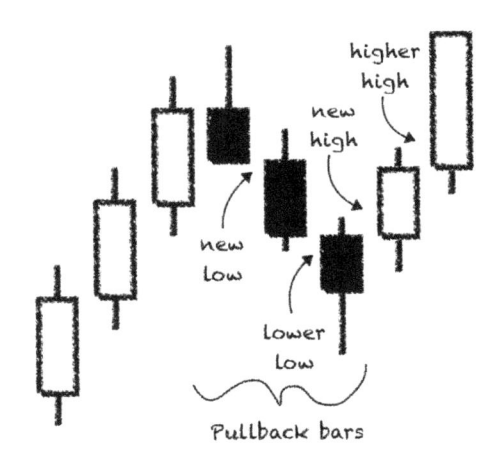

Figure 7.28: Pullback bars depicted in an uptrend.

Continuation Bar, or Surge Bar. A Continuation Bar is a technical analysis tool that can be used as a trading signal. A Continuation Bar is a signal that the pullback is to discontinue. When the price has moved to a certain point, it may start moving even further in that same direction. Continuation Bars are sometimes considered to be reversal patterns, but they are not a signal for change in trend. They are simply a signal that the price is continuing to move in its current direction.

The Continuation Bar is one of the most powerful trading bars in technical analysis. It's used to determine when price will continue higher or lower after it has made an abrupt move. The Continuation Bar might serve as a trade signal after it closes above the high of the Inside Bar or the final bar of the pull back bars. Apple was approaching earnings when it sent price into an upward trend after displaying phenomenal earnings. Examine how price pulls back into a lower high and lower lows formation (See Figure 7.29).

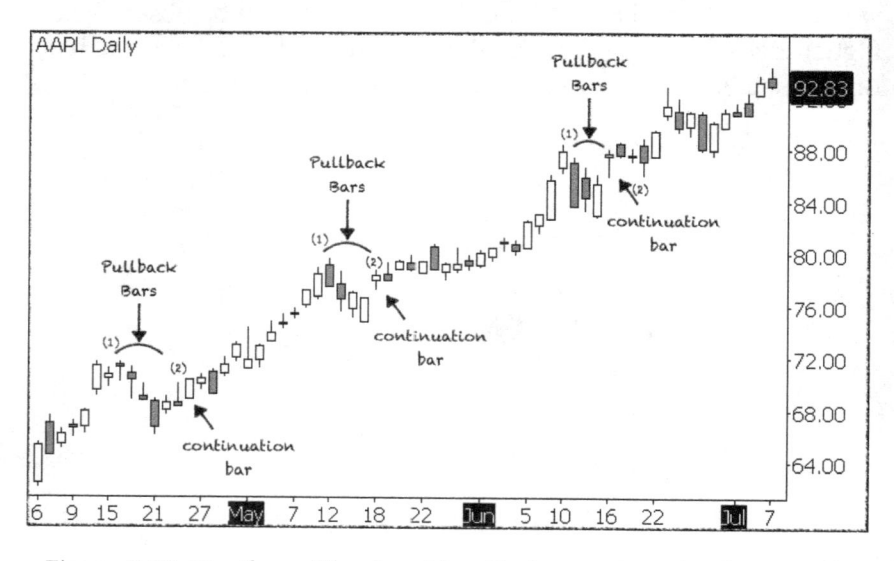

Figure 7.29: Use the pullback to identify the continuation bar signal. Continuation bar at 2. Pullback bars at 1.

When price breaks above the high (or below the low for shorting) of the prior bar, you can enter at that moment, or wait for the end of the day just before the market is about to close. The stop may be set at any of the technical locations beneath the Pullback Bars or elsewhere; it is entirely up to you. It's simple and effective, but it works best when combined with other strategies. To fine-tune this approach, consider trading Continuation Bars that stem from a pattern depicting momentum with retracement patterns that trade in the top portion of the move (See Figure 7.29).

Levels of support and resistance may be established in the retracement pattern, which is where traders are likely to trade both sides of the market. There are bearish traders who are waiting for the price to decline so that they may cover at support to break even. Those who are bullish remain patient and wait for the stock to recover back to resistance so they may break even as well. If price is retracing after an uptrend, take the opening and closing prices of the Pullback Bars; and the first and last bars are Bullish Bars that lie between three opposing bar forming a G-R-R-R-G pattern (See Figure 7.30).The second bar high has a gap open, and the fourth bar low features a closing price at the bottom. A box is drawn around the bars. As you might guess, the line is projected to the right from its mid-point. The downtrend scenario, on the other hand, features resistance sandwiched between bearish trend bars.

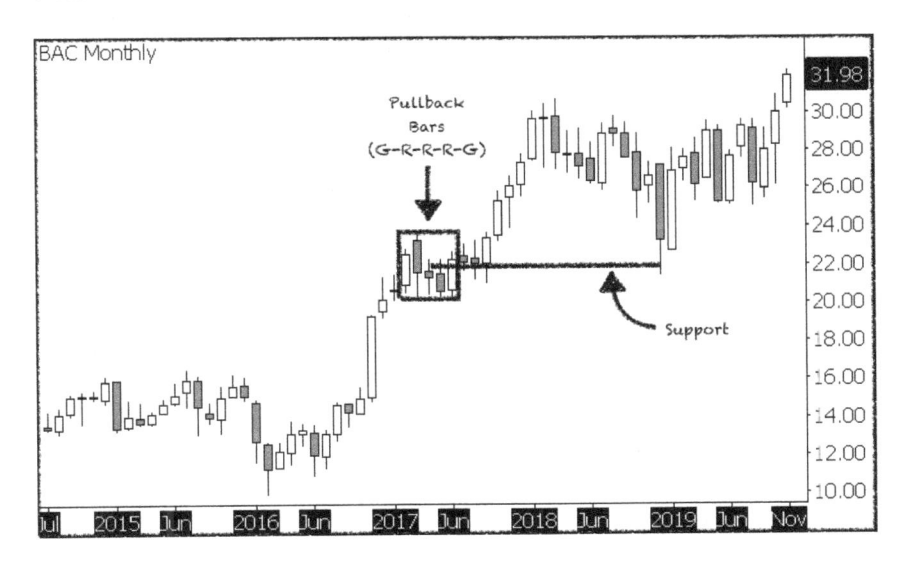

Figure 7.30: Use pullback bars to identify support and resistance.

A pullback is when price moves down for a period of time before continuing its uptrend. This can be caused by many different factors, but it typically occurs because traders on both sides of the market start taking profits or exiting their positions. Identifying a pullback is an excellent method to determine where potential support and resistance levels may be found. The following is a monthly chart of Bank of America that experienced a pullback that lasted for three months before resuming its uptrend. Many investors have flooded in from both sides of the market during this pullback. The price dropped to $22, and those who had entered at that level started reacting once more by pushing the price up into a multi-month uptrend. A large number of investors might place an order at support in the event that the price will drop to retest and reverse direction. In this situation, placing a limit order at $22 in advance provides a good trading opportunity. You may also use the $22 price range as a clue to find better entries in a lower time frame. As a consequence, your accuracy will improve.

In conclusion, one of the most popular technical analysis trading patterns is a bar with a retracement price movement. The retracement pattern is a fairly straight-forward pattern to spot. An understanding of the price mechanics behind this pattern will give a clearer picture. It is important to note that this pattern only works well during periods when there is a clear overall upward or downward momentum trend in price; otherwise, it may indicate nothing more than a temporary pause in price action. You can use this strategy for any time frame and any market—It's used by traders of all levels and styles because it provides an easy entry point into a trending market—so if you want to be more aggressive, make sure you place your stop order just beyond that bar on the left side for some great entries.

GAP PATTERN

Gaps are areas on a chart where the price moves sharply higher or lower, with little or no trading in between. Gaps can occur at the beginning or end of a trading session, or during the session when there is a significant event that causes an influx of buying or selling pressure such as a circuit breaker halt. A stock market circuit breaker halt can create gaps in the market where prices can change dramatically. For example, if a stock is halted due to a circuit breaker, the price may jump or drop when trading resumes. Gaps can also form when there is a sudden change in market conditions, such as a shift in supply and demand dynamics. All gaps share some common characteristics. For example, all gaps have an opening and closing price, with the latter being higher or lower than the former, depending on whether it's an up gap or down gap.

There's always a chance for a gap. Gaps occur when the opening price of a stock is substantially different than its closing price from the previous day, and they can be classified as either "bullish" or "bearish." The key factor that the two types have in common is that they happen unexpectedly and can often determine a long-term trend in your stock. The next factor that must be determined is the direction of the gap. There are only two possible directions—bullish or bearish. This is somewhat self-explanatory, as a bullish gap would be one that is formed with the opening price being higher than the previous day's closing price. However, most traders have special names for each type of gap that helps to identify the bullish or bearish nature.

Common gaps. Common gaps are the most basic type of gap and simply occur when there is a sudden shift in market conditions. This type of gap is not necessarily predictive of future price action, but it can give some clues as to where price might go in the short term. A gap that forms in between two sessions of trading when there is a sudden jump in price. They are the most common type of gap pattern that are also used in intra-day trading. They can be reliable indicators of identifying upward or downward momentum, and usually appear after a period of consolidation. However, they can also appear in the middle of a trend, causing traders to question if momentum has been lost or gain. The pros of common gaps are that they are an indication of a strong move in price and often lead to a period of consolidation or start of momentum. The cons of common gaps are that they can fail, which can lead to an unexpected reversal in the trend.

Various forms of gaps exist, bullish and bearish gaps, along with partial ones (See Figure 7.31).

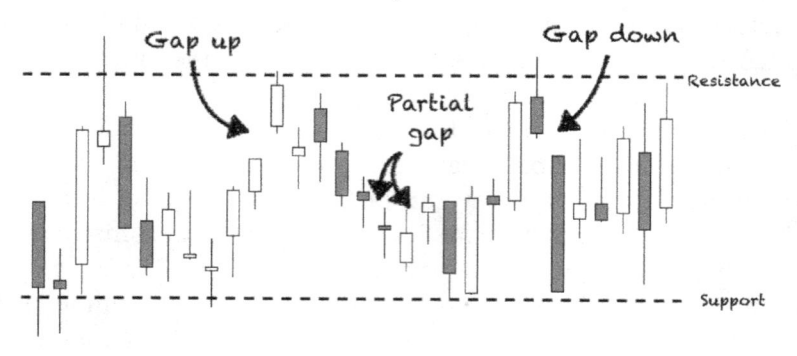

Figure 7.31: Various type of common gaps

Partial gap. The Partial Gap is a very useful signal for traders. It can tell you the possible strength of how far prices would go, which could be a signal that prices are trending into new territory or held back due to uncertainty. By using this signal, traders can take advantage of this gap. They may be able to get into a position that offers lower risk and greater reward potential if they believe the gap will be filled by market close. Partial gaps can be difficult to interpret, so traders should exercise caution before entering into a position based on them (See Figure 7.32 on right).

Bullish gap. A bullish gap is like a big smile on the face of the stock market. It's a very bullish signal that indicates strength in the underlying stock. Large bullish gaps are relatively rare, but when they do occur, they are usually very reliable and profitable trading opportunities. The key to trading a bullish gap is to be patient and wait for the right opportunity to enter. Don't try to trade every bullish gap you see; only trade the ones that offer a clear and convincing setup. When you do trade a bullish gap, don't be afraid to hold on to your position for a while; these trades often have excellent upside potential.

With Japanese candlesticks, a bullish gap is defined as one where the opening price is higher than the close and high of the previous candlestick (See Figure 7.32 on left). In other words, there was some serious demand at the open, which suggests that investors believe that this stock is on the rise. Furthermore, it's also an indication that demand could continue to push prices higher throughout the day. So, if you're considering entering into this stock, the market's open might be a good time to do so.

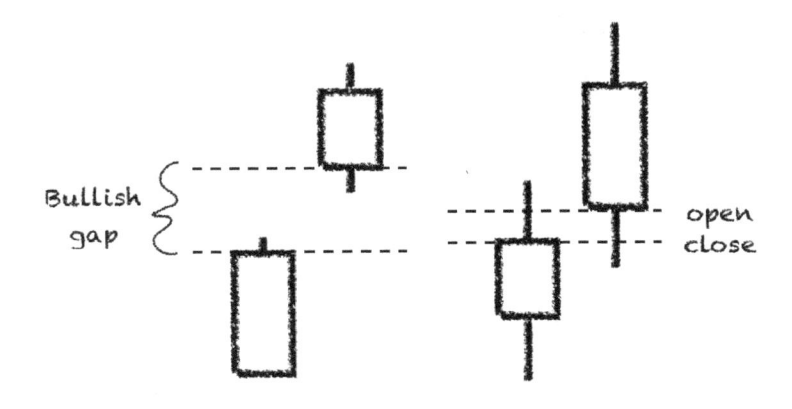

Figure 7.32: Bullish gap and partial bullish gap.

This happens frequently in a bearish trend after some unexpected good news for investors comes out–although it's not as significant as it would be in a bullish trend, it may signal a trend reversal. So, if you see this happen and you're thinking of trading, beware–things might not be what they seem.

Bearish gap. A bearish gap is like a bad breakup—it happens during a downtrend, and it signals further downward movement. This type of candlestick pattern occurs when the price opens lower than the low of the previous candle (See Figure 7.33). When you see this pattern, it's generally a good idea to sell the stock. After all, who wants to keep falling when they're already down? A bearish gap is a type of chart pattern that can signal a potential reversal in prices. This often occurs after an uptrend, and can be seen as a sign that the buyers are losing control and the sellers are taking over. Bearish gaps can be used as a trading signal, but should be confirmed by other indicators before entering into a position.

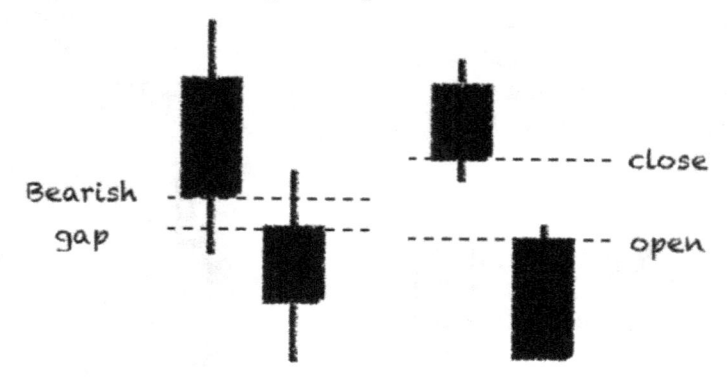

Figure 7.33: Partial bullish gap and bullish gap.

This gap frequently occurs in the aftermath of unexpected investor news. So, if you see a bearish gap emerge, don't immediately panic. Instead, take a step back and assess the situation. It could be a sign that a new trend is beginning.

Technical analysts analyze gap formations into four categories. common, continuation, breakaway, and exhaustion. Each type has its own set of features that may be used to predict the future direction of prices. Also they don't necessarily signal anything about future price movement and are often quickly filled. Continuation gaps occur during an ongoing trend and signal that the trend is likely to continue. Breakaway gaps form at the beginning of a new trend and signal a potential change in direction. Exhaustion gaps occur at the end of a trend and signal that the trend is running out of steam and could soon reverse course. Although there are four types of gaps— Common Gaps, Breakaway Gaps, Continuation Gaps and Exhaustion Gaps—which differ from one another based upon their location within the trend (See Figure 7.34).

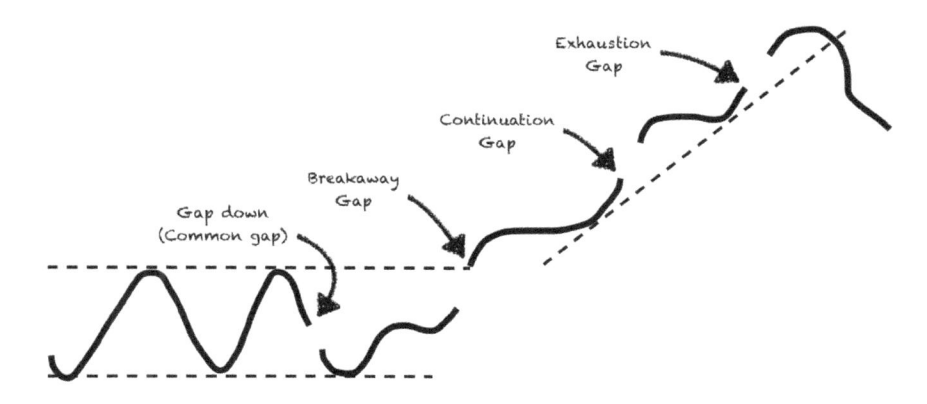

Figure 7.34: Using gap analysis to identify price cycle.

The problem is that there's no easy way to identify which type of gap has formed until after understanding how price moves. As a trader, it is imperative that you are well-versed in the distinction between the four gap patterns. This knowledge can be used as a predictor of where prices may go. Once you have identified these different types of gaps, it will become easier to spot them in real-time market conditions and use them to make better trades going forward. Gap trading strategies can be used in any time frame, but most often by intra-day swing traders who look for short-term opportunities created when gaps occur on higher-than-normal volume.

Breakaway Gap. Breakaway gaps are a technical analysis pattern that signals the end of one trend and the beginning of a new one. They can appear at any time and should be used as a reversal or continuation pattern. When a stock gaps on high volume, it signals that there is strong buying or selling pressure in the market. This type of move can often lead to price continuing in the direction of the gap. Breakaway gaps are an indication of a strong move in price and should be used as reversals or continuation patterns (See Figure 7.35).

Figure 7.35: Breakaway gap after consolidation.

Continuation Gap. Continuation Gaps occur during an existing trend and signal that the trend is likely to continue. These gaps are typically followed by a period of consolidation or pull back before price resumes its move (See Figure 7.36). A continuation gap forms after an extended trend and is followed by more of the same. Continuation Gaps represent a brief interruption in a trend and usually precede another strong move in the same direction. They occur when there is a large increase in volume.

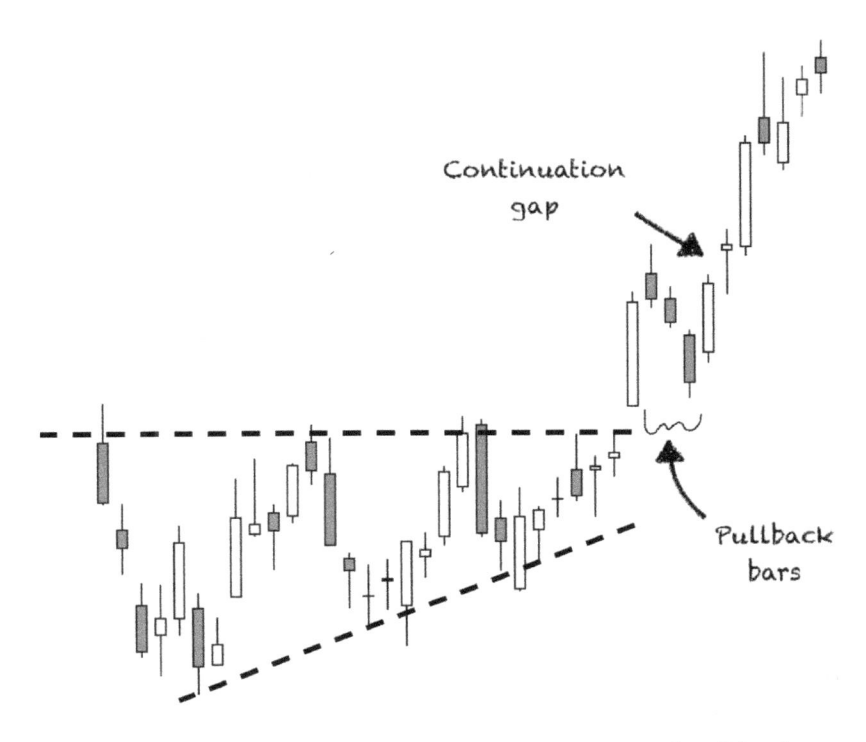

Figure 7.36: Continuation gap after momentum and pull back.

Exhaustion Gap. Exhaustion Gaps occur at the end of a trend and signal that the trend is about to reverse. An exhaustion gap forms at the end of an extended trend and is often followed by a reversal. They are the result of a final burst of momentum. They happen on low volume and usually follow a Breakaway or Continuation Gap. These final bursts of momentum can signal that the trend is over, which also means that the final leg of a bullish or bearish trend is about to end. The climactic activity that occurs during this type of gap allows it to act as confirmation to exit an existing trade or enter into a reversal pattern (See Figure 7.37).

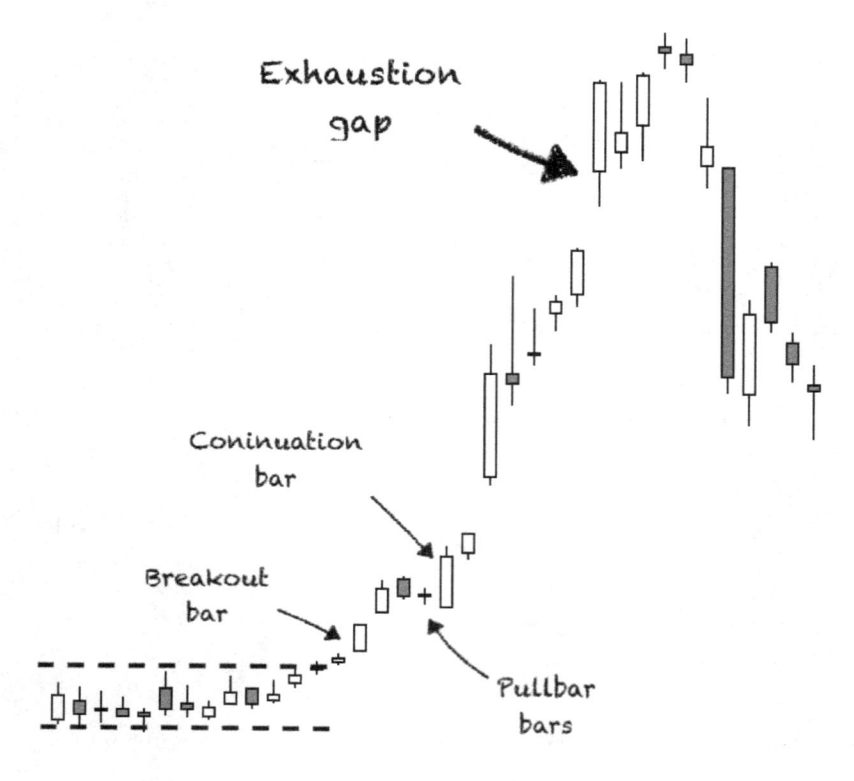

Figure 7.37: Exhaustion gap after a bullish run.

While no one can predict where gaps will form with 100% accuracy, understanding the different types of gaps and what they mean for future price movement can give you an edge in your trading. So, keep an eye out for these different gap patterns in the market and use them to help you make better trading decisions going forward.

VOLUME

If you're like most people, you probably think that volume is just the measure of how loud something is. But in the world of investing, and trading, volume has a whole different meaning. It is a measure of how many shares of a stock are being traded in a given period of time. It can give you important clues about the health of a trend, and can be used to confirm trend reversals, identify price exhaustion moves, and signal potential price reversals. When volume increases as price swings toward one end of a consolidation, it often indicates that a breakout is more likely to occur. However, it should not be used in isolation, and should be combined with other technical analysis tools to get the most accurate picture.

As any trader knows, volume is essential for confirming trends. A rising market should see an increase in volume. With an increase in volume, you can confirm that the trend is sustained—by interest and increasing enthusiasm, which is sure to drive the price of that stock. On the other hand, decreasing volumes with increasing price is a warning signal of lack of interest and may be a sign of an impending trend reversal. The simple fact is that a price rise (or drop) on a small volume is not a strong signal that something in the market has fundamentally changed. A price rise (or drop) on a large volume is a stronger signal that a trend may be ahead. So, if you're looking to confirm a trend, pay close attention to volume!

When analyzing volume, recent history is always the best place to start. After all, data that's even a few days old can be completely irrelevant. And when looking at breakouts vs. false breakouts, volume is key. If there's a big increase in volume on an initial breakout, that's a sign that the move has some serious strength behind it (See Figure 7.38). But if it stays the same or decreases, that's usually a sign of a false breakout. So, pay attention to volume changes–they can tell you a lot about what's really taking place.

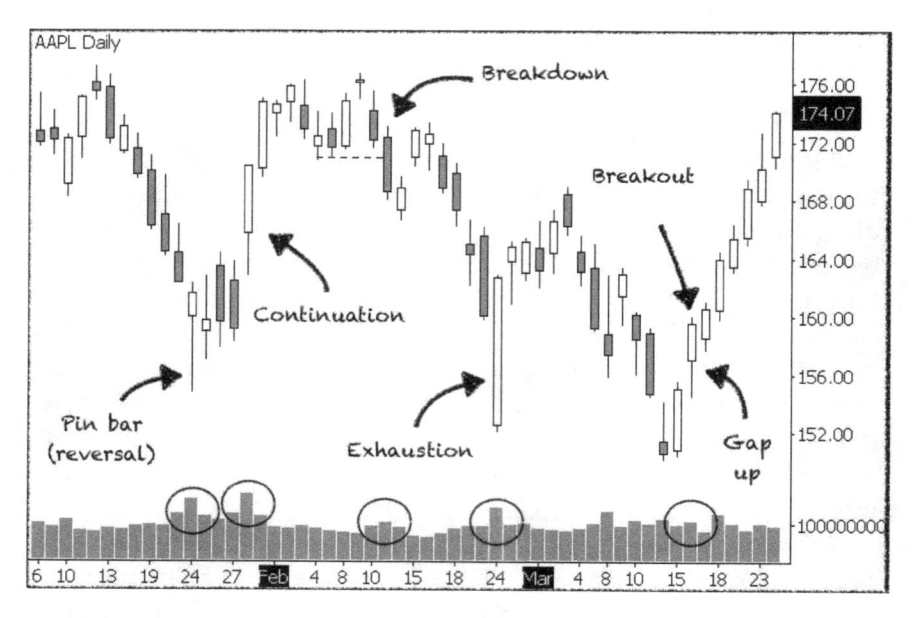

Figure 7.38: Use volume to filter price action.

Exhaustion. We've all been there; that feeling when you just can't do anymore, when you're completely and utterly spent. It's a feeling that's all too familiar in the world of trading. Exhaustion moves are sharp changes in price that are accompanied by a sharp increase in volume, signaling the potential end of a trend (See Figure 7.38). They often happen when traders who don't want to miss out on more of the move pile into the market at tops (in an uptrend), thereby exhausting the trend. In a downtrend, continuous price declines usually force traders out the market at the bottom, resulting in volatility and increased volume. How the volumes play out for subsequent days, weeks, or months can be analyzed using these volume guidelines. So, next time you're feeling exhausted, remember you're not alone. The markets are right there with you.

In conclusion, volume is an important charting tools that primarily gives information about momentum. When analyzing volume, there are a few guidelines that give you hints about the strength or weakness of a move. As a stock trader, you should be inclined toward making trades that show strength and not those showing weaknesses. Alternatively, you could look to enter a position in a direction against the direction of weakness. For instance, if the volume are indicating a very weak bullish momentum, you should look for opportunities to short the market ahead of a trend reversal. You must note: these guidelines may not hold for all situations. They are general and will hold true for most situations.

8 Trend Analysis

Chapter Overview

» Using moving averages for beginners.

» Moving-average method trading strategy.

» Trading consolidation trend patterns.

Tale of William Delbert Gann

Trading can be a confusing and intimidating experience, especially if you're new to it. There are so many strategies and techniques that it can be overwhelming. It is hard to know when to enter into a trade. An American finance trader, William Delbert developed many trading systems and technical analysis tools. He is one of the most renowned traders in history, and he developed a system called the "Gann Wheel" that can help you time your trades for maximum effectiveness. His approach to the markets was based on time, price, and pattern analysis. He believed that all market movements—up, down, or sideways—are a direct result of the time factor and that everything that happens in the market can be explained by geometry, astronomy, and mathematics. His system will ensure that you no longer have to worry about making timing mistakes, such as buying at the highs or selling at the lows.

He was born in 1878 in Texas to a cotton farmer. He was a great student of religion and the Bible, in addition to the knowledge of ancient mathematics, and Greek and Egyptian cultures. Gann began his career as a commodities broker in 1902 and quickly gained a reputation as a skilled investor. His unique approach to market analysis allowed him to make highly accurate predictions about future market movements. In 1908, he founded W.D. Gann & Company, an investment firm that used his unique system of market analysis to guide its clients' trades. The prediction capabilities looked into the political trends, whereby Gann capitalized on his mastery of events to predict political challenges between countries.

The application of the Gann angles to predict the price movement was an important innovation that marked his career. The market events were predicted using astrological events, which indicated how market events repeat in cycles. Gann used this method in 1929 to predict the market crash, and economic depression. This period did not affect Gann, since he had predicted the timelines based on his methods.

Gann died in 1955, but most of his literature has been set for scientific evaluation, given that he used complex ideologies to predict markets. His unique approach to trading made him one of the most successful investors of his time. His legendary status continues to this day, as his ideas and methods are still studied by those seeking to find an edge in the financial markets. Gann's philosophy of predicting financial periods has received criticism, due to its applicability. However, the literature that he left has been used to develop the modern-day investment strategies. Using the Gann method predicted the financial crisis in 2019.

Gann's techniques were based on his theory that there are natural rhythms and cycles in the markets that can be identified and used to make predictions. He believed that by understanding these rhythms, it was possible to forecast market turning points in advance. One of the most famous techniques he developed was the use of what he called "time squares," which were based on a mathematical formula that related price and time. Gann's methods are based on what he called the "Law of Vibration," which he believed was the key to understanding market movements. According to this law, everything in the universe vibrates at its own unique frequency. By understanding the frequencies of different market factors, Gann believed that traders could predict future price movements.

Gann combined science and astronomy to study and describing the financial phenomena. If you find yourself wondering about the purpose of this story and why it's important to your development, understand that having a trading system and tool is key to succeeding. In the next section, I have another tale about the New York subways system that inspired me to develop the Moving Average Method. The New York subway system is similar to following trends in the stock market using moving averages. You've probably noticed where I'm heading with this. As in any other fields, perfecting your skills with the appropriate tools is important. Many will find this story relatable and easily understand the powerful message of having a tool to assist you on your journey. Let's start at the beginning.

INTRODUCTION TO TREND ANALYSIS

The New York subway system is similar to following trends in the stock market using moving averages. This system has been in operation since 1904 and has been a vital part of the city's transportation network. The subway operates 24 hours a day, 7 days a week, and is the more affordable way to get around the city. The following tale is about my first experience with the subway system of New York and how it has influenced my trading approach. I was excited to be visiting my dad for the summer. He was living in an apartment in New York, working as a temporary contractor for an engineering service company. After landing in LaGuardia, we took a taxi to Manhattan. My mother informed me that I'd be able to see my father once he was done with work, but, in the meantime, we would explore the city. To get around the city, we took the New York City subway. The subway is a subterranean railway network that links the city's railway lines to its various areas. The subway system is used to transport around 8.5 million commuters every day. It's also a very cheap form of travel and provides a fast and easy commuting option. When we got on the train, everything smelled like smoke and it was loud with people talking loudly over each other. "Mom, can we please go to Chinatown?" I begged my mom. "I want to see the people and try some of their food," I pleaded with my mother. She hesitated for a moment before agreeing. From Penn Station we took the orange line before transferring over to the green to City Hall before getting to Chinatown. We walked around the busy streets until we found this small restaurant that had all kinds of different dishes on display in the window.

Once done, it was time to see my dad, so we went back to the subway. This time, the train was crowded and we had to stand, but I didn't mind because it gave me a chance to people watch. One of the most interesting things I saw on one of my trips was this guy who made balloon animals. He had an entire backpack full of balloons and he would make them into all sorts of shapes, such as elephants, giraffes, and monkeys, and more. They were so cool! We finally reached the place where my dad planned to meet us. He finally met us at our location, and we decided to go touring around the area some more before heading home. He pointed out some of his favorite sights. On the way home, the subway was practically empty, except for the few people who were waiting on the platform. The train pulled up to the station and we jumped inside, finding an open seat against one of the windows. It had been a long day running around New York City, exploring different places with my family before we went back to his New York apartment to sleep.

The New York subway and the stock market may seem like completely different systems that work in very different ways. Stock markets and their trends are fascinating to watch, but they're even more fun when we understand what we're viewing. When we see stocks on a graph going up and down, one of the first things we want to do is make some assumptions about the trend or if it's reversing. A downward trending stock means that, as time passes, the movement of those stocks between highs and lows is becoming less drastic; similarly, an upward trending stock would show us contractions in those graphs as time goes by. New Yorkers use the subway as a reliable and inexpensive mode of transportation. It's similar to how traders use moving averages for understanding the direction of the market.

The New York subway has several alternative routes to reach the same destination at various times and speeds. The different moving averages are similar to railroad tracks that can be used for prediction purposes to determine the general trend and strength of markets over time. If price is trading along a fast-moving average, it is said to have momentum; and if trading along a slow-moving average, it is said to have a steady trend.

A "moving average" refers to a type of statistic that calculates the average value over an interval, which is usually closing prices. It does so by adding up or averaging all of the prices in some time period and dividing it by how many shares were sold within that period. There are various sets of moving averages, such as short term (20-day), medium term (50-day), and long term (200-day). The trend in stocks generally dictates what kind of moving average should be used because differing types indicate different degrees of volatility.

IDENTIFYING TRENDS

The market is always changing and it's important that you stay in tune with what's taking place. Know what the market is doing before making a trade, otherwise your portfolio could suffer without warning. Trends are a great way of seeing where things are headed. If you don't, you could end up losing money or missing out on opportunities. That's why I identify the price trend first to help me figure out where a stock price is headed next and estimate how much it will move in that direction. This helps me decide whether I should buy or sell stocks at any given time. In this chapter of trend analysis, I will show you when a stock price has reached its peak and when it's about to drop—giving you plenty of opportunity for profitable trades.

What is a trend? Trends are established patterns in which something is moving forward and not changing direction. The trend can have a big impact on your trading results. One simple way of determining what trend a stock is on is by creating a trendline, which is taking price action over a period and connecting each action or series of lows (uptrend) or highs (downtrends). Trend lines are a graphical representation of the price movement over a period. Making use of trends lines in trading could help you to make better trades when buying or selling. If the line connects a series of (though not necessarily consecutive) higher highs, it creates a support level for future price increase that is also an indicator of an uptrend. If the line connects (again, not necessarily consecutive) lower lows, it creates a resistance level for a downtrend. Over time, it shows a line that predicts the most probable price direction. You can see in Figure 8.1 above how a trend line may have given us an indicator of when to buy and when to sell, but how do they work? Support and Resistance are the key components of trend lines. When a price is moving lower toward a level where it may stop and reverse, support is present. On the other hand, resistance occurs when a price is moving higher toward a level where the price will stop and reverse.

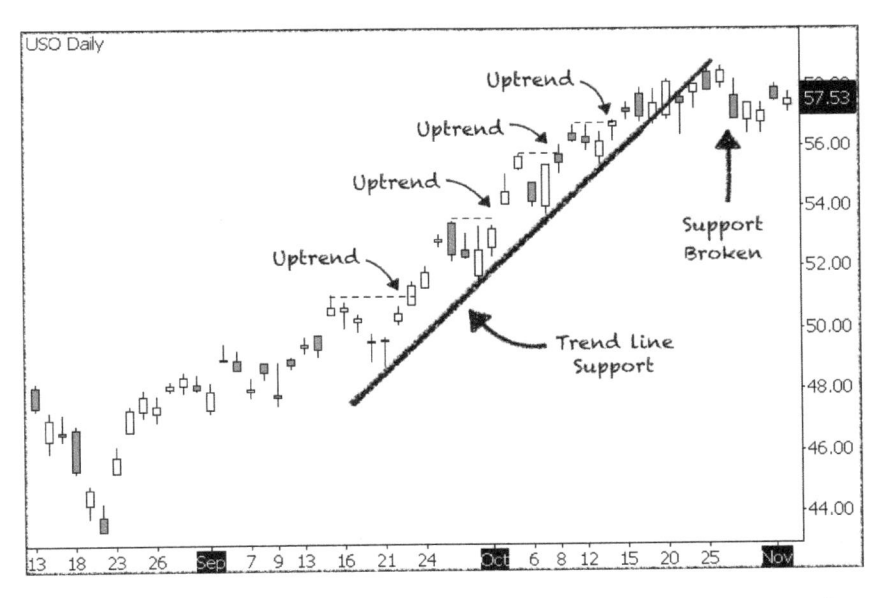

Figure 8.1: Use trend line to signal a trend continuation or reversal.

When a support level is broken, it indicates a bearish movement and the price of the stock may go lower. If you are buying to hold long on the stock, it may be a good time to close to sell short at the current market price, or close the trade all together.The resistance level works the same way in reverse. When a resistance level is broken, it means bullish movement may be coming to a stop and a bearish movement may be in place, as shown in Figure 8.1. In general, the price of the stock will likely go higher. If you are short on the stock, it may present a good time to cover your position and close out your trade. The best thing to do is make use of the trend line's direction, stick with it, and don't question its strengths. If the bull market continues, it will likely run into resistance. If the bear market continues, it will likely run into support. These are just generalities, but can be a successful way to trade the markets.

Most of the time, trendlines will show the general direction of price movements. There are, however, instances wherein we would need to redraw the trendline given certain market conditions. For example: During an uptrend, the price of a stock may fall below the trendline on one instance, but this may not mean the upward trend is over. This one slide in price may be a bleep in the price trend but, overall, the direction of the market is still bullish. During such an event, we just need to redraw the trendline to account for the sudden fluctuations in price.

Trends are not perfect, they will reverse at some point, but they offer a good assessment of where price movement is most likely heading. The direction of the trend is identified by the slope of the trend line. In an uptrend, the trend lines are pointing upward. In a downtrend, trend lines are pointing downward. In a sideway trend, the trend lines are horizontal and pointing sideways.

There are three distinct market trends: an uptrend, where the stock prices rise; a downtrend, where they decrease; and lastly, a sideways trend, which shows no movement in either direction.

Uptrend. An uptrend, also known as a bull trend, is the condition of a financial market where the prices are moving higher. The price movement may be slow and steady or volatile, but it's always in an upward direction. An uptrend occurs when the price is making higher lows and higher highs. The longer it continues, the weaker it may become. An uptrend will have some resistance at each high, but continue making higher lows and higher highs. This indicates that momentum is strong enough to carry prices higher.

For example, Good Company has been in the news lately due to announcements from its CEO about new products and services. The movement in the price of this company over the past few days has been going in a steady upward trend—until reporting a bad earning report. An uptrend can continue to go in a positive direction until it reaches a peak, and then starts going down again.

Downtrend. A downtrend, on the other hand, refers to lower lows and lower highs. When there is a downtrend, the tendency of many traders is to assume that the market will hold the trend until there is evidence that a reversal is about to happen. A downtrend occurs when the price is making lower lows and lower highs.

This is when the value of the trading instrument starts to diminish. Prices also typically become more volatile during the downtrend, which often leads to short selling opportunities. This type of trend can be triggered by any number of things—the company releases bad news, fear over another company acquiring it.

Usually, but not always, downtrends do reverse course at some point, so traders take this as a cue to get bargain prices in the hope of getting profit once the stock prices bounce back. This generally prompts an uptrend later. A downtrend will likely end by prices breaking the resistance level and moving higher, where we see higher highs or higher lows.

Sideways. A sideways trend occurs when the price is moving within a horizontal range. This may happen because the market feels indecisive and is not sure which way to go. The longer it continues, the more likely it may break out to either the upside or downside. There are ways to use support and resistance levels to your advantage.

If the price breaks out of it, it is likely to be significant. Sideways movement can be very frustrating because it looks like the trend will go on forever. It can also be very profitable because it often signals a change in direction, after which the trend resumes. Use these tips to handle sideways movement. Set your stop-loss point just below the support line. If the price goes beyond it, you can relax because that will be the new resistance line.

Failure Swing. A failure swing is a type of technical trading pattern that occurs in a bullish or bearish trend. Failure swings are important to recognize because they signal the end of an existing trend and the start of a new trend. They can be both bullish or bearish, but it's more common for it to be bearish. The prices fail to make a new high in an uptrend and price falls below the previous trough is called " the failure swing high." The top of the failure swing price will then decline below the previous trough, which becomes a new swing low point—this is where the downtrend starts (See Figure 8.2 on left). If prices fail to make a new low and continue to increase until it breaks above the previous peak—this is called "the failure swing low" (See Figure 8.2 on right).

A failure swing is also called a rejection pattern and considered more important than other patterns because it signals the end of an existing trend and the start of a new trend (which is why the pattern is called "failure").

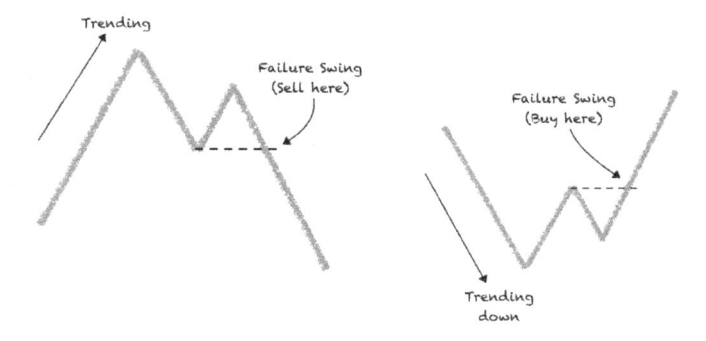

Figure 8.2: Various type of failure swings.

If a downtrend fails to swing lower but instead penetrates to the upside, this also indicates a reversal. On the flip side, if an uptrend fails to swing higher but breaks to the downside instead, this also indicates a reversal. The key to taking advantage of the failure swing is to be able to identify it in real-time. To identify a failure swing, you need to locate the peaks and troughs. First and foremost, a true failure swing must form within the context of an existing trend. This means that the pattern will emerge as the trend begins to lose steam and reversals become more likely.

Ultimately, trend lines are useful in the analysis of trends because they follow general market movements. Of course, some individuals (contrarians) might decide to go against the grain and take their chances by going in the opposite direction of what is expected; however, I prefer taking advantage of the overall trend direction. Once a trend comes to an end, it can either be abrupt or show a false reversal; at which point, I will update my trend line. I also take into account any gaps and/or additional volume that may occur, which could signal a potential shift in the market. In summary, trends are an important tool for analyzing stock market movements and can be used to inform decisions about when to buy or sell.

MOVING AVERAGES

Moving Averages are a very popular indicator used in technical analysis. It's also one of the most misunderstood trading tools ever. Many traders make the mistake of using it as support and resistances levels. The result may provide false signals or may cause the timing of the entries to be inaccurate. I believe that this tool should be used as an unbiased indicator, not as a support or resistance level. They smooth out price action by filtering out the "noise" from random price fluctuations. This makes it easier for traders to see the direction of the trend. As a rule of thumb, moving averages are not a good source of a buying signal. They do not provide accurate entry signals all by themselves. Also it is important to note that while this section has a superior guide to analyzing price trends, other factors are to be accounted for when making decisions on buying or selling.

To get us started, let us first define what is the Moving Average Method. To illustrate this, let's have this analogy. Imagine you are an owner of a stand in a market fair where people can negotiate on the prices of each produce item. Let us say you are selling oranges at a rate of $1.00 apiece and that your stand is open for about 8 hours. During the course of the day, you may find buyers who would ask for a discount and purchase your oranges at a lower rate (let us say $0.80 per piece) while there are buyers who would buy your produce at a higher rate (let's assume $1.10 per piece). Tracking the transactions per day, you could find the range by which your produce is sold and the average of its price for any day. Each day will probably have a different average price per day. So, if we track the movement of the price over a period, you could see how the average changes day per day. That trend is your moving average.

There are three types of moving average that can be used in trading—Simple, Exponential, or Weighted. Each one is based on different criteria but they all do essentially the same thing: help predict future prices by analyzing past prices.

Simple Moving Average or SMA. The most common type of moving average is probably the SMA, which is created by computing the average of a fixed number of the closing prices for a certain number of time periods. For example, if you compute the average closing price over 20 days, the result is the tewnty-day SMA. It takes a sum of each data point over a specific time period (usually 20 days counting back from the current bar) and then divides this total by the number of periods chosen (20). In other words, each day has an equal impact on its value regardless of where it falls within those 20 days.

Exponential Moving Average or EMA. EMA gives greater weight to more recent prices, which makes it a bit more responsive than the SMA. The weighting of each data point is based on an exponential multiplier, so the more recent the price, the greater its influence. That's why it's known as an "exponentially" weighted moving average. The most common version of this is the 20-day EMA, which gives more weight to the most recent prices and less to those further in the past. The EMA is faster than the SMA and it's best used to determine the general trend.

Weighted Moving Average. A weighted moving average assigns more significance to the most recent data points. Its weighting formula is much more complicated than that of the other two moving averages. The most common version of this is the declining linearly weighted moving average. This means that more weight is given to recent prices, but the weights decrease as you move further back in time. This type of moving average is best used to analyze the trend and it's great for eliminating noise on odder price action information.

As you can see, all three types of moving averages are based on the same mechanism. Moving averages are considered lagging indicators since their average merely follows the price with a delay. For example, if the price is decreasing and then rebounds, the moving average may steadily rise after the price rises. While this SMA method may provide some basic direction information, it does not always give the clearest trading signals. EMA is a type of moving average that gives more weight to recent prices in an attempt to make it more responsive to new information. For example, if the price is decreasing and then rebounds, the EMA may start to rise more quickly than the SMA. While the EMA may provide some benefit over the SMA, it is still a lagging indicator. As such, it is important to combine it with other types of technical analysis tools to get a clear picture of what is happening in the market. For example, if the price is falling and the SMA is rising, this could be a sign that the price is about to rebound.

From what I've seen, there's no difference in performance among the three types of moving averages. When the markets are trending, all three of them work well. But when markets are choppy, they stop working so well. Whenever the market is ranging, it'll also make these moving averages unreliable. That's why I don't use them very often. The moving average method is extremely useful when forecasting long-term direction of trends. When used in stock trading, the general averages to use are 8-day, 20-day, 50-day, and 200-day. Now that we have defined what a moving average is and how it is commonly used, we can transition over to discussing how we can distinguish a moving average that is appropriate to use.

LAWS OF AVERAGES

Many traders have no idea when or why to use moving average lines. I have developed simple strategies that will help you understand what the market is doing. The moving average strategies work on all time frames and allow you to choose from among different types of averages. You will learn what different types of moving average exist and which ones work best for each situation, as well as discover practical examples and real-life trading strategies that can help improve your results right away.

A "well-chosen" moving average will also help you identify important price events on the chart. Having one's moving average period too long or too short may result in missing the trend, as well as simplifying noise or filtering out interesting price action. There are many more types of moving averages, but we'll only cover the most popular. You can also use two or three moving averages at once to find momentum, trend, direction, and sentiment of the market. The default setting is a simple moving average. You can also use weighted or exponential moving averages, but the strategy will be the same.

Momentum. Use shorter-period moving averages, such as 5-15 periods, to determine momentum. These moving averages are optimal for short-term movements. This is because they will help you identify when price is accelerating or decelerating, which can help you make better trades.

Trend. Identifying the trend is important to avoid whipsaws. Most traders use momentum moving averages, which are great for identifying short-term moves, but they tend to lose their effectiveness when used over longer periods of time. This is because shorter-term price fluctuations can obscure the actual trend. The solution to this problem is using a longer-period moving average, such as 20-30 periods, to identify the trend. This moving average is also optimal for identifying longer-term trends. This is because they help you identify the overall trend of the market while ignoring shorter movements. You can then use the moving average to confirm that you're indeed in an uptrend or downtrend before entering into trades. Using this method will allow you to trade with confidence and reduce whipsaw risk significantly. Statistically, most lasting trends end up retracing their movements very close to the average of the last 20 periods. This is commonly used by traders and is an accepted benchmark, hence it is to your advantage to use the same when looking for trends.

Direction. While there are many moving averages that traders use, it's still hard to get a quick overview of the market direction. Being able to quickly identify the market direction is essential for successful trading. It also gives you an idea about how long your trade will last, based on its proximity to this moving average line. The 50 is a somewhat longer-term moving average that incorporates the prior ten trade weeks. The 50-day average helps to eliminate noise from the chart on the charts and provides a larger direction view. With a fast scan, you can observe how the market has performed, the long-term direction, and whether the market is moving up or down. For example, if price has crossed above the 50-day line then it means that prices are likely going higher over the next several weeks until they cross back below this key indicator again. Conversely, when prices cross below their 50-day moving average line, it indicates that they may continue lower until they eventually move back above this indicator again. This moving average can help you to determine whether or not to take a trade depending on where the price is in relation to the 50-day moving average line.

Market Sentiment. The big advantage of using a 200-day SMA as an indicator for sentiment over the stock market cycle. Using the 200-day SMA will help keep your investment strategy on track by warning about potential turning points in the market. Because you're only evaluating prices from 200 days ago, this gives us a good indication of the market cycle. This is because stocks are generally more responsive when they're trading close to their 200-day moving average than any other point in their cycle. It acts as support during a bull market and resistance during a bull market.

Death cross. The death cross is traditionally defined as the point where the 50-day moving average crosses below the 200-day moving average. Market sentiment—A bear market is met with pessimism and negative investor confidence about future prospects. This is a signal that a bear market may be coming or has already begun. The markets can expect to see sentiment change for Bull to Bear Market.

Golden cross. The golden cross is a chart pattern that is created when the 50-day moving average crosses above the 200-day moving average. It signals an increase in volatility, often followed by higher prices. A bull market is met with optimism and increasing levels of confidence for investors. There are increasing chances of a corrective bullish trends, called "bull rallies," popping up to restore some risk appetite among bulls.

In conclusion, the first few questions that traders always ask are: at what time frame are we looking, and which moving average should we use? The most popular are the daily, weekly and monthly charts. Stock traders use a variety of time frames, ranging from and use multiple time frames to create your strategy. I recommend using at least two moving averages on the same chart, such as a short-term and long-term. And while the data sets look different because of the differences in the periods of measurement, you will eventually realize that some periods are equivalent on a lower time frame. There is no right or wrong period to use because the volatility of the market would dictate at what time frame you should be looking, depending on the desired result you are after.

TREND FOLLOWING

Trading is hard. You have to make a lot of decisions and sometimes it feels like you're just guessing. Most traders only make money when the market is going their way. This means they're constantly guessing, and when they guess wrong, they lose money. Moving average pivotal points are key to successful trading. These price points identify where buyers or sellers are likely to enter the market, which can help you time your entries and exits for maximum profits. There are a few ways to skin this cat. The first would be to look at the overall direction of the market. This can be determined by looking at moving averages. If the market is trending up, then the market direction is bullish. If the market is trending down, then the market direction is bearish.

You can also use a momentum-moving average to determine the current state of the market. Momentum measures how fast the market is moving in a particular direction. If the momentum is increasing, then the market is said to be breaking out. If the momentum is decreasing, then the market is said to be breaking down. Finally, you can also use a market sentiment-moving average to determine the current state of the market.

Market sentiment measures how bullish or bearish investors are. If investors are feeling bullish, then they are more likely to buy stocks, which will push prices up. If investors are feeling bearish, then they are more likely to sell stocks, which will push prices down. All of these indicators can be used to determine the current state of a trending market.

The point where price touches the moving average is known as the equilibrium point. Price equilibrium is the term used when price equals a point on the moving average. If the moving average is moving upward when price crosses from above, price is expected to continue up at a later time. Same for if the moving average is declining when price crosses from below, price is expected to continue down at a later time. For example, if the moving average is rising and price crosses below but then immediately rises back above, that could be a bullish sign and indicate that prices will continue to rise in an uptrend. Similarly, if the moving average is falling and price crosses above but then immediately falls back below, that could be a bearish sign and indicate that prices will continue to fall. So, while the general rule of thumb is that prices will move in the same direction as the moving average, it's important to keep an eye out.

The crossing of price is a pivotal point beyond which price is expected to continue. This can be helpful for determining when to enter or exit a trade. We can use the pivotal point as a signal for determining when to enter or exit a trade. If the price is expected to continue beyond the average, it can be a good time to enter the market. Conversely, if the price is expected to drop below the average, it may be time to exit the trade. Of course, averages can be tricky to interpret, and there is no guarantee that the price will behave as expected.

The moving average is a good indicator of the direction in which the market is moving. When the moving average has an increasing slope, this indicates that the average price is moving up at a constant rate. At the point where price crosses or touches the moving average line, with a certain level of confidence, we can predict that price should continue to move up in the near future. The temporary decline in the price is a pullback before continuation. There are many different strategies that traders use when trading with the moving average (See Figure 8.3), but the most important thing is to always be aware of the trend. By following the trend, you will be able to make profitable trades and avoid costly mistakes.

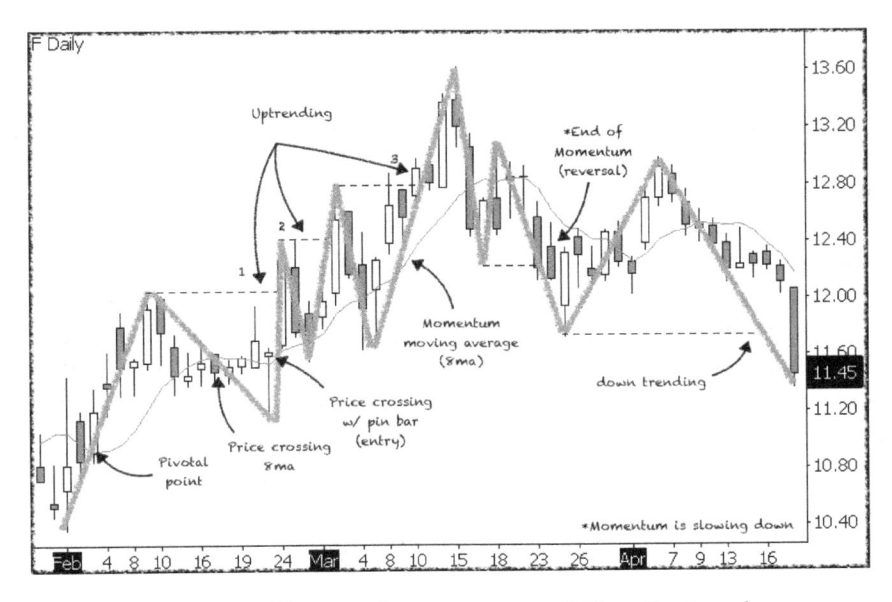

Figure 8.3: Use moving averages to follow the trend.

In conclusion, trend analysis is an important tool for traders, and identifying support and resistance levels is a key part of this discipline. Simply put, the support level is the price at which demand is thought to be strong enough to prevent the price from falling further. The resistance level is the price at which selling pressure is thought to be strong enough to prevent the price from rising further. The equilibrium point is the price at which supply and demand are in balance for that period, and it represents the point at which traders are most likely to place their orders. Being able to identify the equilibrium point can help you make more informed and profitable trades. However, researching historical patterns can give you a better sense of how the market typically reacts to different levels of support and resistance. With this information in hand, you can make better decisions about when to enter and exit trades. Learning how to trade using this technique can give you an edge over other traders in the market.

THE MOVING-AVERAGE METHOD

The problem with most moving-average strategies is that they are too slow or too fast. They're either not sensitive enough to short-term trends, or they lag behind and can't anticipate big moves in a stock. And if you want to trade multiple time frames using the same strategy, then it's even harder because you need an entirely different set of rules for each time period (like crossover signals). Also, many trading systems require lots of parameters and fine tuning, which makes them difficult to implement consistently. The moving-average methods are easy to apply to any time frame, from a daily up to a monthly chart; you can choose among different types of averages.

The length of the moving average is determined by the analytical objectives. These moving averages can be used to identify the direction of the trend or turning points in the market. When choosing a moving average, chartists should consider their analytical objectives and the characteristics of the underlying security. A shorter moving average will react faster to changes in price but may also produce more false signals. A longer moving average smooths out the price action and filters out the noise, but may lag behind the recent price action. When prices are above a moving average, it indicates bullish price action. When prices are below a moving average, it indicates a bearish price action. Short moving averages of 8 and 20 periods are best suited for short-term trends and trading. Chartists interested in medium-term trends would use longer moving averages that could span 20 and 50 periods. Long-term investors will prefer moving averages with 100 or more periods.

The moving average method is a tool that I developed to help identify opportunities. Using this method, I take into account all simple-period moving averages for momentum, trend, direction, and sentiment. Remember the story of being in New York City and traveling through the subway system, transferring between train lines to get to Chinatown. I had to transfer lines at least two times before finally arriving at the location. By using the concept of the subway system of transferring between lines, I was able to see how a stock goes from a period of momentum to a period trending in a particular direction. After identifying these changes, I can then go over and identify critical price levels where the bias of direction is likely to change. By using this method, I have been able to successfully trade and make a profit. It is a useful tool in trading and has help me immensely. If you're ever lost in the New York City subway system, just remember to use a moving average!

After a long period of downward trend, the United States Oil Fund (USO) started to exhibit momentum by moving along the 8-period SMA—just like railroad tracks. Momentum, or a "power trend," is what I call it when prices rise and fall along an 8-period average. This could be a good opportunity to buy USO as it moves along the 8-period average, as this is a strong indication that the trend will continue. The buy point would be when USO moves above the 8-period average, which would be a good time to enter into a long and hold position. At the peak of momentum, USO starts to show weakness by displaying a reversal pattern. A reversal pattern is when prices start to move in the opposite direction of the previous trend. This can be a good time to exit a long position or enter into a short position. In this case, USO has started to move below the 8-period average, indicating that the momentum has reversed and it may be a good time to sell.

USO prices have been dropping and are predicted to fall even more significantly when price cross the 20 simple-period moving average. This is because the 20 SMA is a key moving average used by many investors. When prices cross this level, it is a strong indication that the direction of the trend has changed. In this case, USO has crossed the 20-period moving average to the downside, indicating that the downtrend is likely to continue. This would be a good time to enter into a short position. USO price crosses the 50 simple-period moving average. It quickly recovers (30 days later) and goes into another uptrend with momentum that follows the 8 simple-period moving average (See Figure 8.4).

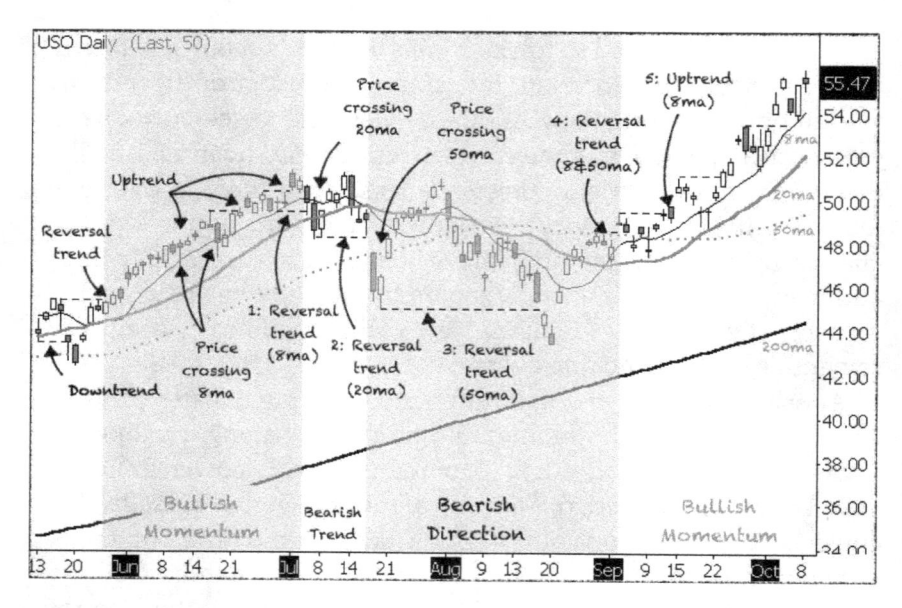

Figure 8.4: Daily chart of United State Oil recovering after a brief bearish trend.

In conclusion, by using the moving average method and trend following strategies, I was able to successfully identify these key points in USO's price action and profit from them. This method can be especially useful in rapidly changing markets. To use the character traits of moving average, you first need to identify the trend, direction, and sentiment of the stock. The trend can be easily identified by looking at the 20-day moving average. If prices are rising and falling along an 8-period average, then it is exhibiting momentum and is likely to continue in that direction. The direction can be identified by looking at a reversal pattern along the 50-day moving average. The sentiment can be identified by taking into account bullish or bearish crossings near or at the 200 moving average. In the example above, we can see how the moving average method helped me identify an opportunity to enter into a short and long position in USO.

CONSOLIDATION TRENDS

With moving averages, it's important to know when they're helpful—and when they're not. After all, no one likes getting burned by a false signal. And while moving averages can be great tools for spotting upward or downward trends, they're not so useful when the market is sloppy or moving sideways. In these cases, moving averages can actually give false signals. For example, if the market is moving sideways and the moving average is pointing down, this could lead traders to believe that the market is in a downward trend. In reality however, the market may just be experiencing a temporary pause before resuming its trend. So, next time you're considering using a moving average as part of your analysis, make sure you take into account the potential pitfalls.

As any trader knows, charts are essential tools in market analysis. They allow us to visualize price performance over time and identify different patterns and shapes that can help us predict future price movements. Another benefit of using charts is that they can help us spot potential stock breakouts and reversals. By keeping a close eye on the formation of these patterns, we can gain an edge over the market and make more profitable trades. So, if you're serious about stock trading, then learning how to read and interpret chart patterns is essential. Take the time to understand the different patterns and shapes that form on charts and you'll be well on your way to success in the markets!

Pennant. A pennant is a triangle-shaped technical chart pattern that is created when price consolidates after a strong move up or down. The two sides of the pennant are formed by trend lines that converge at a point, also known as the apex. Pennants typically form during periods of market indecision as traders pause to assess the direction of the trend before continuing in a direction. Because they are often seen as continuation patterns, pennants can be used by traders to identify potential entry and exit points. When combined with other technical indicators, pennants can be a valuable tool for making trades.

There are four different types of pennants: ascending, descending, symmetrical, and wedge triangle. Each type of pennant has a different meaning and can be used to signal different things to traders. Ascending and descending pennants are continuation patterns that signal a continuation of the current trend. Symmetrical triangles are consolidation patterns that often signal a breakout in either direction. Wedge triangles are also consolidation patterns, but they have a bit of a different meaning. They often signal a breakout in the direction of the wedge. So, if you're ever feeling indecisive about which way the market is going to go, just remember that you can always look for a pennant to give you some clues.

Ascending triangle. Triangles can be a fickle mistress. Some days the patterns make perfect sense, while other days they seem like nothing more than random squiggles. But if there's one thing on which technical analysts can agree, it's the importance of the ascending triangle. This bullish chart pattern is often seen as a continuation of an uptrend, signaling that a breakout is likely to occur where the triangle lines converge. So how do you actually draw this pattern? First, you'll need to place a horizontal line (the resistance line) on the resistance points. Then, you'll draw an ascending line (the uptrend line) along the support points (See Figure 8.5). Once you have both lines in place, you'll be able to see the potential for a breakout at the point where they converge. So, keep your eyes peeled for this formation next time you're looking at charts!

Descending triangle. The descending triangle is a bearish pattern that signals a potential downward breakout. It is formed by a horizontal support line and a descending resistance line, creating a triangle shape. The descending triangle is typically seen as a continuation pattern in a downtrending market. When the price breaks below the support line, it can signal a further decline (See Figure 8.6). The descending triangle is usually considered a relatively reliable pattern, but like all chart patterns, it is not foolproof. Traders should watch for confirming signals before making any trades. So, if you're seeing this formation on your charts, beware! The bears might be taking over soon.

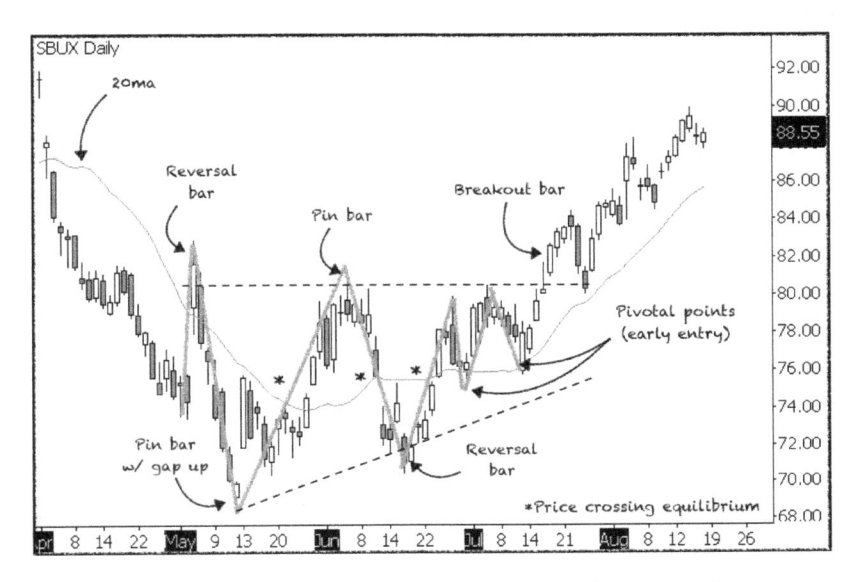

Figure 8.5: Daily chart of Starbucks with ascending triangle pattern

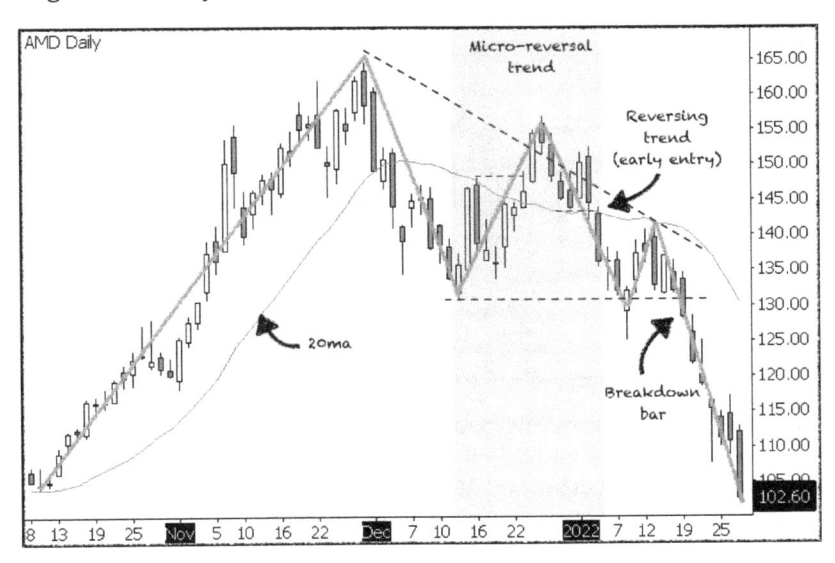

Figure 8.6: Daily chart of Advanced Micro Devices with descending triangle pattern.

Symmetrical triangle. Have you ever noticed how two trend lines start to meet in a symmetrical triangle? No, not those kind of triangles—we're talking stock market trend lines. This pattern is almost always a sign that a breakout is about to occur in either direction. But which direction will it be? Here's a hint: it often follows the general trend of the market. So, if the market is currently trending upward, you would expect the symmetrical triangle to break out upward as well. Makes sense, right? After all, if the market was trending downward, it would likely continue to do so even after the symmetrical triangle forms. There are a few exceptions to this rule, but, for the most part, you can expect the symmetrical triangle to break out in the same direction as the overall market trend (See Figure 8.7).

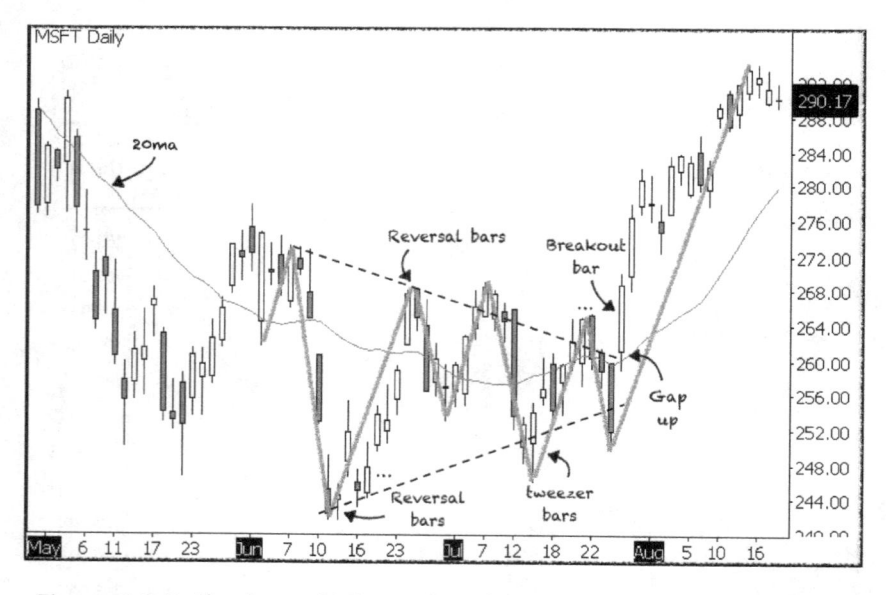

Figure 8.7: Daily chart of Microsoft with symmetrical triangle pattern.

Wedges. As any experienced trader knows, wedges are important patterns about which to be aware. A wedge represents a tightening price movement between the support and resistance lines, which can be either a rising wedge or a falling wedge. Unlike the triangle, the wedge doesn't have a horizontal trend line and is characterized by either an upward trend lines or a downward trend lines. For a falling wedge, the price is hypothesized to break through the support. This means the wedge is a reversal pattern in the opposite direction to the general trend (See Figure 8.8). So, next time you see one of these bad boys on your chart, make sure to pay attention.

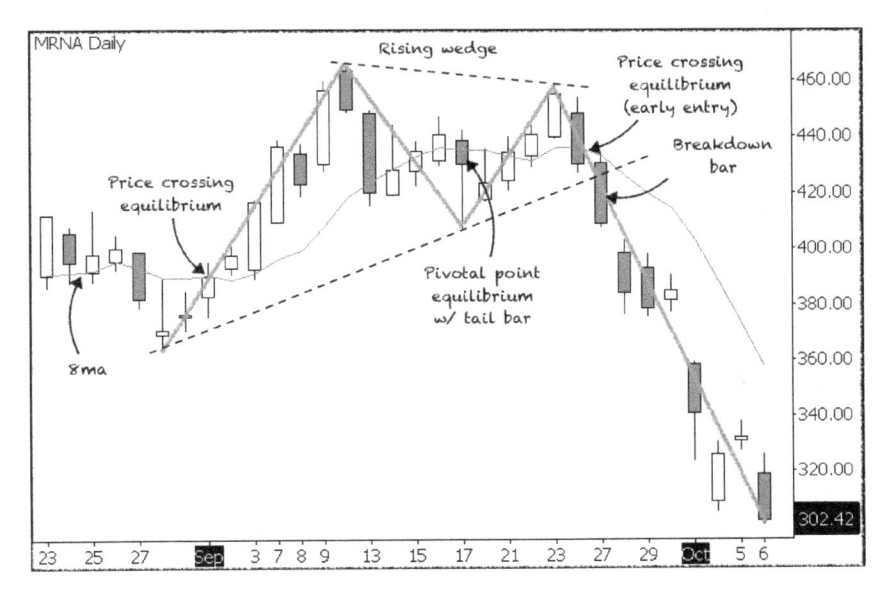

Figure 8.8: Daily chart Moderna with raising wedge pattern.

Double top. Just as the name suggests, a double top looks like the letter M. This reversal pattern forms after the price fails to break through the resistance level twice. After that, the trend follows back to support and starts to downtrend, breaking through the support line. So, if you see an M-shaped pattern forming on your charts, it might be time to start thinking about short selling the market (See Figure 8.9). While this may not be the most glamorous way to trade, it can certainly be profitable. And, let's face it, making money is what trading is all about. So, if you see a double top forming, don't be afraid to take advantage of it.

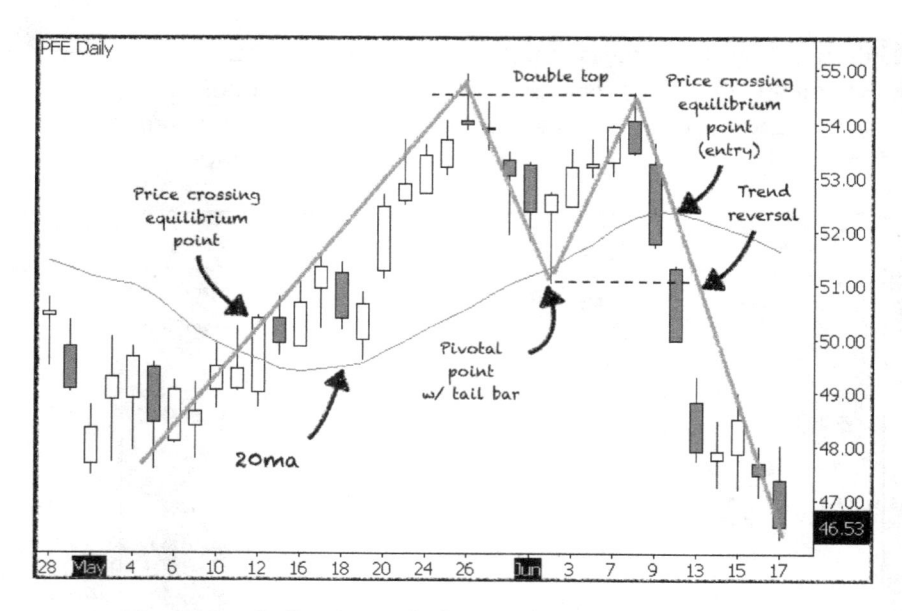

Figure 8.9: Daily chart of Pfizer with double top pattern.

Double bottom. The double bottom is a frequently occurring market pattern that can be useful for identifying potential reversals. As the name suggests, this pattern occurs when the market price makes two unsuccessful attempts at breaking through a support level. However, after the second failed attempt, the market price typically shifts toward an uptrend (see Figure 8.10). While this pattern can be useful for identifying potential reversals, it is important to remember that it is not perfect. There may be times when the market continues to fall after two failed attempts, and there may be times when the market does not turn around even after the retest fails. Therefore, it is important to use other indicators and analysis techniques in combination with the double bottom pattern to confirm one's suspicions.

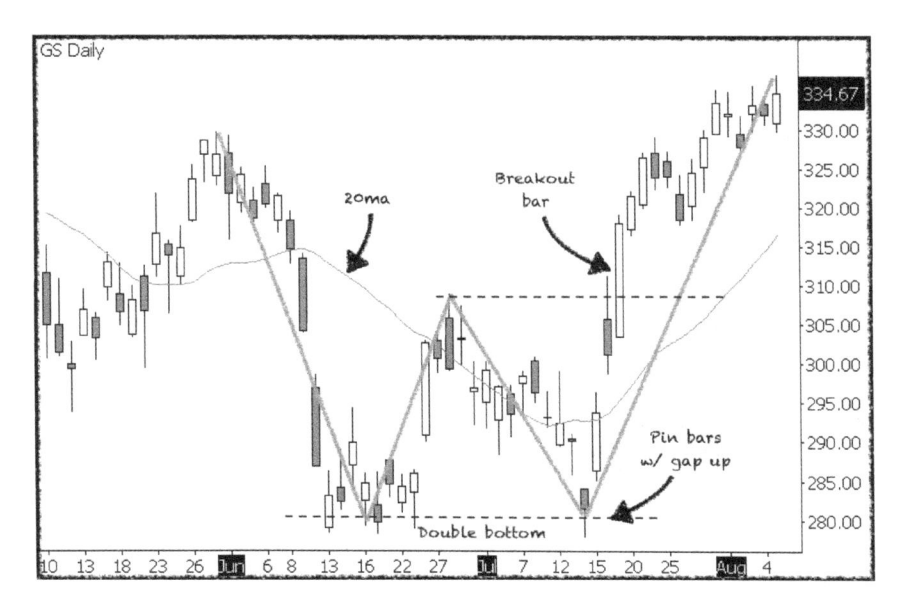

Figure 8.10: Daily chart of Goldman Sachs Group with double bottom pattern.

Head and shoulders. The head and shoulders pattern is one of the more well-known analysis chart pattern. This three-part formation occurs when there is a large peak followed by two smaller peaks, with all three levels falling back to the same support level. Once the pattern is complete, the trend is likely to break out in a downward direction (See Figure 8.11), or in an upward direction in the case of an inverted head and shoulders pattern. While this pattern is often associated with bear markets, it can also occur during bull markets. For this reason, it's important to confirm the head and shoulders pattern with other indicators before making any investment decisions. Despite its well-known status, the head and shoulders pattern is notoriously difficult to identify in real time. More often than not, investors only recognize the formation after the fact. As such, it's important to exercise caution when using this indicator alone. Instead, consider using it in conjunction with other technical indicators to get a more accurate picture of market conditions.

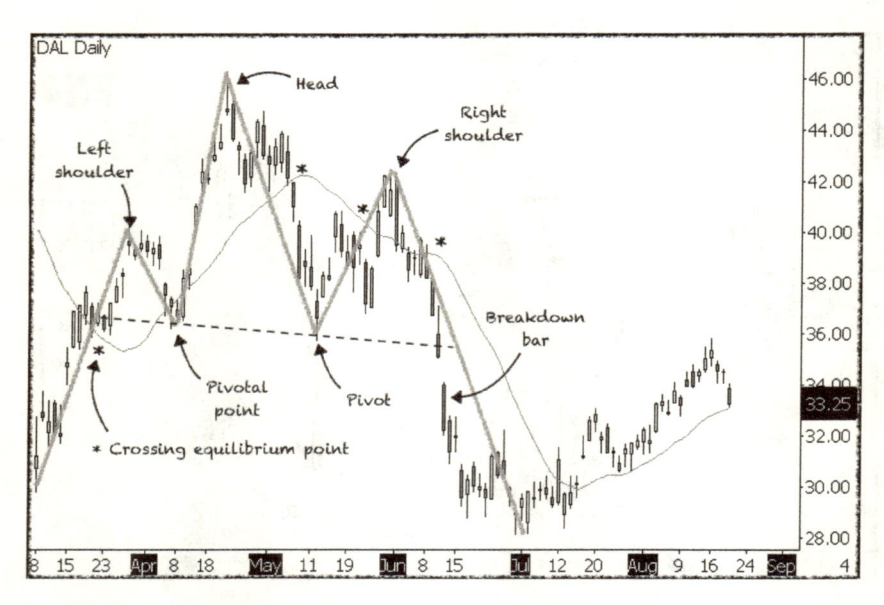

Figure 8.11: Daily chart of Delta Airlines with head and shoulders pattern.

Cup and handle. The cup and handle is another well-known reversal stock chart pattern. It is formed when the price of a stock rounds bottom and then forms a handle. The handle resembles a wedge and, once completed, you can see the market breakout in a bullish upward trend. Some investors believe that the cup-and-handle pattern is a reliable predictor of future market movements, while others believe that it is merely a reflection of past market behavior. Regardless of its predictive ability, the cup-and-handle pattern is an important tool for technical analysis. The cup-and-handle pattern is named for its distinct shape; the "cup" part of the pattern is created by the rounded bottom, while the "handle" part is created by the pennant that forms afterward. Investors use the cup-and-handle pattern to predict when a stock is likely to break out in an upward trend. While there is no guarantee that the pattern will be accurate every time, it is still useful to consider when making investment decisions.

In conclusion, the moving average tool is a fantastic way to assess price movements without all the complicated charts. It is a simple, yet powerful tool that can replicate most of the functions of other methods with high accuracy and minimal skill sets. The main advantage of moving averages is that they smooth the data and thus provide a clearer visual picture of the current trend. In addition to that, signals can give a precise answer as to what the trend is. The main disadvantage is that they are lagging rather than leading indicators, but this should not be a problem to longer-term investors. When used properly, the moving average method is a great way to stay in a rising trend during pullbacks. Recognizing a change in the direction of the moving average is a strong clue that what has been working is starting to weaken and may be signaling the end of a trend.

9 Market Cycles

Chapter Overview

» Drivers of market cycles.

» History of Dow theory

» Modern market cycles.

Tale of Charles Dow and Edward Jones

Wall Street is known for being cutthroat. It's a place where people will do almost anything to get ahead. So, it should come as no surprise that financial journalism is one of the top competitive fields in journalism. To be successful in this field, you need to have a strong background in statistics. Dow and Jones are two examples of successful financial journalists who got their start by working at the Wall Street Journal. Charles Henry Dow was an American journalist with interests in financial evaluations and literature. Dow was born in Sterling, Connecticut, on November, 6 1851. When he was six years old, his father died. Although he did not have much education, at 21 he got work with the Springfield Daily Republican in Massachusetts, working as a city reporter.

Dow had a ringside seat to the birth of modern finance. In 1879, he went on an adventure that introduced him not only into new worlds, but also changed his life forever—traveling with some America's wealthiest individuals and gaining knowledge about how money worked outside just being involved in stocks or trading bonds at Wall Street firms like Goodbody & Co. Dow's big break came when he co-founded The Wall Street Journal, which has become one of the most respected financial publications in the world. His investing strategies quickly gained popularity, and by 1890 he was one of the most respected financial analysts in the country.

Dow believed that stock price movements are primarily based on the law of supply and demand. According to Dow, when there is more buying pressure than selling pressure, stock prices will rise. Similarly, when there is more selling pressure than buying pressure, stock prices will fall. To determine whether there is more buying pressure or selling pressure in the market, Dow developed the theory of price movements.

The theory states that stock prices will move in three directions: up, down, or sideways. When stock prices move up, it indicates that there is more demand than supply in the market. Similarly, when stock prices move down, it indicates that there is more supply than demand in the market. Finally, when stock prices move sideways, it indicates that there are equal amounts of demand and supply in the market. While the theory of price movements is a key determinant of stock prices, Dow also believed that the change of time is a factor that explains the fluctuations that the stock prices have.

In other words, Dow believed that stock prices are constantly changing and that this change is a normal part of the market. As such, investors should not be alarmed by these changes, but should instead use them to their advantage by investing in companies with strong fundamentals that are likely to weather any storm. In addition to his work in finance, Dow was also an accomplished writer, and his literary works includes several poems and short stories.

Edward Jones was an important partner who influenced and helped Dow to develop the various theories and models. Jones was born in 1856 and was a statistician and journalist in the USA. He developed a passion for reading and understanding financial literature and processes at a young age. This helped him accurately identify trends in financial strategies. He graduated from the Worcester Academy, before attending Brown University, before dropping out of the school. The first job came as an editor at the Providence Morning Star and Evening Press, where he met with Charles Dow. The reporting processes and aspects have been influenced by his approach on the various issues affecting the stock market. What started as a partnership soon led to a close friendship, as both men shared similar interests in business and economics. Together, they would go on to change the way the stock market was analyzed and reported on, laying the foundation for modern financial news media.

Dow Jones & Company is a financial news and information provider that has been in operation since 1879. The company was founded by Dow, Jones, and Bergstresser, who started it as a small news agency that served banks and brokerage houses. Since then, Dow Jones & Company has grown into a publishing powerhouse, providing critical financial information and analysis to investors around the world.

The company's flagship product is The Wall Street Journal, which is published daily and features two full pages of financial news and commentary. In addition to The Wall Street Journal, Dow Jones & Company also publishes Barron's, a weekly investing magazine, and provides data and analysis. Given its long history and experience in the financial markets, Dow Jones & Company is a trusted source of information for investors worldwide.

Dow and Jones were two journalists who developed the Dow Jones theory, which focused on the trends in the markets. This theory was based on the averages that existed in the various markets. In the theoretical Dow Jones indices, the high and low pricing of equity uses the daily trends, which helps to create a consistent and precise way for evaluating the various stock markets. The determination of the most-traded stock in the market was another publication that helped in understanding the markets and guiding investors on the best ways and strategies that could influence the market developments. The two journalists played an important role in influencing the statistical approaches of the financial markets, while using the publications to highlight their advancements. Thanks to their work, we have a better understanding of how the stock market works.

Dow died on December 4, 1902, at the age of 51. Though he only lived a short life, his legacy continues to this day through the work of the company that bears his name. The theories and ideas that they developed have been important in modern-day stocks, despite the adjustments in the various factors that could affect stock trading.

INTRODUCTION TO MARKET CYCLES

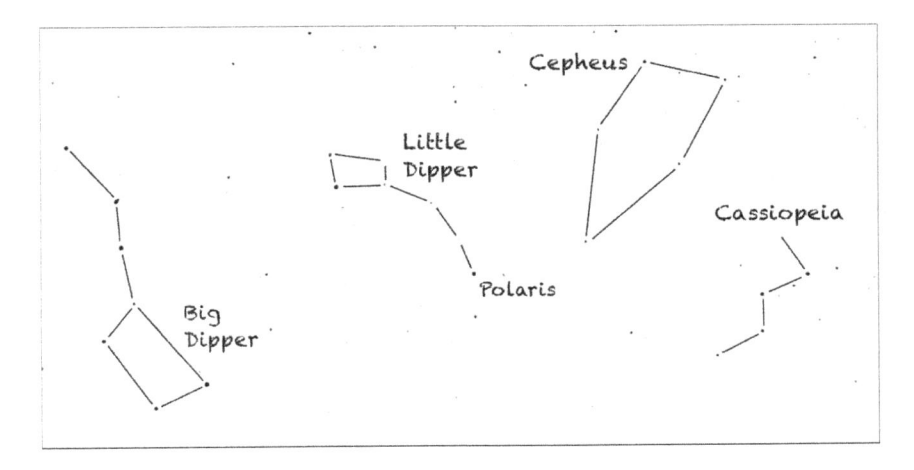

Since it's difficult to teach kids about our galaxy in the classroom. Once every year, the astronomy dome is inflated in my elementary school. I remember being captivated by this experience as a child. The astronomy dome is an inflatable igloo that includes a starry night light projector of our night sky. This high-quality projector is able to accurately show the night sky in sharp detail as it would be seen by your eye, with all its brightness and clarity.

I entered the dome with my teacher and other classmates. We could see all of the stars above us projected on the canvas. I had never seen anything like it before. The stars were gorgeous, bright and alive, even though they seemed so far away. I could see the Milky Way and other galaxies as if they were right there in front of me. It was all a bit overwhelming at first, but when my teacher helped us find Orion's Belt, I felt more connected to the sky than ever before.

The outlined shapes are galaxies that resemble humans, animals, and shapes. Most constellations don't have scientific names at all, but only common names that come from old legends and mythology. Over the years, I have been able to identify many constellations. But more importantly, I could identify their galaxies that were so far away that they seemed like points in the sky.

I never thought I would think of the stars above me as a map to guide my trading, but that's what they became. When I first noticed the connection between stock movements and constellations, it was like seeing a light shining in the dark. All of sudden everything made sense. It was like when you see something for the first time and suddenly you start noticing it all around you. If I follow price charts closely, it will become easier and easier to spot common price patterns because suddenly my eye will see patterns after patterns that were previously hidden to me. Every night I studied more charts, looking for clues about how markets will move to profit from them.

You need to learn how to read the patterns of price action to increase your odds of profiting on trades. There will be a time when your trades catch you completely off-guard. The market twists and turns as stocks rise up and back down. However, if you are able recognize patterns, then trading becomes easier because there's no guessing involved.

The stock market goes through different phases, just like our field of view of galaxies in the night sky. By understanding the four phases of the stock market and the shapes that correspond to them, traders can make better trades. Finally, just as astronomers use telescopes to study galaxies, investors can use technical analysis tools to study stocks.

WHAT ARE MARKET CYCLES

The stock market is a great example of how cycles operate in our lives. The stock market goes up and down in cycles, with periods of growth followed by periods of decline. When the stock market is doing well, people are more likely to invest money in stocks, and when the market is doing poorly, people are more likely to sell. The stock market is a perfect example of how human behavior can create recurring patterns that demand our attention.

Humans are creatures of habit. We like to stick to what we know and with what we're comfortable. It's why we often stay in relationships even when they're bad for us, why we keep going back to the same unhealthy foods even though we know they're not good for us, and why we keep investing in the stock market even though it seems like a roller coaster ride. We see a stock go up and we think it's going higher, so we invest. Then it goes down and we panic and sell. Then it goes back up again and we buy back in, only to see it go down again. And, so the cycle continues.

It's like a never-ending ride that we can't seem to exit. But why do we do this? Why do we keep going back for more even when we know it's not good for us? The answer is simple: because we're human. We're hardwired to seek out patterns and to latch onto anything that looks like a sure thing. It's how we've survived as a species for thousands of years.

Legendary investors know how to identify and master the governing stock market cycles. By understanding the rhythm, they are able to make the best calls on when to stay in and when to pull out. These investors have a keen eye for spotting opportunities and are not afraid to take risks. They are always on the lookout for new investment opportunities and are quick to take advantage of them. By understanding the market cycle, they are able to make a lot of money. These investors are true masters and are always one step ahead of the competition.

It is also possible to use technical indicators to recognize market cycles. However, this approach is more difficult, as cycles are the result of, and not the cause of, changes in the market itself. The main drivers of market cycles are changes in the fundamentals of the economy. These changes can be either leading indicators or lagging indicators. They are also strongly influenced by psychological factors, such as investor sentiment.

The market is always changing, and there's always talk of the next big thing. But what a lot of people don't realize is that these changes often happen for a reason. Cycles are formed when the trends in a particular industry or sector develop in response to new products, innovation, or even the regulatory environment. During a cycle, the net profits and revenues of companies in that industry tend to follow similar patterns.

A new cycle can be formed when something disrupts the existing trends and creates new ones. These changes are usually specific to an industry, which means that not every sector will be affected. To properly identify them, you need to look at both economic indicators, like natural disaster, and political climate, and interest rates. With this information, you can be prepared for whatever the market throws your way.

Cycles have no set duration and can last for different time periods, from minutes to decades. They are mostly difficult to determine as they hardly have a beginning or an ending that can be clearly identified, thus leading to confusion and controversies while assessing the economics and the policies.

Experienced investors are thought to be successful because they follow strategies that allow them to predict before the market shifts direction in its cycles. It is difficult for investors to determine their current cycles because the market do not have beginnings or endings that can be identified clearly in most cases; the cycle go on without a set duration that can feel like forever.

WHAT DRIVES MARKET CYCLES

The bear and the bull markets are both secular cycles. These cycles are long-term and can last for 4-10 years or more. In these secular cycles, there exists the sector rotation. When the bull market begins, technology, consumer, and financials outperform. When the bull market is at its middle, telecommunication, energy, raw materials, and industrials outperform. When the bull market ends, the bear market starts, which is characterized by the success of utilities, health care, and consumer staples. The rotations of this sector thus provide a hint on what really drives the cycles.

Sector rotation is a method of forecasting changes in the market, suggesting when it might be time to invest in a new sector, and selling the other. Sector rotation is the process of moving money among between different sectors of the stock market to take advantage of changing conditions. For example, if an investor thinks that the stock market is in a boom period, they may move money into sectors like technology and energy, which are expected to do well in a boom. Alternatively, if they think that the stock market is in a recession period, they may move money into sectors like consumer goods, which are expected to do well in a recession. This is because different sectors perform differently at different stages of the market cycle, and by rotating money among different sectors, an investor can take advantage of these different performances.

The market cycles are driven by different factors, such as interest rates, fluctuation of the exchange rate, and current events, among others. These factors have possible effects on the investor's behaviors. The main reasons are the macroeconomic factors, which include inflation, unemployment levels, and the economic growth rates. A drop in the rate of interest will result in a rise in markets and reflects economic growth. A rise in the inflation rate indicates is typically followed by an increase in the rates of interest which results in a slower growth, and thus results in a contraction of the market. High rates of unemployment also foretell a slowing in growth. However, a clear understanding of the key drivers in the market cycles helps an investor in deciding the best time for buying or selling their stocks.

The key drivers include:

Inflation. Inflation can affect the stock market in a few ways. First, it can lead to higher interest rates, which can make it more expensive for companies to borrow money. This may cause them to lay off workers or cut back on their investment plans, which could lead to a decline in stock prices. In addition, inflation can erode the value of people's savings, and this may cause them to buy more assets to protect their money. Finally, high levels of inflation can lead to stagflation, which is a dangerous combination of high inflation and high unemployment. This occurs when the economy is unable to grow because of the high levels of inflation, and it can be very difficult for businesses and consumers to cope with it.

Interest rates. During a recession period in any economy, the interest rates are lowered by the federal reserves, which adds more money to financial systems so as to outgrow the business and the consumer spending with an objective of moving the economy from the recession. The consumers and business borrow money that have low interest rates and spend more money. The banks are able to lend, the consumers are able to buy goods, and the businesses are able to buy new technology. As a result of the spending, corporate earnings increase. Prices of stocks normally increase where there are good earnings.

Economic Data. There are a few different ways that news or information can affect the stock market. For example, if a local government announces good news, the price of its stock may go up, and if it announces bad news, the price of its stock may go down. This is because investors react to news by buying or selling stocks, and this can cause the stock market to fluctuate. In addition, economic data can have a big impact on the stock market. For example, if the unemployment rate rises, it may cause the stock market to go down, and if the inflation rate increases, it may cause the stock market to go up. This is because investors use economic data to make decisions about whether to buy or sell stocks, and these data can be interpreted in different ways.

Company Earnings. Information that relates to individual companies such as a report on earnings, has the potential to influence on the stock prices. For instance, information that shows strong earnings in a particular stock will result in an upward movement of price while information that shows weak earnings on a particular stock will result in a downward movement in price. However, some companies that have low earnings can still show some rocketing stock price. This is an indication that the investors have great hope that the company will have greater earnings in the future. However, it is worth noting that fulfilment of the investors' current expectations by a company is not certain as the company might not have future earnings as high as predicted.

Natural disasters. Natural disasters, such as fires, rains, winds, and earthquakes, can drive the market. In most cases, seasons of natural disaster are accompanied by a decrease in the stock index on the days that the disasters occur. During this period, the investors are forced to sell their index for the days that the disaster is on or hold their index for more days.

Political influence. Political events can also have an impact on the stock market. For example, if the president of a country is elected who is perceived as being unfavorable to business, the stock market may go down. Political influence over the stock market can come in a few different forms. For example, the government may try to boost the stock market by bailing out banks or by providing tax breaks to investors.

Alternatively, they may try to depress the market by selling its own bonds or by imposing taxes on investors. In addition, the government may pass laws that regulate industries, and these laws can have a big impact on how the market behaves. For example, after the stock market crash of 1929, the US government passed a number of regulations that helped to stabilize it.

Taxation. The stock market is a fickle beast. Its ups and downs are influenced by a variety of factors, from global events to the weather. But one of the most important drivers of market activity is taxation. Changes in tax rates can have a significant impact on earnings, and, as a result, the stock market will often give its own response in the form of a rally or a sell-off. Higher taxes may be weighing on earnings, while lower taxes could be provide a shot in the arm. Either way, it's important to keep an eye on how taxation is affecting the markets.

When the economy is booming, companies can maximize their production and boost revenue. This means that borrowing decreases significantly, resulting in a surplus of money from both businesses and consumers. As this supply increases exponentially, inflation takes effect; market analysts, therefore, keep an eye on money flow as an indicator of when the bull market cycle will take off again.

The Federal Reserve has a mandate of controlling inflation by increasing the interest rates, as well as removing money from the system. Higher rates of interest discourage borrowing, thus resulting in a decline in both consumer and business spending. Higher rates of interest also result in an increase in business costs and a decrease in customer demand, which translates to lower earnings. Stock prices are proportional to the earnings and thus a decrease in earnings results in a decrease in the prices of stocks.

In conclusion, market sentiments can be explained as the psychology of the market participant, which can either be collective or individual. Market sentiments are often biased, obstinate, and subjective. For instance, solid judgements on the growth of a stock in the future can be made where the future can confirm the projections. However, the market can be currently working on some other projections that may keep the stocks low or high. This can make the investors wait longer while hoping that other investors will realize the fundamentals.

HISTORY OF DOW THEORY

In finance, there's a theory that every major trend has three phases. The first phase is when the trend starts and few investors are paying attention. The second phase is when the trend really takes off and everyone jumps on board. The third phase is when the trend peaks and then starts to reverse. The theory was developed by Dow Jones founder Charles Dow, and it's still used by market analysts today. While it's mainly used to predict stock-market trends, it can also be applied to other areas, like fashion or technology.

The concept of Charles Dow, who was the first editor of the Wall Street Journal has formed the foundation of today's technical analysis. Dow developed an industrial average of the highest blue stocks and second average of the top railroads. Dow believed that the averages' behavior echoed the fears and the hopes of the whole market. The patterns of behavior that Dow observed are applicable to the markets all over the world.

Dow theory refers to a financial theory that explains the market as a rising trend if one of the theories averages advances directly above the preceding important high and is followed by a similar increase in other averages.

The theory is made up of six tenets and every investor who wishes to use the technical analysis must have an understanding of the tenets, which will help them understand the working of the market. The theory is based on a hypothesis that stock markets do not operate at a random basis, but have some specific trends that guides the performance. Dow theory gives an explanation on how the investors can use the stock market to know how healthy a business environment is.

There are three main market trends that the Dow Theory looks at. the primary trend, the secondary trend, and the minor trend. The primary trend is the long-term direction of the market, and it is usually determined by looking at a chart of the DJIA over a period of years. The secondary trend is a shorter-term movement that runs counter to the primary trend, and it is typically measured using a DJIA chart spanning several months.

Finally, minor trends are small fluctuations that occur within the primary and secondary trends. These are usually measured using a DJIA chart spanning days or weeks. By analyzing all three of these market trends, investors can gain a better understanding of where the market is headed in the future (See Figure 9.1).

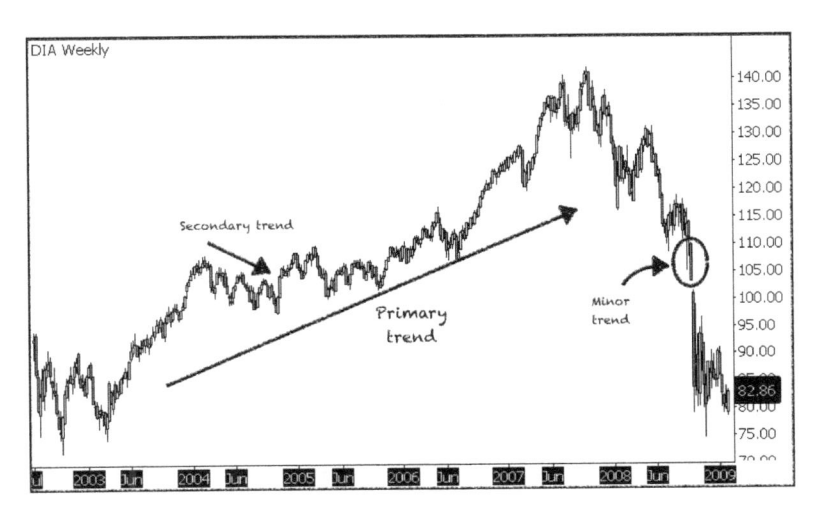

Figure 9.1: Three main market trends of the Dow theory.

Three major phases—The three phases of Dow's theory are: accumulation, public participation, and distribution (See Figure 9.2). The accumulation phase refers to the first stage where informed investors begin joining the market with the belief of a foreseen turning point. The public participation phase is the stage where a rapid rise in prices is experienced and an improvement in the economy is noted. More investors join this market as there is evidence of positive sentiments and an improvement in business conditions. This is the phase where most investors focus their attention. It is during this phase that the trend becomes widely known, and public investors begin to participate, driving prices even higher. While some investors may choose to cash out at this point, others see this as an opportunity to buy even more, hopeful that the trend will continue. The distribution phase is the final phase of the trend, where the smart money begins to cash out and take profits. Prices typically peak during this phase and then begin to decline.

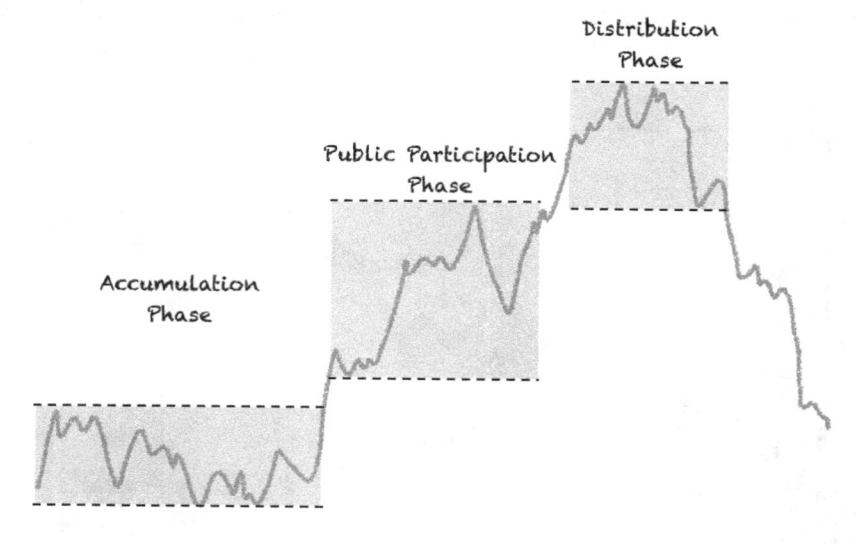

Figure 9.2: Three major phases of the Dow's theory.

While most investors focus on the public participation and distribution phases, it is the accumulation phase that is of utmost importance. This is the phase where the smart money is buying up assets, driving up prices, and laying the groundwork for the trend. By understanding and identifying this phase, individual investors can get in on the first floor of a major trend and ride it higher. So, keep your eyes peeled for accumulation patterns in the markets you follow; they could be your ticket to profits.

The averages must confirm each other. As any investor knows, the stock market is a complex and ever-changing beast. Trying to predict which way the market will turn next can feel like a fool's errand. However, there are certain indicators that can give you a good sense of which way the wind is blowing. One of these is the relationship between the rail and industrial averages, for example. According to Dow theory, if these two averages are moving in opposite directions, it's a good sign that the market is about to change direction. However, if they are both moving in the same direction, it's a strong confirmation of the current trend. So next time you're wondering which way the market is headed, be sure to take a look at the relationship between two separate averages. It just might give you the insight you need to make your next move. This theory remains relevant to this day with the age of finance, energy technology, and vehicles.

The averages discount everything. It has been famously said that "Wall Street discounts the future." This, in a nutshell, is the principle of reflexivity as applied to markets. Simply put, it means that stock prices reflect not only underlying fundamentals, but also the expectations and perceptions of market participants. These expectations and perceptions can be based on anything from earnings reports to rumors. As a result, stock prices can sometimes move in strange and unpredictable ways. The key to successful investing is to try to understand why prices are moving in a particular direction rather than simply following the herd.

One of the most famous examples of reflexivity in the markets is the Dot-Com Bubble of the late 1990s. During this time, investors were so caught up in the frenzy of new Internet companies that they were willing to pay absurdly high prices for their stock. They were convinced that these companies would change the world and make them rich. Of course, we all know what happened next. When the bubble finally burst, many people lost a lot of money. The principle of reflexivity can also be applied to individual stocks. For example, let's say that Company A announces it is going to enter a new market. The news will likely boost the stock price in the short-term, as investors bet on the company's future success. However, the stock price may not reflect the true underlying fundamentals of the company.

The volume must confirm the trends. There are a lot of different theories out there about what drives prices and how to predict changes. The theories focus on the idea that price movements are the main indicator of market trends. According to Dow, volume is a secondary indicator whose role is important in confirming signals for prices. In other words, the volume should expand in the same direction as the primary trend. So, in an upward trend, the volume should rise along with prices, and vice versa. This theory can be helpful in giving traders an idea of when to buy or sell. However, it's important to remember that all theories are just that—theories. The stock market is complex, and there's no sure-fire way to predict what it will do next.

The trend is assumed to be in effect until it gives definite signals that it has been reversed. The trend is your friend, until it's not. Such is the Dow theory, which assumes that trends exist regardless of any outside influences (aka "market noise"). Sometimes the market will move in the opposite direction of the trend, but it will always eventually return to its original path. Dow believed that any trend lasting longer than average is likely to change soon, and offers some reversal signs for which investors need to be on the alert. Dow also believed that market trends are created by the collective actions of all market participants, and that it's impossible to predict when a trend will end. So, keep an eye on the market noise and be ready to buck when the trends change.

In conclusion, Dow theory has remained relevant for a long time and is also important in the current market. Understanding the theory can help traders to exploit market trends and also take advantage of spotting good opportunities. It is important for each investor to have in mind that technical analysis is an essential component in trading and that a better understanding of the process helps in making the appropriate decisions and in avoiding possible losses. So, next time you're trying to decide whether to jump on a bandwagon or not, remember the Dow theory—it just might help you stay ahead of the curve.

MODERN STAGES OF A MARKET CYCLE

The Dow theory is one of the most well-known approaches to market analysis. Originally developed in the late 1800s, it argues that stock prices move in cycles and that these cycles can be used to predict future market movements. However, the theory has come under criticism in recent years, with some arguing that it is no longer relevant to today's markets. There are several reasons for this. First, the theory assumes that all market participants have access to the same information and act rationally. However, this is often not the case in today's markets, where information is asymmetric and emotions can play a major role in decision making. Second, the theory relies on a mechanical approach to market analysis, which is no longer feasible given the increased complexity of the financial markets. Finally, the theory fails to take into account the impact of global factors on market movements. As a result, many modern market analysts believe that the Dow theory is no longer an accurate representation of how markets actually work.

Market cycles are created by the interaction of two forces—human psychology and market fundamentals. Psychology drives markets in the short term, while fundamentals drive them in the long term. In the short term, investors are driven by emotions like fear and greed. This can lead to bubbles and busts. However, in the long term, stock prices are driven by earnings, dividends, and other company fundamentals. This section provides a more modern approach to market cycles. So, let's begin.

The markets are always in motion, and there's no telling what will happen next. The prices of stocks might appear to be random, but the price cycles keep on repeating. The cycles are mainly driven by involvement of large financial institutions in this market. Traders should have strategies that will enable them to take advantage of the price action as they occur.

The four main stages of a stock market cycle are expansion, peak, contraction, and trough. Expansion is characterized by rising prices, economic growth, recovery, and boom, or market recovery. Peak is marked by high prices and slowing economic growth in a period of stagnation. Contraction is characterized by falling prices and economic recession. Trough is characterized by low prices and economic depression (See Figure 9.3).

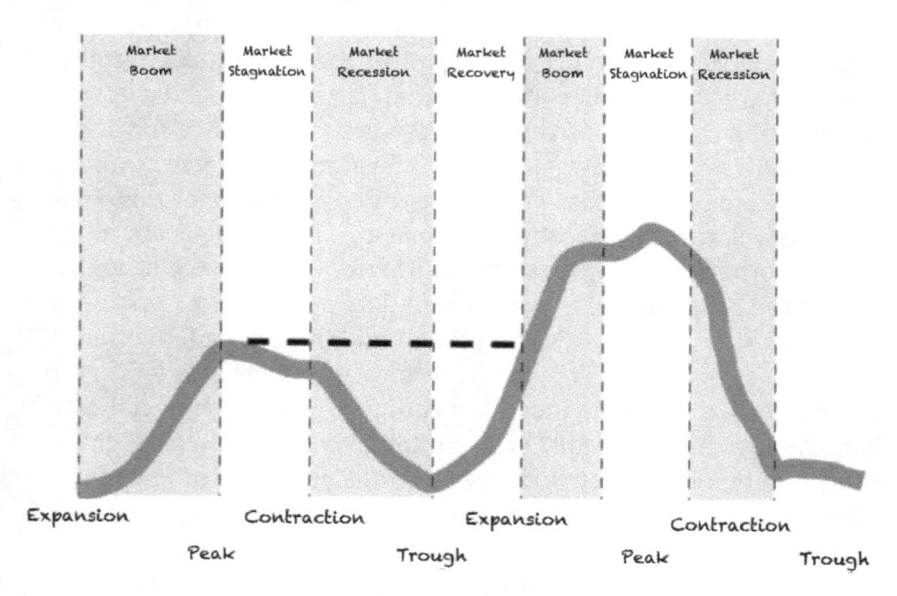

Figure 9.3: The modern stages of the market cycle.

Trough stage. The trough stage, which is also known as the accumulation stage, starts when the institutional investors, like pension funds, large banks, and the mutual funds, purchase a significant number of shares of a given company. This means that institutional investors accumulate stocks over time to avoid causing the stock prices to increase too much. The prices form the base because the stock shares are accumulated and prevent price from dropping further. The early adopters and the investors also start purchasing as they assume that the worst seasons are over.

The accumulation stage occurs immediately after the market gets to the bottom. When the investors, experienced traders. and money managers figure that the worst seasons are over, and company valuation becomes important. This occurs because of economic growth, which leads to a bull market. In this period, the sentiments of the markets switch from negative to neutral.

The accumulation stage can last longer in an economy that is well managed. This stage is not lucrative to buy as a retail investor because capital becomes tied up or the trader may face a large drawdown of their capital. However, it is important for traders to recognize the accumulation stage signs so as to get insight of the future opportunities. There is a potential for the investor's capital to wear down over time in this phase because the prices is moving sideways.

 A trough market pattern can form with an ascending triangle, double bottom, or cup and handle. A double bottom is a bullish chart pattern that occurs when prices fall to a new low, rebound, and then fall to the same low again. This indicates that buyers are starting to take control of the market and push prices back up. The second low forms what looks like a W connected by a horizontal line. A cup and handle is a bullish continuation pattern that forms after a downtrend. The cup is shaped like a bowl or rounding bottom, while the handle looks like a short downtrend or consolidation phase before breaking out of the cup. As buyers start to take control of the market, prices will break out from the cup and continue on their upward trajectory (See Figure 9.4).

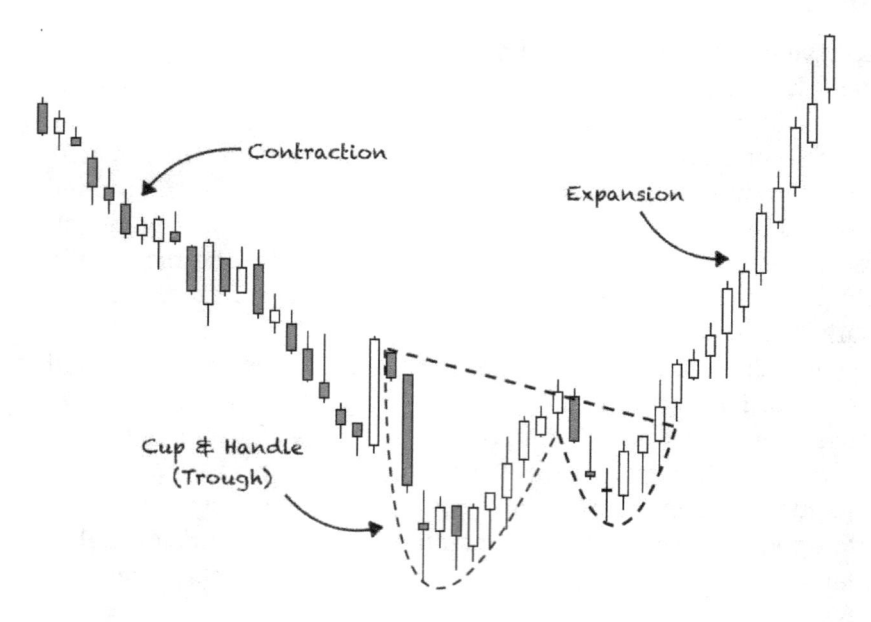

Figure 9.4: The trough stage forming a cup and handle pattern.

Expansion stage. The expansion stage cycle is where prices get to the highest point and marks the shift to the stage of increasing prices. This stage mostly occurs when the market has been stable for a while, and it starts to go up in price. At the stage, a switch of the market sentiment is experienced from neutral to bullish. The stage is marked by investors jumping in large numbers, hence a significant increase in trading volume is observed. The climax of buying usually takes place during the stage when prices start to go up quickly. This happens because more people are getting interested, including risk-averse investors and fence sitters. Basically, in the expansion stage, the price breaks out of the range and start an uptrend that is sustained. The prices start to move up and the big money has positions that have already been established. The retail traders are invited at this stage to invest and join in the profit party. This is the most profitable stage for investors and provides an opportunity to make a lot of money. If you want to make the most money as the market is expanding, you should enter the market early into this stage.

An expansion market pattern can form with a rising wedge or uptrend pattern. A rising wedge is a type of bearish chart pattern that indicates a reversal in the current trend. The trend lines drawn on the chart are angled and symmetrical, with a downward sloping trend line connecting several lower highs and an upward slopping trend line connecting several higher lows. As the selling pressure increases, the price will break out of the wedge formation to the downside. An uptrend can be explained as a succession of higher pivot lows and higher pivot highs. This indicates that the price is steadily increasing over time (See Figure 9.5)

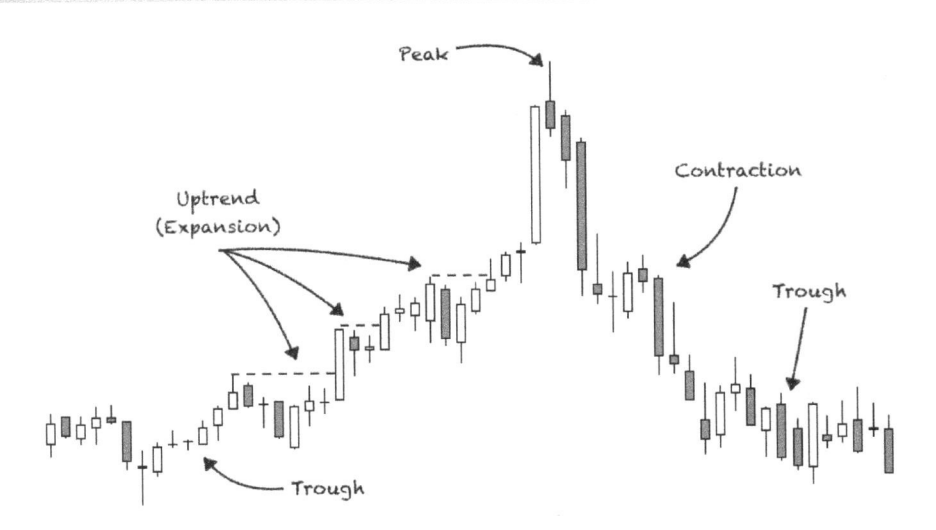

Figure 9.5: The expansion stage forming an upward pattern.

Peak stage. The peak stage, also known as the distribution phase, begins after the expansion stage, where the prices get into another trading range. In this third phase of the cycle, the sellers are in control as the traders sell. The shares are sold over a period of time, with the seller wanting to keep the price high until all their shares are gone.

When the market is at the distribution stage of its cycle, it demonstrates a weakening in demand. This happens when there are more sellers than buyers, and can result in lower prices for stock as well as decreased popularity overall. The market's sentiment changes over time from optimistic to neutral. The market's direction also changes over time by economic stagnation. The prices at this stage tend to remain a bit constant for several months. These changes may last for an extended period of time. Chances of market decelerating are also high, which may result from bad economic news, like the pandemic lockdown or a negative change in the political environment.

 A peak to market pattern can form with a double top, descending triangle, or head and shoulder patterns. A double top is a bearish chart pattern that occurs when prices fall to a new low, rebound, and then fall to the same low again. This indicates that sellers are starting to take control of the market and push prices down. The second high forms what looks like an M connected by a horizontal line (See Figure 9.6). A descending triangle is a bearish chart pattern that indicates a reversal in the current trend. The trend lines drawn on the chart are angled and symmetrical, with a downward sloping trend line connecting several lower highs and an upward sloping trend line connecting several higher lows. As the selling pressure increases, the price will break out of the triangle formation to the downside. A head and shoulder is a type of bearish reversal pattern that forms after an uptrend. The head is shaped like a peak or shoulder, while the two subsequent lows form what look like arms or shoulders. As sellers start to take control of the market, prices will break below the neckline and continue on their downward trajectory.

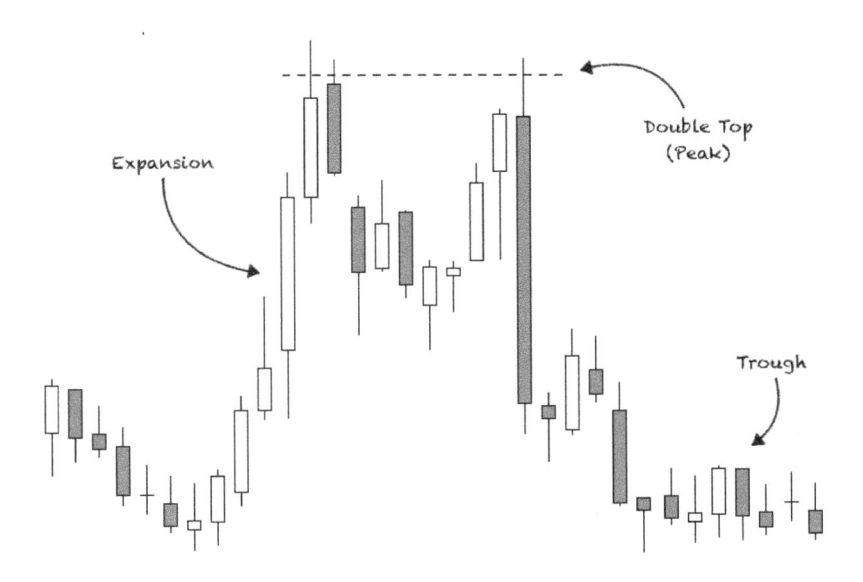

Figure 9.6: The peak stage forming a double top pattern.

Contraction stage. The contraction stage or recession, which is defined by a sharp drop in value and economic downturn, is a procedure that frequently leads to a market crisis. Some people are waiting for the price of stocks to go down. Investors who still have a position are usually in a terrible stage. The prices of the stocks fall and are below what the investors had initially paid. The larger investors are not fools; they can see that these stocks have been overvalued and, thus, are not worth their investment. Company layoffs and unemployment continues to grow despite government efforts to stimulate the economy. The market starts at its peak and ends at its trough in a downtrend. This indicates that the price is steadily decreasing over time. The prices for stocks are starting to go down. The institutional investors who have a lot of money have already sold their stocks. The people who are selling stocks now are the small investors. When investors sell, the price of the stock goes down. This being the last period and also marking the beginning of the accumulation phase where new investors will purchase stocks that have depreciated, these investors are planning for another recovery and new market cycle.

 A contraction market pattern can form with a falling wedge or downtrend pattern. A falling wedge is a type of bullish chart pattern that indicates a reversal after a bearish (contraction) trend. The trend lines drawn on the chart are angled and symmetrical, with a downward sloping trend line connecting several lower highs and an upward sloping trend line connecting several higher lows. As the selling pressure increases, the price will break out of the wedge formation to the downside (See Figure 9.7). A downtrend in price is often represented by a succession of lower pivot lows and lower pivot highs.

Figure 9.7: The contraction stage forming a falling wedge pattern.

In conclusion, it can be hard to stay on top of the market and know when to buy and sell stocks. Markets go through four distinct phases, and each phase has its own opportunities and risks. Understanding the four phases gives an investor an opportunity to optimize profit. Investors who understand the four market phases can make more informed investment decisions that result in consistent profits with minimized drawdowns. Being aware of the current stage of the market will help you make better trades.

PART IV

RISK MANAGEMENT

The stock market is a risky place, and people can lose their capital in seconds. Fortunately, there are some rules that, if followed, will help you to minimize the risk of losing your hard-earned capital in this casino. These rules were formulated after many years of research and by top financial analysts. They are not only used by professional traders to consistently beat the odds and make consistent profits over time. These rules are simple and, if applied correctly, would greatly increase your chances of winning this game called stock trading.

Unfortunately, most traders don't follow any set of rules because they simply lack knowledge of them nor know how to apply them properly. For instance, having a mentor is an effective way to learn how to trade and achieve your trading objectives more quickly. That's why I wrote this section for you, which contains everything you need to know about beating these odds and making consistent profits from stocks. The stock market is similar to a casino because, in both places, people are taking risks. And what they need is to think rationally, think in probabilities, and count on their odds. Often, we have falsely instinctive behavior about our bets—we often make emotional decisions instead of calculated risks. We gamble on emotions like fear and greed, which if not curbed can only negatively impact us. Emotions also don't just exist when making decisions; we can make up "fantasy" scenarios or build up hope for future success that may never come to fruition—pulling justifications out of thin air for everything that happens to justify our actions.

There are three very important processes that successful traders use to secure their capital. These are position sizing, stop losses, and psychological biases. Each of these processes is different in the long run, and each has an impact on your success while trading. The section will cover what each process is and how it functions. Risk management is about controlling your exposure to loss, which prevents disasters from happening. It involves limiting the amount you invest in any one investment, while also determining what price levels would release your commitments. This protects you from total loss of all the money you have invested or added to this trade so far. You can also decide what percentage of investments you take on based on an account balance or the amount of money with which you're trading.

Position and share sizing. This section will discuss how position sizing is the most essential of the processes because it determines how much you can invest in any given trade. This is important because it determines how much you can lose in each trade, but also what your profits might be on the other side of the market.

Stop loss placement. This section will discuss different strategies to determining how much you can risk using stop loss placement. Stop losses also go hand-in-hand with position sizing because they are used for determining when to get out of the market. They act as rules that determine whether you give up on a trade before it destroys the capital you've put into it. Most traders use a combination of position sizing and stop losses to determine how much they can invest in a trade or when to get out of the market.

Psychological biases. Psychological biases are about using your ability to think in ways that will reduce losses and maximize profits. This management section will discuss how you should avoid making mistakes that are caused by cognitive biases, which can result in lost money. There will come a moment when we will suffer a loss as a result of our decisions.

Emotions should not have a role when making decisions about investments in stocks. Gambling may not seem like such a big deal until you face financial ruin or lose your entire life's savings. This risk management section of this book is intended to assist you by offering tools and information that you can use by understanding: gambling mentality, trader discipline, and how to mitigate risk-averse behaviors with trading plans and journaling trades.

Gambling mentality. The idea of gambling and the stock market is very similar. In both, it's about predicting the odds and then either winning or losing based on those odds. There are a lot of factors that can go into determining if you win or lose. However, the emotions and stress that come with these decisions may be much less extreme from day to day than what we see when people gamble—but they exist all the same. What should your trading decision-making framework teach you about making decisions?

FUN FACT Winning isn't everything. Poker players often enter tournaments for which they have no chance of winning, or they will spend time and money playing in a game that has no money as the prize. They do this because of their love for poker, and the thrill of playing supersedes everything else. The same is true for traders who are willing to go into risky trades because they love trading. There is no better feeling than making the right trade at the right time and then watching your hard work pay off in handsome dividends. Again, the stock market is a risky game, but there are ways to mitigate the risk involved and ensure that you have an edge over your competition. Not only that, when you have a solid trading system in place and the ability to execute it correctly, you'll find that your success comes much more easily.

Trader discipline. A large part of trading discipline is being able to take the correct action at the time it's needed. To do this successfully, you must practice taking these actions so it becomes second nature. Having a trading plan before embarking on your journey as a trader will help provide the discipline to follow it and increase your chances of success. But what is discipline? It's doing something even when you don't want to do it. Making sure you follow your trading plan and reevaluating trades when you get in them are just a few of the ways to increase your trading discipline.

Trading Plan and journaling. By sticking to a set of rules and following a set plan, traders are more likely to see favorable results in terms of money flow. It takes a lot of self-control to stick to a plan, especially when the market is moving against you. But, in the long run, it's worth it to trade with discipline if you want to be successful. The market rewards you for your discipline. The most important risk management practice is to take calculated risks. Steps need to be taken when journaling the trade, to document the odds of success and failure, analyze if lost if unsuccessful; and whether that level of loss is acceptable.

People frequently lose because they are obsessed with becoming rich quickly. They make a trade and risk their entire capital in the hopes of making a huge profit. When we are wrong about our trades, it is crucial to stop out as quickly as possible and not allow them to grow. And, we should constantly be mindful of how much risk we have taken on in each trade so that we may quit immediately and limit losses if things go wrong. So, remember, there is no shame in admitting that you made a mistake and taking steps to protect your capital.

10 Risk-to-Reward

Chapter Overview

» How to use risk-to-reward ratio

» Common traps of cognitive and psychological bias.

Tale of Richard Wyckoff

Richard Wyckoff was an American stock market investor and founder of the Magazine of Wall Street. He has primarily conducted research on the technical aspects, with a focus on generating wealth, and has earned accolades for his expertise in this area. Wyckoff, who was an expert in stock investing, observed that there were gaps in knowledge and experience on Wall Street that prevented people from creating wealth. As a result, he published books like "Studies in Tape Reading" and "How I Trade and Invest in Stocks and Bonds." He strived to bridge this gap through education, teaching, and publications.

Wyckoff was born in 1873 and died in 1934, within which he influenced the teachings and understanding of the various concepts in stock market approaches. Wyckoff was one of the most prolific and successful investors of the early 1900s. He made a fortune by investing in bonds, stocks, and commodities. His investment strategies were based on timeliness and patterns that he observed in the markets.

In 1922, he wrote an article for the Saturday Evening Post called "Bucket Shops," which highlighted the problems and offered solutions. Wyckoff's insights have had a lasting impact on wealth-generation strategies and continue to be used today. Thanks to his foresight, we are better equipped to create and maintain wealth. His insights helped to shape the way that investors view the markets.

Wyckoff's main goal was to develop the technical analysis of stock prices to better understand how the stock market works and what implications it has on investors. He did this by studying the movements of price data over time and evaluating the various factors that influence stock prices. This enabled him to identify trends and make predictions about future stock prices.

Wyckoff's philosophy was that markets are constantly falling and rising, and that the key to success is to focus on the external forces that influence market movements. Wyckoff believed in the importance of understanding the psychology and movement of the market before making a trade. He developed various strategies to help investors maximize profits and minimize losses, such as using stop-loss at certain percentage of its value. He thought that it was best to identify the potential risks and rewards when trading.

The theories and models he developed regarding the stock market have had an impact on the way we trade today. Consequently, his work has been revolutionary in shaping how people understand and study the stock market. Without a doubt, Wyckoff was a brilliant mind whose work continues to be essential for anyone wanting to understand how the stock market works. Wyckoff's work was instrumental in helping modern investors understand the stock market.

Being a successful trader takes more than just riding the wave of good fortune. In addition to having nerves of steel and the ability to think fast on your feet, you also need to have a firm understanding of market trends and how to interpret data. With so many factors influencing price changes, it can be difficult to make sense of it all. Fortunately, Wyckoff was here to help. A pioneer in the field of technical analysis, Wyckoff developed a system for understanding market trends, risk-to-reward, and the psychology behind them. He also believed that the study of market changes could help investors make better decisions about their portfolios. Thanks to Wyckoff's pioneering work, we have a better understanding of how the stock market works—and how to make money from it.

INTRODUCTION TO RISK-TO-REWARD

I don't know how to describe this feeling I get every time I see the numbers go up on my screen. Sometimes, when I'm away from it all, say at a restaurant with friends or something, and somebody texts me about their trades going well—my stomach tightens and butterflies take over my chest. It's an adrenaline rush like no other. And then there are times when everything is just too much. The market crashing out of nowhere or someone else in a trade doing so poorly that they're bankrupting themselves by chasing after losses. Then again, if you want something worth living for in your life, nothing will ever compare to trading as far as excitement goes. There are ups and downs in trading, similar to a roller-coaster ride at a theme park.

Trading is a highly lucrative venture, but it can be dangerous if you don't know what you're doing. It's important to understand why you are trading before diving in headfirst; otherwise, your livelihood could be at risk due to psychological challenges or an inability to manage the risks of dealing with different market environments. The fear of missing out is another psychological challenge that you need to overcome during high market volatility.

I had a friend who was trading stocks. She would spend all day reading the news, following trends on social media, and asking people about what she should buy next. At first, it seemed like she was doing well, but then the market turned south, and the value of her portfolio plummeted. It got so bad that I started telling others not to talk about stocks around her because she would instantly panic if their conversation went into financial territory for more than five minutes. I have come across people before who lead themselves into panic-buying mode because they are afraid of missing out on the next big mover.

Trading is a difficult business, and it takes discipline to stay on track, even when we're in the middle of a tricky situation and even if my trading has been going well for weeks or months at that point. There's still always the possibility of getting knocked off balance by an unforeseen event, like being caught up in one bad trade after another. Most traders struggle with keeping their rules, especially when they are faced with potentially losing days that can affect them psychologically. When they listen to your thoughts about what you believe may happen but hasn't occurred, this complicates trading tenfold!

It's not uncommon for traders to get too bold and expose themselves to unnecessary levels of risk. We know that we don't want to be reckless, but it can be hard to find the right balance between safety and growth. I will teach you how to easily manage your risk by analyzing how much exposure you have in terms of capital as well as time horizon, which is key when managing risk. Our biggest asset is our capital. We must protect it from unnecessary risks. We are all aware of the fact that there are many kinds of risks in today's market environment, and they can be very dangerous to you and your capital if not handled properly.

Risk is the chance that something will happen and is seen as a double-edged sword. There is the possibility of loss, but it can also mean opportunity. We are always taking some level of risk in our lives—whether it be financial, emotional, physical, or social. When we take risks, we often reap rewards. The key is understanding what your tolerance for risk is and how much you're willing to lose if things don't go as planned. Risk management is the process of assessing, analyzing, and minimizing potential negative impacts. Managing risk is all about minimizing losses when markets are generally bearish (down) and maximizing gains when markets are generally bullish (up). In other words, it's all about timing. If you can time the market correctly, you stand to make a lot of money. Of course, timing the market is easier said than done. It's a risky business, but that's why they call it gambling. And like any good gambler will tell you, the key to success is knowing when to walk away. So, if you're feeling lucky, go ahead and take a chance. But remember, always know your limits.

SHARES SIZING

Although catastrophe losses are extremely uncommon, they may be devastating if they happened to you—such as an asteroid striking the Earth or you are struck by lightning. As your investment gets bigger, it becomes more expensive to "loose" than with a smaller account. One of the most popular strategies for managing risk is called "share sizing," (also known as position sizing) which conceptually has a lot in common with wearing a belt before you go into battle—this way, if you lose your shirt, at least you won't end up losing your pants, too. When you buy shares of stock, you are putting money into the company. When you trade stocks, the share sizing is how much money you want to risk on each trade. The decision of how much to risk per trade requires substantial thought.

Many factors go into setting your risk parameters, such as how much you're willing to lose and what kind of returns will make up for those losses. There isn't one perfect answer because no two traders have the same situation or goals, so it's important for each person who wants in on this wild ride to do their due diligence before they get too deep with any trade. The problem with most traders is that they are not aware of how much money they can afford to lose. As a result, many traders lose their entire account balance within days or weeks. This leads to them giving up on trading altogether.

Your maximum dollar risk will tell you the maximum amount of dollars that can be lost if the market goes against you. It does NOT tell you how many shares to buy or sell, but rather helps you determine an acceptable risk level of loss before entering into a trade. When using share sizing for managing risk, it's important to know what portion of your portfolio is exposed in any single trade and not exceed 2% of the total available value. The max amount at risk ensures that you do not lose more than 2% of your total capital on each trade by limiting each position to a specific maximum.

A good rule of thumb is to calculate risk before the start of the trade. If you are starting, we would recommend starting with a conservative amount (1% is what we would recommend). The importance of using share sizing to manage risk can be seen in the following example. If you enter a trade at $1.50 and you have put a stop at $1, then your risk is 50 cents per share. Determine the absolute number of shares allowed to be traded. To do this, take the risk amount per share and divide it by your maximum dollar risk. For example, if your account size is $25,000, and your maximum dollar risk is $500 (which is within 2% of your account size), then your maximum position size is 1,000 shares (See Figure 10.1).

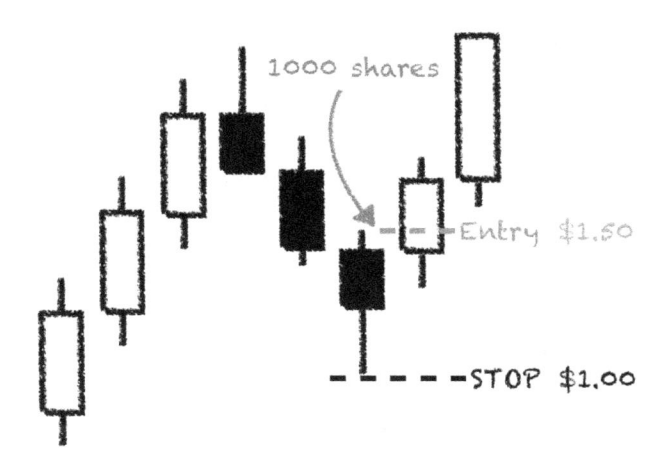

Figure 10.1: The maximum position size is 1,000 shares for $500 risk.

Dollar-cost averaging. Instead of committing to a trade all at once, why not consider adding in increments? Dollar-cost averaging can be the perfect way to trade because it allows you to spread out entries over time. Not only does this strategy help reduce risk, but additionally it takes away the need for constant monitoring because this strategy can be easily automated. More importantly, this strategy gives you more control over when and how many shares to add at regular intervals regardless of stock prices.

If you want to start dollar-cost averaging, pick how many shares (or contracts) you want to buy each week. For example, you could buy 100 shares every week.

Generally, prices drop more quickly in market downturns, opening an opportunity to acquire more shares on the way down, which in turn decreases your overall average cost per share. This is beneficial because it allows you to take advantage of changing market conditions while still minimizing the risks associated with trading. Therefore, instead of committing a considerable sum all at once, consider investing in increments.

However, it is not without its risks. For example, the timing of entries could lead to missed opportunities or potential losses. Additionally, it can be difficult for traders to predict the future direction of the price or when to exit a position. Therefore, traders need to understand the risks involved before committing to this strategy.

Fade. Fading is counter-intuitive yet advantageous; traders buy when prices drop and sell when they rise, thus allowing them to capitalize on both bullish and bearish markets. With the potential for sizable returns, this approach can be highly profitable if done strategically. For example, trading with an oscillator indicator can be a great way to time your entries (See Figure 10.2).

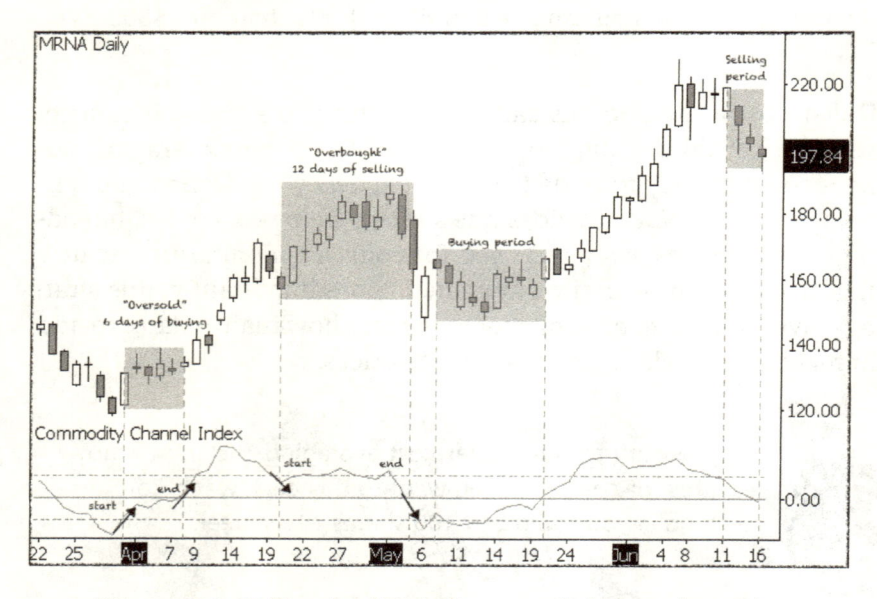

Figure 10.2: Utilize the CCI indicator to fade into the trade.

We can utilize technical indicators like the RSI or CCI as a means of assessing periods of opportunities in Moderna, Inc. This strategy helps to take the guesswork out of when to buy and sell, by taking advantage of indicator conditions that represent overbought and oversold situations. When a stock is oversold, its price has fallen beyond what may be considered normal or fair value, and so the odds of price rising increase. By waiting to buy the stock until it has been deemed oversold, the traders can potentially purchase at the right time and price.

In general, fading is a proven strategy popular with both amateur and professional traders alike. It's an easy way to start building your trading portfolio without needing extensive market knowledge or having too much capital upfront. This strategy will also ensure that you do not miss any opportunities, whether the market is up or down.

Averaging down. Averaging down is a technique used by traders to reduce their average cost per share. It involves buying additional shares at lower prices than they had originally paid. The idea behind averaging down is that more shares are purchased at progressively lower prices. If the price eventually goes back up, then you stand to make a larger reward due to the lower average cost basis. This tactic is very risky. Should you attempt this strategy without due caution, it can prove hazardous to the inexperienced trader.

Scaling. Did you know that using Fibonacci Price Levels can also reduce your risk? It uses sophisticated mathematics to help identify potential support and resistance levels, so you're not blindly relying on luck. Plus, when using Fibonacci price levels to scale into a trade, it reduces your average price paid per share. With this strategy, traders can buy additional shares of a stock at the support level and wait for its price to rebound, thereby increasing the likelihood that they will make a profit from their trade (See Figure 10.3).

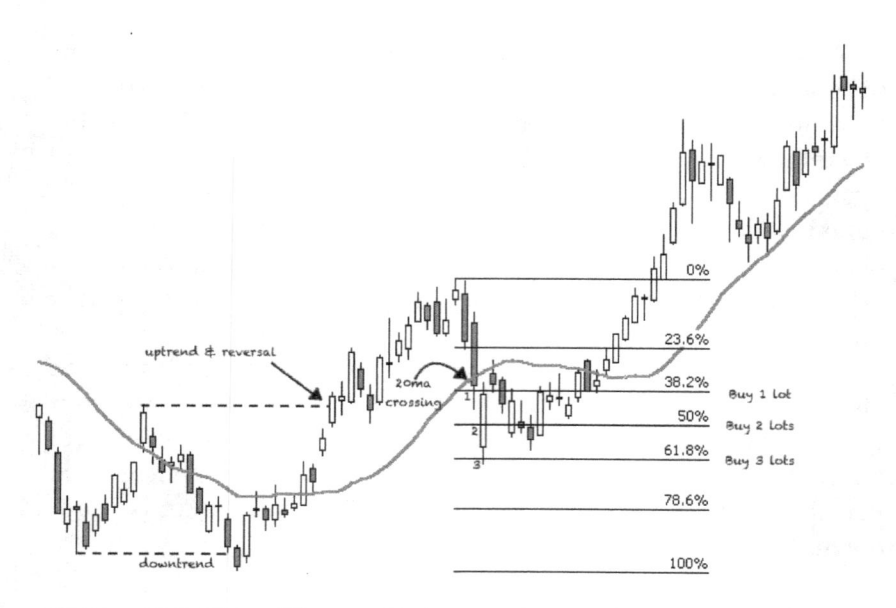

Figure 10.3: Using Fibonacci Price Levels to scale into the position.

Fibonacci price levels, also known as Fibonacci retracement levels, are popular strategies used by many traders. These levels are created by drawing a trend line between two extreme points (high and low) on a chart, then dividing the vertical distance by the key Fibonacci ratios of 23.6%, 38.2%, 50%, 61.8%, 78.6%, and 100%. On many occasions, experienced traders often scale into their position with increasing share size while maintaining a fixed risk and multiplying their reward.

Overall, scaling at each Fibonacci price level can be a useful strategy for those who are looking to reduce their average cost per share and risk to potentially increase your profitability.

Dangers. It is important to note that while averaging down and scaling can provide trader with larger reward, there is an inherent risk involved as well. If a stock continues to fall in price, the trader will end up buying more shares at lower and lower prices, potentially leading to a loss. If the stock does eventually go back up but not enough to cover the cost of all the additional shares purchased. Therefore, treader should always consider their risk tolerance before employing these strategies. Additionally, they should research the company to ensure you have a good understanding of the fundamentals.

Consider setting a limit on how low the stock must go before adding more to your position. This will help you avoid unnecessary loss. All in all, these are useful strategies but they should always be used with caution.

When not having a plan, the problem with this is that you are at risk of losing your capital in a snap. In other words, if you don't have a plan, you're essentially gambling with your money. And we all know how that tends to end. So, if you want to be a successful trader, make sure you have a solid plan in place before you implement share sizing. Otherwise, you're just asking for trouble. The bottom line is that share sizing is a crucial part of managing risk. By knowing how much you're willing to lose and what kind of returns will make up for those losses, you can set yourself up for success. Just remember to do your due diligence before getting too deep into any trade. And always, always have a plan.

STOPS LOSS PLACEMENT

Many factors can determine your success. There are a lot of traders out there who have tried and failed at trading. It's not easy to succeed in this industry because it takes hard work and dedication to be successful at what you do. The problem with most traders is that they don't know how to trade profitably or even if their strategy will work when put into action in real markets. This section teaches you how to find profitable trades by using stop-losses so you never take too much risk with any trade again. You'll also learn about the market risk/reward ratio that will help you figure out whether or not the time is right for making a trade based on the current market conditions and price movement patterns. However, one thing is for sure—a good strategy is crucial to your success in this business. A profitable trading strategy is determined by market circumstances, such as the entrance point of trade, as well as well-placed stop-loss.

Being a successful trader in the stock market is all about stop-loss placement. The risk/reward ratio is one of the most important things to consider when share sizing. This is because it helps you to weigh your potential losses against your potential gains. If the risk/reward ratio is skewed, then it's probably not worth taking the trade. However, if the risk/reward ratio is in your favor, then share sizing becomes a whole lot easier. You can use price action to help you decide where you want to place your trades. By analyzing your potential winnings versus losses, you can make sure that you're always getting the most out of every trade that you make.

Price Action Stop. Stop-loss placement is a very important concept. By making sure that you're always getting the most out of every trade that you make, you can protect your investment while still allowing yourself to make a profit if the stock moves in the direction that you anticipate. When I use price action as my strategy to compute risk and reward, I place a stop underneath the candle pattern (See Figure 10.4).

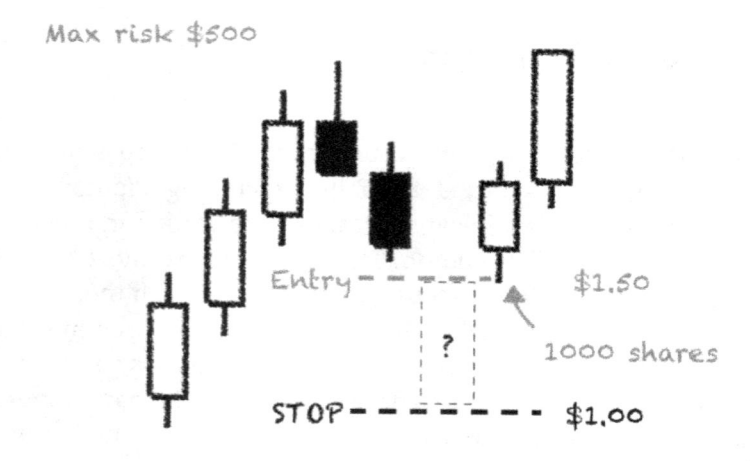

Figure 10.4: Place stop underneath the bullish candle pattern.

This is a very important method to use when share sizing since it can help you to make sure that your losses are always kept to a minimum. If the stock price moves against you, then you can simply exit the trade and only lose the amount that is under your maximum dollar risk. However, if the stock moves in the direction that you anticipated, then you can keep your position and potentially make a large profit. Thus, by using share sizing and stopping underneath the candle pattern, you can maximize your chances of success while still limiting your risk.

Average True Range. Are you having trouble setting the right stops because the market is constantly hitting your stop-loss? Average True Range (ATR) is an amazing technical analysis indicator that can help you identify the best level at which to place their stop losses. It considers the range of price movement for a given period by computing the average range and percentage change. By using this valuable information, you can choose the right price to place stop losses underneath your trade. Ultimately, this helps traders to allow room for their trade to move in their favor without being triggered out of the trade too soon.

The advantage of using ATR for placing stop-loss orders is that it considers the potential volatility of the market. This means that you don't have to guess how far the market could move against you and you can set more accurate stop-loss orders. By combining ATR with a trailing stop order, trading can be drastically simplified.

Moving Average Stop. The moving average method is a technical analysis strategy used to identify the direction of price trend, as explained in an earlier chapter. This strategy can then be used to help traders set stop losses that are aligned with the market's overall thesis. If price moves up and crosses the moving average, the stop loss should be placed underneath the pivot (See Figure 10.5).

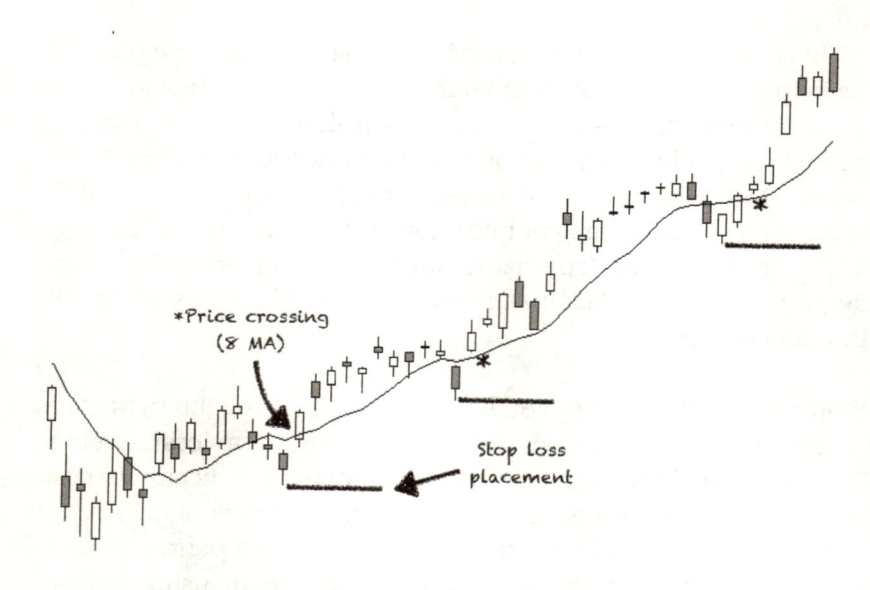

Figure 10.5: Stop loss placed underneath the trough.

In conclusion, losing trades are inevitable, but this doesn't mean you should take the hit and move on. The stop-loss is a tool that can help you minimize your losses in case of a downward slide. However, it is also something that needs to be used correctly if you want to avoid bigger losses. If not used properly, the stop-loss can end up being more dangerous than helpful. Many traders have been known to get into trouble because they don't know how to use it properly or when not to use it at all. You'll need to set a stop-loss price before making any trades so you know when you're going too far with your investments and can cut them off before they go south. This will help keep your losses manageable while still allowing for some growth in case things work out in your favor!

PSYCHOLOGICAL BIAS

So, you want to be a trader, huh? You're in for a wild ride. The market is full of irrational people who are just looking for the next quick win. You're not going to find any magic bullets or get-rich-quick schemes here; instead, you need to focus on a long-term strategy of building consistency through small wins over time. This type of trading takes patience, discipline, and consistency, which are all qualities that successful traders possess. Don't worry if you don't have them yet, as they are learnable skills. The bottom line is that if you want to be a profitable trader, then you need to know where the risks are and how many shares before entering into any particular trade. It's also important for traders to remember that risk management should always come before looking at potential returns because your main goal as a trader is to be consistent. So, if you're thinking about getting into trading, make sure you have a solid risk-management strategy in place first and foremost. And always remember: the market is full of irrational people, so don't let yourself become one of them!

When managing stock positions, many traders are susceptible to loss aversion. This is the tendency to avoid losses, even when the profit potential is great. As a result, traders may hold on to losing positions for too long, hoping that the stock will rebound. However, this often leads to even greater losses. Another common bias is confirmation bias. This is the tendency to look for information that confirms our existing beliefs while ignoring information that contradicts them. For example, a trader may hold on to a losing position because they believe that the stock will eventually rebound. However, if the stock doesn't rebound, the trader may continue to hold on to the position, despite all evidence to the contrary.

Availability heuristics is another common bias. This is the tendency to base our decisions on information that is easily accessible, rather than on more reliable information. For example, a trader may make a decision based on what they saw on TV, rather than on research they have done themselves. Finally, anchoring is another common bias. This is the tendency to fixate on a particular number or price point and then base our decisions around that number. For example, a trader may buy a stock because it is trading at $10 per share, even though it may be overpriced at that level. These are just some of the psychological biases that can affect a trader's decision-making process. If you are not aware of these biases, you may be doomed to fail as a trader. However, if you are aware of them and take steps to avoid them, you will be well on your way to success.

When stock prices are falling, there's a psychological trap into which we all fall. It's called the "endowment effect," and it means that we value something more highly simply because we own it. So, when the price of a stock starts to drop, we convince ourselves that it's not really falling, or that it will rebound soon. And as the price continues to drop, we go through different stages of anger, denial, bargaining, depression, and, finally, acceptance. But by then, it's usually too late and we've lost a lot of money. The key is to learn how to manage stop-loss orders and trailing stops so that when the price does go down, it doesn't take all of your money with it. With a little bit of discipline, you can avoid the psychological trap of falling stock and keep your portfolio healthy.

Anger. Anger is a psychological bias that can lead to big problems in trading. When we get angry, we tend to blame others for our misfortune and this can lead to resistance to change. If we're losing money, it's easy to become frustrated and take our anger out on the market itself. This is unproductive and will only lead to more losses. The key is to recognize that we can't control what the market does, so there's no point in blaming it for our mistakes. Instead, we should focus on what we can do differently to improve our odds of success. This might include diversifying our portfolios, sticking to our trading plan, or cutting our losses early when trades go against us. Recognizing and managing our anger is essential for successful trading.

Denial. It's no secret that humans tend to deny reality when it's inconvenient or harmful. We see this all the time in everyday life, whether it's people refusing to believe they have a drinking problem or denying that their relationship is in trouble. This psychological bias is known as denial, and it's a defense mechanism to which we resort when we're in danger. When faced with stressful situations, our brain automatically starts looking for ways to protect us from pain. One of these mechanisms is called dissociation, which is when we start thinking about something else or paying attention to anything else to avoid stress. This might seem like a good idea in the moment, but it's a problem because the stress will remain and continue to get worse until we come to terms with it and deal with it. So. next time you're feeling overwhelmed, take a step back and ask yourself if you're really in denial about what's going on. It might not be pleasant, but it's better than living in a state of constant stress.

Bargaining. Bargaining is a psychological bias that can lead to costly mistakes. One of the biggest psychological traps that traders can fall into is known as the sunk-cost fallacy. This is when we convince ourselves that a stock is going to rebound in value simply because we have already invested so much money into it. We think that since we have already lost so much, it would be foolish to sell now and lock in those losses. However, this is often a costly mistake, as the stock may never rebound and we end up losing even more money. The key is to cut your losses early and move on to greener pastures. Otherwise, you risk falling into the sunk-cost trap and losing even more money.

Depression. There's nothing quite like the feeling of impending doom when you're staring at a loss. Your heart races, your palms start to sweat, and you feel like you might just lose it all. This feeling is known as "depression" in the trading world, and it can be a real problem if you let it get the best of you. The key is to remember that depression is just a psychological bias, and there are plenty of other things that can contribute to a loss. When traders realize that they are in danger of losing money, they start to feel helpless. The risk still exists and the trader is not able to prevent it even though he or she knows what's happening. When this occurs, it's important to remember that the risk wasn't the only thing that went wrong. There could be plenty of other things that contributed to the loss, which will help you focus on an area of trading where you might be more successful. Don't focus on the one thing that went wrong; try to learn from your mistakes so you can be more successful in the future.

Acceptance. It's natural to feel attached to our trades and to want them to succeed. After all, we've put a lot of time and effort into making them happen. But when a trade doesn't go our way, the acceptance phase of trading is not the same as the acceptance that someone might experience after a breakup or the death of a loved one. Acceptance in trading means acknowledging the situation and coming to terms with it so you can move on. This is easier said than done, of course, because we're all prone to psychological biases that make us see what we want to see. For example, if we're in a losing trade, we might start seeing "evidence" that the market is about to turn around. Or if we're in a winning trade, we might convince ourselves that we're smarter than the rest of the market and that we can ride it to the top. Neither of these views is realistic, but they can be hard to release. The key is to accept that all trades are a gamble, and some of them are going to end up being losers. It's part of the game, and as long as you keep your losses small, you'll eventually come out ahead in the long run.

In conclusion, there's a simple rule of thumb that I like to follow: never put all your eggs in one basket. That is, don't put all your money into one stock, no matter how confident you are in its potential. Unfortunately, far too many people fall into this trap, and they often do so because they believe they are in control of the stock price. They think that if they make the right decision based on what they see, everything else will take care of itself. But the reality is that we are not in control of the stock market; it's a giant beast that does whatever it wants. So, if your trade is initially performing badly, it's important to resist the temptation to get out as soon as possible. Sure, your emotions may be telling you that your investment is doomed and there's no hope for recovery. But, if you sell too early, you could miss out on a rebound. And that, my friend, would be a costly mistake.

RISK-TO-REWARD RATIO

As a trader, the important thing you need to understand is the risk/reward ratio. This refers to how much risk you're taking relative to the potential rewards you could earn. If the risk is too high, it means you're exposing yourself to too much risk for the potential rewards. On the other hand, if the reward is too low, it means you're not taking enough risk to potentially earn high rewards. Finding the right balance is crucial to success in trading. Trader probability also plays a big role in this. If you're too anxious about risks, you'll never make any profits. But if you're too reckless, you'll quickly blow up your account. So, it's important to find a balance that works for you and stick to it. The less risk there is in trade, the more reward a person is going to make, especially in the long run. Knowing your statistics can help you focus on high-probability trades instead of wasting your time with bad ones. Your statistics also show the probability that the target will be reached in black or white. This eliminates guesswork and helps you focus on high-probability trades. Finally, the Reward-to-Risk ratio is an important concept in trading that any individual trader must learn to be able to trade profitably.

As traders, we are always looking for an edge. One way to get an edge is to have a clear understanding of risk-to-reward ratios. What is a risk-to-reward ratio? It is simply the amount of money you are willing to risk in order to make a potential profit. For example, if you are willing to risk $100 to make $200, then your risk-to-reward ratio is 1:2. In other words, for every $1 you risk, you stand to make $2. There is no magic number when picking a risk-to-reward ratios; but, as a general rule of thumb, most traders look for trades that have a minimum 1:3 risk-to-reward ratio. This means that for every $1 they risk, they stand to make at least $3. Of course, this is not set in stone and some traders are comfortable with a 1:2 risk-to-reward ratio while others may even go for 1:4 or higher. It all depends on your trading style and Risk Profile. So, what is an ideal risk/reward ratio? Well, that depends on your win-rate probability. If you have a high win-rate probability, then you can afford to take on more risk because you have a higher chance of winning. Conversely, if you have a low win-rate probability, then you need to take on less risk because you have a lesser chance of winning. At the end of the day, it's all about finding the right balance for you. If you're comfortable with a higher risk/reward ratio, then go for it. But if you're someone who wants to play it safe, then make sure you adjust your ratios accordingly. Ultimately, it's up to you to find what works best for your trading style.

Maintaining your expectation is equally as important. If you're expecting to win every single trade, you're setting yourself up for disappointment. The reality is, it's impossible to win 100% of the time. In fact, if you're only winning 70% of your trades, that's actually pretty good! Instead of fixating on a win rate that's unattainable, focus on finding situations where the risk/reward ratio is in your favor. If you can do that, you'll be well on your way to success. If you're thinking about getting into trading, there's one thing you need to know: your numbers. I'm not talking about the stock market ticker or the latest news from Wall Street. I'm talking about win-rate probability. You see, the key to making money in trading is to be right more often than you're wrong. And the only way to do that is to know your win-rate probability for a particular setup. When you know your win-rate probability, you can make better decisions about when to buy and sell. So, if you're serious about trading, get out a piece of paper and a calculator and figure out your win-rate probability. It just might be the most important number on which you ever trade.

The last, and arguably most important, thing you need is to find your trading competency. In other words, you need to figure out "how much money you're making" and "What sort of losses you're sustaining?" What is your best trading setup? Once you have these questions answered, it will be much easier to make money. But don't worry, if you don't have all the answers right away, that's completely normal. It takes most people years to find their trading competency. So just keep at it and eventually you'll find your sweet spot. Trust me, it's worth it. Making money in the stock market is amongst the most exhilarating feelings in the world. So go out there and find your trading competency so you can start making some profits.

In conclusion, if you find yourself struggling with your trading, it is best to not dwell on the negatives; but rather focus on what has proven to be working. To do this, you need to first find out how profitable you are as a trader. Second, look at the frequency that you have won, and then also weigh your losses accordingly. Once you understand where your strengths lie, practice them until they become second nature.

11 Trading Psychology

Chapter Overview

» Psychological factors that influence trading decisions.

» Trading discipline.

Tale of Jesse Livermore

Trading can be a very profitable career, but it's also incredibly risky. It is all about taking risks, but if you don't know what you're doing, those risks can quickly become disastrous. One mistake can lead to a massive loss, as Jesse Livermore found out. Livermore was one of the most successful traders of all time, and he wrote several books on trading that are still popular today. Livermore was an American stock trader and speculator who made his fortune in the early days of the stock market. His story is an inspiration to anyone who wants to achieve great things through stock trading.

Jesse Livermore was born in 1877 in Shrewsbury, Massachusetts, in the USA. He was born to a poverty-stricken family. At age five, Livermore could read newspapers, which highlighted his excellence in self-taught skills and concepts. Livermore was always a gifted trader. After leaving home, Livermore was employed at age 14, working as a stock brokerage with a payment of $5 per week. In 1892, when he was 15 years old, Livermore bet $5 at a stock gambling shop called a bucket shop, which earned him $3.12. The entry into the bucket shop marked an important part of his success in the financial markets.

By 1897, he had accumulated $10,000 in trading profits. Livermore had few choices for places to trade because he believed that the bucket shops were fixing the trades. He moved to New York in 1900, where he traded $10,000, leading to over 400% profits, since he earned $50,000. However, he lost the entire stake in New York, triggering his return to the bucket shops. Jesse made his first big trade when he was just 24 years old, buying stock in Northern Pacific Railway. The stock rose, netting Jesse a profit of $250,000. But he wasn't done yet. In 1907, he shorted Union Pacific Railroad and made a profit of over $1,000,000. Jesse's success came to an abrupt halt in the cotton trade of 1908, which led to his bankruptcy.

Despite this setback, Jesse Livermore is still considered one of the greatest traders of all time. A notoriously savvy investor, Livermore filed for bankruptcy twice in the early 1900s before making a comeback in the 1920s. His success came to an abrupt end in 1929, when the stock market crashed and he was forced to declare bankruptcy for a third time.

Livermore then became a financial advisor, selling a system of technical analysis that he claimed could predict future stock prices. While his skill as a trader is undeniable, Livermore's legacy is somewhat tarnished by his repeated bankruptcies and controversial dealings with the bucket shops. Nevertheless, he remains one of the most influential figures in the history of American finance.

Livermore was known for his achievements in the stock market as well as his involvement in several publications, which helped him to solidify his place in trading history. In 1923, Edwin Lefevre contacted Jesse about writing the "Reminiscence of a Stock Operator"— although Jesse wasn't the direct character in the book, his ideologies and business savvy were certainly captured within its pages. He also had success with other publications, including "How to Trade

Stocks" and "Analyzing the Market Key System"—both of which cements his legacy as one of the most well-known and respected financiers in history.

Livermore's life was a roller coaster of successes and failures, both in his trade and in his personal life. His high-stakes gambles often paid off, but they also took their toll, both financially and emotionally. He made and lost several fortunes over the course of his career, but his biggest fall came in 1940 when he lost everything in a series of bad trades. He was despondent and bankrupt, so he took his own life by shooting himself with an Automatic Colt Pistol in the Sherry-Netherland hotel's cloakroom, where he usually had cocktails.

Jesse Livermore will forever be remembered as a cautionary tale about the risks of trading on margin. His life is a reminder that even the most successful traders can make fatal mistakes. While Livermore's story ended tragically, his legacy continues to teach generations of traders about the importance of risk management. He was a stock trader who lived fast and died young. Thanks to him, we know that even the most experienced traders can make mistakes that cost them everything.

In conclusion, it's hard to know where to start and who to trust. Most people give up before they even get started because it seems too complicated and risky. They don't want to lose their hard-earned money. Livermore is the perfect example of someone who overcame all the odds to become successful in the stock market. He started with nothing and made millions by understanding the concepts behind gambling and stock trading. It is attributed to his mental capabilities in financials and mental mathematics Livermore's successes are an inspiration to many people who aspire to achieve great things. His story is one of rags to riches, and proves that anything is possible if you set your mind to it. If you want to learn how to trade like a pro, there's no better source than Livermore himself.

INTRODUCTION TO PSYCHOLOGY

I'm just starting out on my own, and the market has crashed. I'm scared of what's ahead of me—but I came too far to turn back now. I was looking at my computer screen and I had a sinking feeling that something bad would happen. It was like the air itself became heavy with anticipation. When it finally happened, there was no warning whatsoever; one minute everything seemed normal and then in the next instant I saw prices drop lower than expected, as if they were being pulled down by an invisible force. I knew what to do immediately because of my trading plan.

If you acquire all of the basic and technical aspects, but you don't possess the moral trading psychology, you won't be getting all that far, especially if you plan on having trading as a career. Self-care is another subject that should not be overlooked. Your trading psychology is very important, especially if you're a novice. The financial markets are extremely complex and dynamic, which means that the specific return on investment is not guaranteed. No matter how solid your strategy is, the other element that will always affect your outcomes is your own emotions. So, it is very important to be aware of your own emotions if you're new to trading.

What you need is patience and discipline, two very important elements in trading that are utilized by the best traders around the world. You need to maintain a strategy and follow your plan of action, no matter how difficult the markets make it for you. If you can do that, then you will be able to trade profitably. You need your own style of trading and not copy other traders' styles. It is important to know your own personality and understand at what you're good, so that when the time comes for a certain trade, you can make the best choice.

A very interesting question to ask yourself would be, "What am I after?" And this could be answered by asking, "What are my goals in life? What do I want to achieve with the money that I earn?" This is a great way to start off if you want to make money and be successful in the financial market. Trading psychology, as the term implies, is the emotional and mental control that helps decide success or failure. It's all about making decisions founded on tested facts and working strategy, rather than being scampered by emotion. The importance of having an ethical psychological attitude to trading shouldn't be downplayed. It's crucial that you have a proper and clear understanding of your own psychology.

EMOTIONAL TRADING

There are two opposite emotions, that are prominent conditions that have a serious influence on our lives. And unless you're a human computer, dealing with risk-averse behaviors is inevitable in trading. These human emotions are the two biggest factors that affect a trader's decision-making, but it is how you control these elements. If you can successfully control greed and fear, nothing will be able to stop your success.

When you start losing a few trades, doubts arise in your head as you lament your losses. You become a little more risk-averse and suspicious about opening new trades because you are concerned that you will lose more money. This is a common occurrence, and it will happen to everyone at some point. The best thing that you can do when things are not going well is to just put your head down and continue trading. Make sure that you are consistent with what you do, the approach that you take when trading, and the amount of money that you invest into each trade. Keep your emotions in check and stay focused on your trading activity. Even if you are not making money, continue to train yourself and trade.

Fear of taking risks. Fear is probably the most notable emotion for traders. Fear is the opposite of greed and it is a very strong emotion. When you're feeling fear, your mind will be dominated by negative thoughts that can have a very negative effect on your decision making. It can stop you from making the right choice and cause you to lose control over yourself, which can lead to disastrous results. Almost every trader battle with this emotion. It can cripple you from referring to your hard-earned skills. Important losses can lead to emotional distress and unrest; and if you don't address them, you may repeat such mistakes. Yes, the trader would be bewildered amid these anguishing losses, unable to join the trade or rule in other fear-based ways. Although the enthusiasm to trade may be active, the mental comeback should be stronger. In fear of suffering, you begin to avoid seizing possibilities by circling around them. You start to lose track of your strategy. You need to look at your trading system and interrogate if it still works for you.

Surrendering to greed. Greed is the desire for more of something than one needs. The object of a person's greed is always his/her own self-interest and never other people's interests or the common good. And greed is what makes people become selfish and self-absorbed. Greed can come in when you successfully trade and have gained a considerable amount of profit. You might think about waiting longer before selling your shares, to get a higher price, even though the market doesn't look promising right now. This is where greed begins to meddle with your trades, this is the reason you should have a system to assist indicating when the good time is to take profit. Furthermore, you'll need a money management plan to manage your investment. This is to avoid over trading and getting greedy when you should be out of the market.

Most traders often decide to leave the trade out of fear that the market will keep moving against them. These are the same trades they would have taken had fear not been in their way. Being paralyzed by fear is never a good thing, but it is always better than not taking any risks. If you are paralyzed with fear about your investments, start taking smaller-risk trades and build up to bigger ones as you feel more comfortable. Be aware of the natural tendency to avoid risks with investment strategies; work to concentrate on finding strategies that will allow you to take on calculated risks, which will maximize profits while minimizing losses.

In conclusion, despite the analysis pointing toward a strong entry, traders may find themselves embroiled by the fear of missing out (FOMO) and end up losing immediately at the market open. This usually results in a string of poor trades and the trader spends more time trying to recover than learning from their mistakes. To be a profitable trader, one must first learn how to limit their risk taking. It is therefore essential to manage risk and ensure you know your entry point before making the trade. If you are wrong, the damage is minimal.

GAMBLER MENTALITY

You will often hear of so-called experts who could argue that gambling and trading are very similar. I would agree to a certain extent that there are some aspects that very closely resemble each other. However, the motivation for gambling is not the same as our motivation for trading. In gambling, your motivation is to entertain yourself with the possibility of gaining some wins. That is not how we should look at trading. Our primary purpose is to earn profit, and it takes due diligence to do so. If this is not what is motivating you, then we would need to consider if you can do this for the long term.

Imagine a man walking into a casino with chips on hand. He sits at a Baccarat table and decides to gamble a little. He loses his opening hand and says to himself, "the next hand will be a winner..." and bets again. He loses his hand again and he assures himself by saying, "I am going to win the next hand..." and again places his bet on the table. Seeing that he has lost a considerable amount of money at the table, he doubles up on his bets and thinks he can get back what he lost this way. Assuming he plays this way until he finally wins one hand, how do you think he fared over the course of the night? In fact, he still can't believe that he lost all his money. All it took was one bad hand and poof, gone!

Many times, an inexperienced trader falls into the same trap as the Gambler's mentality. Many traders would double down on their trades after losses in the effort of recovering lost money. They assume (and this goes along with the premise of many gamblers) that if something is happening more frequently than normal, then it should get to a point where the opposite will happen eventually. So, staking progressively big bets after a streak of losing will eventually get them a winning hand and recover all previous losses. By assuming that everything eventually evens out by rule of averages, they fall into a scenario where they continuously bet on losing propositions in the assumption that they will eventually win in the end.

It is not something you can do in the long term and it most likely than not breaks the bank. Remember that each trade is disconnected from your previous trade. Whether you traded on a gain or loss, the outcome of each trade does not determine the next, which is why we need to follow these guidelines. Again, it boils down to what our initial objective is. If you always keep that objective in mind, you can avoid falling victim to the gambler's mentality.

TRADER PSYCHOLOGY

There's an old saying on Wall Street that the market is like a toilet. And, just like a toilet, some days the market is prettier than others. But whether the market is up or down, there are always people trying to predict which way it's going to go next. Some people say that the market is more likely to go up than down in the long term. That may be true; but in the short term, the market can be pretty volatile. And even in the long term, there are always going to be ups and downs. So, if you're thinking about investing, you need to be prepared for both the good times and the bad.

Some people say that some stocks are better investments than others over a given period. Again, that may be true. But you need to remember that past performance is no guarantee of future results. Just because a stock has done well in the past doesn't mean it's going to keep going up. And just because a stock has gone down doesn't mean it's a bad investment. You need to do your research and make your own decisions about which stocks are right for you. Some of these findings can be applied to help you in your own investing decisions. However, by avoiding losses, you may come up with damaging findings, such as not losing money is more important than making money; or don't put all your eggs in one basket; or diversify your portfolio; or don't invest in anything you don't understand. All of these may be sound advice, but they won't make you rich overnight. If you're looking for get-rich-quick tips, you're better off going to Vegas and playing the slots. At least there you'll have some fun while you're losing your shirt and pants.

As any trader knows, one important aspect of success is understanding loss. After all, losses are an inevitable part of trading, and the ability to take them in stride is essential to long-term success. However, many traders struggle with this concept, and the fear of taking a loss can often led to hesitation and ultimately blowing up their trading account. This is because they fail to realize that a loss is not the end of the world, but rather an opportunity to learn and grow. By understanding this, traders can approach losses with a more positive outlook and eventually overcome this psychological obstacle.

Trading is a funny thing. When you're up, you feel like you can do no wrong. But when you lose a few trades in a row, suddenly you become hesitant to pull the trigger. The fear of losing more money starts to set in, and you start second-guessing your every move. As a result, you miss out on profitable trades that could have made up for your losses. So, next time you're feeling reluctant to trade, just remember that even the best traders lose sometimes. And the only way to get back in the game is to keep trading. That's why it is important to not to hesitate when you see a good opportunity. If you're waiting for the perfect moment, you'll probably miss it. And if you're afraid of losing money, you'll never make any profits. Instead of agonizing over every trade, just pull the trigger and let the chips fall where they may. In the long run, you'll be glad you did.

Risk. It's the trader's kryptonite. We all know we should take it, but, we just can't seem to do it. We see a risky trade, and our heart starts racing, our palms start sweating, and, all of a sudden, we're frozen. We can't pull the trigger. We tell ourselves that we'll just wait for a better opportunity; but deep down, we know that we're really just afraid of losing money. The problem with avoiding risk is that it constricts your trading account. You miss out on profitable setups because you're too scared to take a chance. And the more you avoid risk, the more your account shrinks. Sooner or later, you'll find yourself in a death spiral of small losses and missed opportunities, all because you were too afraid to take a risk. So, what's the solution?

The first step is to understand your psychology. Why are you afraid of risk? Is it because you're worried about losing money? Or is it because you're worried about making a mistake? Once you understand your fears, you can begin to work on overcoming them. Take baby steps at first. Enter a small position on a risky trade and see how it goes. If you lose money, don't beat yourself up. Just take it as a learning experience and move on. Slowly but surely, you'll build up your confidence and become comfortable with taking risks. And as your comfort level grows, so will your trading account.

These are some of the common mistakes that traders make, and you should avoid them at all costs. These are how to handle the fear of losses. If you're in a situation where you must trade with money that is required for living, it's not a smart idea. When you trade with money that is required for your day-to-day survival, such as rent and food, it will keep you from taking good trades for fear of losing it. When trading stocks, never risk more than two percent of your account on any given trade. When you risk more than that, it will place excessive pressure on your trading account. The risk should be small and the reward bigger so you can minimize your risks as well as maximize the returns that you get. Recognize that trading is dealing with odds that are never certain. You should accept the fact that you will win some and lose others. You must accept the reality that not every trade is likely to give you a winning outcome.

Another thing to do is create a trading strategy that has simply defined entries and exits, and follow up your strategy. This will help you to minimize your risks and increase your profit potential by having a predefined plan for where the market is going. If you're feeling hesitant to take a trade, ask yourself if you have the necessary information about the stock to take it on confidently. If not, wait until you have enough evidence from which to make a decision. Become disciplined by having an entry for everything; so that when the time comes you know what trade to take or not take at all costs. By having a clearly defined strategy, you will be more factual rather than trading based on emotions. You have to commit a lot of time to the research process.

TRADER DISCIPLINE

Most traders are not disciplined, and they end up losing money. Have you ever entered a trade that didn't work out? Have you exited a trade too early or waited too long to exit it? These are the most common problems for any trader. It can be very frustrating when this happens. But if we take an objective look at our trading behavior, we will see that discipline does play a big role in our success as traders. The lack of discipline leads us to losing trades and money. It's important to understand how important discipline is and why it's so hard for most people to practice it consistently when trading stocks. You have the opportunity to trade every single day, but you don't have to. The market gives you unlimited opportunities, but only a few provide great profit potential. Every time you start trading without discipline, your profits decrease and your losses increase. Discipline is an essential quality for traders of all levels; it's what separates winners from losers in this game. Traders must improve their discipline by preventing themselves from taking trades they shouldn't take or missing out on good ones. So, before we talk about how to become disciplined as a trader, let's first discuss why it's hard to master discipline.

What is discipline? It's doing something even when you don't want to do it, but the easy thing to do is nothing. Many traders do not have the discipline to follow their trading plan. Most traders start with good intentions, but then they fall into bad habits that lead them astray from their original trading plans. The result is that they are unable to consistently make money. Discipline will help you overcome your weaknesses and bad habits so that you can trade according to your own rules no matter how tempting it might be to stray from them. You will learn how to develop a strong sense of self-discipline, which is a characteristic for success in any endeavor, including trading.

Have you ever started a trade and then abandoned it because the profit potential wasn't what you expected? Or, did you take a trade without giving it any thought and lost on it? These are signs of a lack of discipline. A large part of trading discipline is the ability to take the correct action at the time it's needed. To do this, you must practice taking these actions so that they become second nature. The more you repeat a given behavior, the more likely you are to execute it correctly in a tough situation. For example, if you're not constantly checking and double-checking your trade setup and entry points because you're afraid of missing out on a profitable opportunity, then chances are that when you finally do execute trades, either too quickly or too slowly, then those bad habits will carry over to other aspects of your trading.

Discipline is key to success in trading. By following these guidelines, you can become more disciplined in your trading. There is one golden rule that you must always follow: Stick to your trading routine! Enter and exit trades immediately when trading opportunities occur, without hesitation, heeding your trading plan and acting on it immediately. This may seem like a no-brainer, but you'd be surprised how many people let emotions get in the way of making trades. It is crucial to be disciplined and do nothing when there are no openings, but always be vigilant for possible opportunities. After all, the market can turn on a dime and you don't want to miss out on a good trade because you were too hesitant. So, remember, stick to your routine and you'll be sure to find success.

Stick to your trading routine. Discipline in trading means sticking to your plan no matter what happens, and this includes when you have a bad losing streak or a winning streak. Discipline is the ability to do what you need to do, even when your emotions are pushing you to do something else. Discipline is what separates successful traders from unsuccessful traders because without it they won't be profitable. This is why you should always have a trading plan before embarking on your journey as a trader. A trading plan will help provide the discipline to follow it and increase your chances of success. Think about it, if you were a bear and wanted to hibernate as soon as the first snowflake fell, would you stay up all night to look for food? No, of course not. You'd go into hibernation mode and save your energy for those long winter months. But now, if you were a hibernating bear and someone wanted to wake you up for some early-season food, would you be able to get out of bed, or go back to sleep? You'd have no choice but to wake up. That's discipline.

Be vigilant. It's important to always stay vigilant and reevaluate your trades regularly. This is especially true when market conditions change. For example, if you notice that the market is currently trending upward, then it would be a good idea to buy stocks/shares in companies with shares priced under their intrinsic value. Alternatively, if you notice that the market is currently trending downward, then it would be a good idea to buy stocks/shares in companies with shares priced above their intrinsic value. Remember, stock-market trading is a highly risky business, which can result in significant losses if not approached with the necessary care and attention. So, if you're thinking of getting involved in this type of trading, make sure you dedicate a substantial amount of time to acquire the necessary skillsets.

There's an old saying in the stock market: "Cut your losses and let your profits run." In other words, if you're losing money on a trade, get out quickly. And if you're making money, don't be too quick to exit. This advice is especially relevant when it comes to placing stop-loss orders, and also placing orders to take profits.

Place stop-loss order. The idea is to limit your losses on a trade gone wrong. There are a couple of things to keep in mind when placing stop-loss orders. First, don't put your stop-loss too close to the current price of the stock. If it's too close, you'll get "stopped out" of your position prematurely. Second, don't put your stop-loss too far from the current price. If it's too far, you'll give up too much ground if the stock does continue to fall. The best way to find the right place for your stop-loss is to use risk-to-reward techniques. This will help you determine the appropriate level for your risk tolerance. So, remember: always have a stop-loss in place! It's an important rule for successful trading.

Always take profits. One of the most difficult things to do in trading is to take profits. When a trade is going well, it's easy to get caught up in the momentum and start thinking about all the money you're going to make. However, it's important to remember that greed is one of the biggest enemies of traders. If you start letting your profits run too far, you open yourself up to the risk of giving them all back—and then some. So, if you're ever in the fortunate position of being up on a trade, make sure you allow yourself to take some profits off the table. That way, even if the trade does eventually turn against you, you'll still be ahead. And, who knows, maybe by taking some profits early you'll even set yourself up for an even bigger win down the road.

In conclusion, trade rules are like the rules of the road—you need them to get from point A to point B without getting into a wreck. And just like on the highway, there are always going to be rule breakers. Maybe they go a little too fast for the conditions or they don't use their turn signal. But just like with driving, if you break your rules, you're only asking for trouble. So, whatever you do, don't second guess yourself. If you're tempted to hold a losing trade longer than you should or take a profit too early, just remember that it's not worth risking your account just to save face. Stick to your plan and follow your rules—it's the best way to stay safe and keep your account in good health. Discipline is not something with which you are born, it is something that you develop through hard work and practice. Discipline is the key to success in any area of life, whether it is your studies, your career, or your personal life. Without discipline, it is very difficult to achieve anything. So, if you want to be successful at anything, make sure you are disciplined! The market rewards those who are disciplined. In the next chapter I will discuss why It's essential to be disciplined and follow your trading plan.

12 Being Profitable

Chapter Overview

» Education and mentorship are key to success in trading.

» Planning trade and journaling to become a profitable trader

Tale of Cathie Wood

Cathie Wood is an American investor with interests in investments and capital management. She has developed and promoted innovative financial strategies and management approaches that have influenced and inspired many others. The CEO and CIO of Ark Invest is a woman who advocates for diversity in an industry that is mostly male-led.

Wood was born in 1955 in Los Angeles, California, in the USA. She studied at Notre Dame Academy until 1974. She graduated from the University of Southern California in 1981 with a Bachelor of Science degree in Finance and Economics. As the daughter of a successful real estate developer, Wood was exposed early on to the world of finance and investing. This experience laid the foundation for her future career as an investor and financial analyst. After graduation, she began her career as a research analyst at Alexandra Investment Research.

In 1980, she provided strategic and major insights on the development of interest rates and helped in realization of the baselines for boosting economic development and success for investors. The economist analysis has always focused on the real-time itemization and processes that could help investors to have the best push for managing the investment needs and process. In 1998, Wood joined hands with Lulu Wang to establish Tupelo Capital Management, which is a hedge fund with baselines in New York City.

Wood is no stranger to managing money. She's worked as the chief investment efficiency of global thematic strategies at Alliance Bernstein and, as a result, has managed over $5 billion in investments. However, she faced challenges during the 2008 financial crisis. Despite this, Wood remained resilient and developed an idea that could influence the disruptive innovation technologies and their utilization across the various processes that could impact growth—positive or negative. Today, her company continues to be part of the strategic inputs in the management of investments that target growth and development—an area in which they clearly have expertise.

After being laid off from her job, which was the pioneer in developing the procedures for managing the fund investments, in 2014 she launched Ark Investment Management, an aggressive growth-oriented asset manager with a focus on disruptive innovation. Under her leadership, Ark has become one of the fastest-growing asset managers in the world, with over $50 billion in assets under management as of 2020. Thanks to her keen eye for spotting market opportunities and her willingness to take risks.

In late 2020, she was named as the best stock picker of the year by the Bloomberg-News editor in chief, which was part of the accolades to appreciate her role and inputs in the management of ARK investments. Thanks to her keen eye for spotting trends and her willingness to take risks, Wood has been extremely successful in her new venture. Wood has earned a reputation as one of the most successful investors of our time.

Wood has always been an important voice in the world of economics. She is known for her work on market development and investment strategy, and her influence has been instrumental in shaping the way businesses operate in the 21st century. In addition to her work in the private sector, Wood has also served as a mentor to Arthur Laffer, one of the most renowned economists of our time. She has been a constant source of wisdom and guidance for Laffer, and their relationship has had a profound impact on the world of economics. Thanks to Wood's insight and expertise, businesses around the globe are better equipped to navigate the ever-changing landscape of the marketplace.

Wood has been at the forefront of innovation and financial management for many years. And in 2021, she was part of the Forbes 50 over 50, with her achievements being identified in leadership, creation, entrepreneurship, and scientific inputs. She is a respected voice in the world of finance and investing, and her insights on managing hedge funds and investments are invaluable. We are lucky to have her as a resource on these matters.

She has been making strides in the investment world and leads one of the top 10 largest fund management firms owned by women. She's been an important part of developing literature on modern stock investments and has recently been able to keep up with the changes in the market despite some challenges. Wood is clearly an intelligent and successful woman who knows what she's doing. However, she's also human and has faced some challenges in her personal life. Despite this, she remains an inspiration to many women who are looking to achieve success in the male-dominated world of investing.

INTRODUCTION TO PROFITABILITY

I've been trading equities profitably for many years now, and I'm now sharing my expertise with you and others like you who want to earn money from their trades while reducing risk exposure at all times. You don't have to learn everything from scratch because I already did that for myself years ago and now I am helping you to become successful as quickly as possible. I want to share my experience with others so they don't go through the same struggles that I did: Focus primarily on downside or upside risk potential rather than larger gains, as many people tend to do today, which only leads them into trouble later.

Trading is a tough business and if you don't know what you are doing, it can be very difficult to make any money. I have been trading for years and the best way to learn how to trade is by learning from someone who has done it before. That is why I created this book—so people like you can learn from me instead of having to figure out everything on your own. The first step in this process should always be understanding your personal tolerance for risks. Once you know a risk strategy that makes sense for you, the next step is to prepare ahead by determining which trades will perform well in various circumstances based on your past winning statistics. Building a trade journal is an excellent way to track your winning and losing trades to be able to calculate your trading statistics.

Most people lose a lot of money because they don't have a plan or strategy for managing risk. They trade without regard to what might happen if their trades go wrong and end up losing their money. I am going to show you how you can create your own personal trading plan by knowing which setups will work well during various scenarios based on past performance. This will allow you to manage your risk while maximizing your profits over time. If you follow my advice, you should be able to maintain profitability even when the markets are difficult and volatile, like they have been recently.

TRADER EDUCATION

Again, most traders lose money. Most people think that trading is about making a lot of money in a short period, but this isn't true. Trading involves risk management and patience more than anything else. You need to be willing to accept losses as part of the process if you want success over time. The key to becoming a profitable trader lies in understanding the basics first.

Traders learn from their mistakes and improve with experience over time. Learning the basics of trading is a good place to start. Once you have mastered them, it's important to learn advanced techniques and strategies that can help you become successful in your trading. The basics of trading is knowing which order types are appropriate for the strategies and knowing which trading tactics are appropriate for the current market conditions. The more advanced techniques are tracking your results and trading tactics that best suits you as a trader. Furthermore, it's important to be realistic with yourself. There is no perfect trading style technique that always produces winning results. But if you learn how to discriminate valid trades from those which are invalid or misleading, then you know where to spend most of your time.

The goal of this book is to introduce the basic concepts and principles behind trading stocks, with specific focus on traders, including topics like technical analysis for stock trading, the use of leverage in trading, understanding support and resistance levels in stock prices, identifying trend reversals in stock prices, managing risk in trading through stop-loss levels, understanding the different types of orders for online trades (market vs. Limit), and time.

Find a mentor. Mastering the trading tactics with practice is important for traders who hope to be successful in the stock market. If you want to learn how to trade stocks, it's important that you have a mentor. Having a mentor shows you what steps to take next, so you can avoid making mistakes. They share their expertise with mentees who are looking for someone to guide them. Mentors are typically known for being skilled in certain types of trading—and they may have one-on-one sessions with mentees who are interested in one specific type of trading.

Once you've mastered these skills, there is no limit as far as where your future can take you. There are many traders out there who have made millions from their knowledge. If you are looking to get into the world of trading, it is important to find an experienced mentor who can teach you the ropes. Several online resources can provide you with information on how to trade, but having a personal mentor to guide you through the process can be invaluable. The problem with reading books is that you can easily forget what you read. It is difficult to remember the important details and even more challenging to put them into practice without guidance. Learning to trade is already hard. You have to learn a lot of new skills to be successful, and this takes time. If you are looking for a faster way to get started with trading, then the best option is to learn from someone with experience. This means finding the right person or resources that can teach you what you need in an easy-to-understand format, without being too basic or too complex. I offer just that. I offer courses, and I know how difficult it is to get started in the world of trading. My goal is to help others avoid common mistakes and speed up their learning curve so they don't waste valuable time or money on ineffective methods. I want my students to start making profits as quickly as possible so they can focus on more important things, like family, friends, and hobbies.

There is no one-size-fits-all approach to trading in the stock market, as each trader has their own strategies and preferences. However, you only need a few tactics and techniques to help improve your trading results. The best way to get ahead of other traders is by learning from those who have been there before us, but not all resources are created equal. Some may be outdated or just flat-out wrong. I compiled a list of trading systems and techniques I believe can help you become successful in any market condition while avoiding common pitfalls along the way. Each strategy has been proven effective over time with consistent results for many years now, so it's up to you if you want to take advantage of them. You can start your journey to becoming a Modern Price Action member today at <www.modernpriceaction.com>. By taking my course, not only will you gain valuable insight on how to trade, but also discover some great tips that are sure to improve your skills as well as give you an advantage over other traders out there. The information contained within these pages is priceless and could make all the difference between success or failure.

If you want to become a profitable trader, you need to seek out and learn from skilled traders. The best way to do this is by reading books and talking with other traders on forums or social media. Find mentors who will teach you the basics and provide guidance as you begin your journey. Some of the most important things that you'll need for teaching yourself how to trade with trade journaling, charting, and detailed educational content.

TRADING PLAN

A lot of traders fail because they don't have a trading plan. Without a plan, you can't measure your progress and make changes to improve it. Trading is a skill and, like any other skill, you need to practice and be dedicated. But it's hard to stay motivated when there are no clear goals or results. A good plan will help you to trade better and more consistently. It will also provide a structure for your thinking as well as an outline of the rules that govern your decisions.

When I started, I didn't have a plan, and I traded without a stop-loss. This can be a risky strategy because if my trades go against me, it could end up costing a lot of money. So now, before I take any trades, I make sure that I have a clear goal in mind for each trade, and I have a stop-loss in place to limit the amount of money that I could potentially lose. A trading plan is a document that outlines how you will trade, what stocks you will trade, and when you will trade. The plan should include the time frame as well as your exit strategy. If you're still unsure as to whether or not this is the right way for you to trade, then do some reading on other people's trading plans or even try writing one by yourself.

Writing your trading plans is important because it will help you to discover if this is the right way for you to trade. If, at any point during your writing process, you decide that it isn't for you, then that's great. You can take trash the plan and/or change it. The problem with most trading plans is that they aren't written to be effective because they fail to address certain aspects of trading, such as psychology, risk management, etc. Your trading plan will come in handy in all scenarios, but especially during the difficult times of your trading career. When everything appears to be going in the wrong direction, your plan becomes critical to the activities you want to take. Your strategy will keep you on track, focused, and help you avoid repeating mistakes while also preserving your long-term goals.

I've gathered some of the critical components and thought processes that should be included in your trading plan to help you. There are three parts to any trading plan: the entry rules, the exit strategy, and risk management. All three of these things are important, but the exit strategy is arguably the most important. Trading is an art and a science.

Entry rules. Have you ever seen a great trade, but then hesitated because it didn't meet your criteria? If so, you're not alone. Most traders don't have a setup, and they trade on impulse or emotion, which usually leads to losing money. When traders wait for perfect conditions to enter a trade, they miss out on opportunities. This is why traders must learn to use setups as their trigger points instead of waiting for confirmation from price action or indicators. The Trade

Setup gives you all of your setup requirements in one place so that you can stop missing trades! It's like having your trading coach with you every time you're in front of your computer screen. So how does the Trade Setup work? First, you need to identify your entry, stop loss, and target areas. Then, once you see a potential trade meeting all of your criteria, you take the trade! It's that simple. Using a Trading Setup will help you avoid emotions and make objective decisions, which will lead to more successful trading.

 There's a reason why trading is often compared to gambling. Like casinos, the house always has an edge in trading. And, like gamblers, traders are always looking for that one perfect trade that will make them rich. The problem is that the best time to enter a trade can be different for each trader. There are many signals and indicators available, but they all have their flaws. Some of them only work in specific market conditions, while others are not very accurate or reliable. As a result, traders typically find themselves chasing their tails, trying to find that elusive perfect trade. But the reality is that there's no such thing. The best a trader can do is to try to stack the odds in their favor by using multiple signals and indicators. Even then, there will always be some element of luck involved. That's why trading is so exciting—and so risky.

Exit strategy. A stop-loss is like a seatbelt for your trading account. It's there to protect you in case of a crash, but it can also become a liability if you don't know how to use it properly. Many traders have no idea how to place a stop-loss, and, as a result, they often end up losing more money than they would have without one. The key to proper stop-loss placement is to find the right balance between protecting your profits and limiting your losses. If you are a trader, your goal is to make money. In your trading plan identify your profit targets. This eliminates guesswork and helps investors focus on high-probability trades instead of wasting their time with bad trades.

Risk Management. The vast majority of traders are not profitable because they take too many trades with insufficient reward potential. We all know that trading is risky, but it's also an incredibly rewarding way to make money. However, most people don't have a strategy for how much risk is acceptable per trade. They just assume their gut feeling about the trade will be correct and then get angry when they lose money on bad trades. Reward-to-Risk helps you determine if your trade meets your criteria for success by comparing the potential profit to the cost of entering the position. If there isn't at least 1 ½ times more possible profit than what you'll risk entering the position, don't take it! This simple concept has helped you become consistently profitable in trading while avoiding unbalanced losses.

A trading plan is an essential tool in the toolbox of any aspiring trader. Regardless of your trading habits, you should treat it as a business; you're investing time and money, and a detailed plan is essential to success. Your trading plan should be written in the same manner as a business plan, offering a framework for the decisions you make. While having a strategy does not ensure success, it will assist you in trading responsibly and understanding how to manage both good and bad outcomes.

TRADING JOURNAL

A trading journal is also extremely helpful when tracking your performance. I will go back to my journal and look at past trades so that I can see what was going on in the market when I took those trades. I do this because it helps me to understand what happened during the trade and why I made that particular decision. It allows me to review my trading performance and see if there are any patterns that emerge, or things I do which will help improve the quality of trades. If, for example, I notice that whenever there is a news release during the trading day, on average my trades are unsuccessful, this gives me an idea of when to expect volatility in the market and allows me to plan my trades accordingly.

A lot of traders have a hard time keeping track of their trading activity. The problem with this is that it makes it difficult to learn from mistakes and improve strategy over time. They can never be sure if you are improving or not, because they don't know what the exact results were before. Trading journals solve this problem by providing a place to record all trades and keep track of them in one place. This way, no matter how many trades you make throughout the day or week, they will always be recorded for future reference. I frequently see traders enter a process, complete the cycle, and then forget the lessons of their mistakes or are unable to identify the actions that impacted the success or failure of a specific trade. They are unable to replicate their achievements or prevent their faults because they failed to record the hows and whys of the process. This is why keeping a trade journal is important.

The false idea about trading journals is that traders believe it requires too much work and time investment. This is understandable because so many traders have already spent countless hours in front of charts trying to learn as much as possible about each market. It's hard enough for them to focus on one thing at a time without having another task added into it. That's why I created simple effective solutions to help them with building a trading plan. It should contain honest assessments of trade values and results so that we can determine which strategies worked and which did not. All of this information becomes embedded in your trading habits and helps you better understand your trading patterns and psychology.

My goal is providing simple ideas to allow traders keep track of all necessary information about each trade without requiring any additional effort than what's required by default. Here are some suggestions to keep in mind when building a journal to guarantee that we do it correctly:

Keep up-to-date. Always begin and end your trading day by updating your journal. It's critical that your journal helps you document and keep track of your trading technique, so it's important to keep it up to date every day. This way, you get to understand yourself better: what motivates you to trade, how external forces impact your ability to or your willingness to make certain decisions, and you get to note why. Traders are always looking for ways to improve their trading. To do so, they have to document what is happening in their lives and how it affects them when they trade. Understanding these aspects of yourself will get you farther into your career as a trader. Many traders don't take the time to journal because they feel that it's not necessary. A trading journal helps you easily organize your daily trades in one place, with no need to worry about forgetting anything or having information scattered across areas.

Document everything. Most people are not keeping a journal. It's not hard to keep track of your trades and how they are performing. Most traders don't record their trading activity on a regular basis, so they have no way to review their performance or make adjustments when needed. This can lead to poor results over time. The Trading Journal is the solution for keeping track of all your trading activity in one place. Each day you enter the following details about each trade into your journal: start date, end date, entry price, exit price, units traded and whether it was a winner or loser. If you had multiple entries during that day, list them separately with the same information as above, but just list them by entry number instead of date/time. Don't forget to indicate if this was an intraday trade (traded within 1 day) or overnight trade (traded at least 1 full business day). You need to know why you took the trade, what were your indicators at the time, and how much did you risk and why? If this information is missing when looking back on past trades, it will be hard for someone to improve their trading skills. By writing every detail in your trading journal, you can look back in 5 years and see exactly where things went wrong or right. A good trading journal should have all these details recorded so that when reviewing them in the future, you can learn from their mistakes and successes.

Track your emotions. Another important factor that many new traders overlook is their emotional state when trading. We'd have to consider how our emotional condition influences our business judgments. When we are excited, do we make fast and impulsive trades? When we are angry, afraid, or depressed, how frequently do we forget our stop-loss prices? Knowing these tendencies will help us remember that we can control our outcomes by recognizing and regulating our emotional state while making trade decisions. Being aware of how your emotions affect your trading decisions is critical to your success. As a trader, you are responsible for the outcome of every trade you make. Ineffective trade management can be attributed to emotional instability or being out of touch with our feelings during trading sessions. A trading journal will help us stay in touch with our feelings and improve awareness of what's going on inside us when we make trades. Journaling about my emotions helps me identify patterns that I might not otherwise notice if I'm focused only on the numbers instead of myself as an individual trader. It also gives me a record that I can go back to later and see what worked well at certain times, and what I felt didn't work so well at other times—and why! This makes it easier for me to repeat my successes while avoiding repeating mistakes.

Track global news events. Most traders don't journal major news events. This is a big problem because you need to know what happened in the past when making future trades. You can't rely on your memory, especially if it's been weeks or months since you made a trade. Keeping a trading journal allows you to record significant events that occurred during the trade that may have affected its outcome. A trading journal will help you remember any relevant global events that occurred during your trade so that next time around, when it comes time to make another trade, you'll have all of the information and won't be relying on your faulty memory for reference material.

Include screenshots. It is impossible to make good trading decisions without knowing what happened before you started. Many traders often miss out on trading opportunities because they don't have a clue what is going on. "How can I tell if the price action is trending? How do I know when to buy or sell?" Capture screenshots of previous trades and save them directly into your journal for later review without having to remember or write down what was going on at that moment in time. Also include quick notes about what happened prior to entering trades, during entry, exit points, as well as other key pieces of information, such as support/resistance levels or news events that may have influenced your decision-making process while in action.

Analysis of a losing trade will help to reduce your losing trades and increase your winning trades so that, in the long run, you'll have more winners than losers. Again, many traders fail to keep a journal of their trades. Without one, they are blind to what is working and not working in their trading. They cannot analyze the reasons for success or failure. And without this critical information, they can't improve as traders. A trading journal will help you stay focused on your goals, identify problem areas that may need attention, and track progress toward achieving those goals over time. It's also an invaluable tool for analyzing your results after each trade so that you can learn from past mistakes and successes.

PROFITABLE TRADER

The market can be a scary place for those who don't have a plan. It's like going into a haunted house without a flashlight. You may bump into some things, but you'll never really know what's behind the door unless you have a plan. Trading is a lot like gambling. The goal is to make money, but the risk is always there that you could lose money. That's why it's important to approach trading with a clear head and an eye for opportunity. Over-trading, or taking too much risk, is one of the biggest mistakes you can make. It's also crucial to have your game face on at all times and stay calm under pressure. Becoming a profitable trader is learning how to check your emotions at the door. If you can do all of that, then you might just stand a chance in this crazy market. Let's take each concept mentioned, and discuss it in more detail.

Over trading. Over trading is one of the top common mistakes made by novice traders. They see a good opportunity, and they go all in without understanding the risks involved. This is a recipe for disaster. Over-trading can wipe out your account in no time. When you over trade, you're not taking advantage of good risk-and-reward opportunities. You're simply gambling with your money. And we all know that the house always wins in the end. If you're looking to make money on the stock market, be smart about it. Understand the risks involved and only trade when there's a good opportunity for profit. Otherwise, you'll end up like most novice investors and traders—broke and out of the game.

Taking too much risk. If you're a trader with a small account, you may be tempted to over-leverage to boost your returns. Unfortunately, this typically leads to blowing up your account rather than achieving consistent growth. The thing is, when you take on too much risk, you're more likely to encounter financial losses you can't easily recover. So, if you want to avoid quickly blowing up your account, it's important to be mindful of how much risk you're accepting. Taking on too much risk is often the root cause of account blowups, so by being aware of this and keeping your risk in check, you'll be better positioned for success in the long run.

Changing the approach. I know what it's like to feel like you're never going to find a trading method that works for you. I've been there, hopping from system to system without any real success. But I'm here to tell you that it doesn't have to be that way! This book has everything you need to know to be a successful trader. Changing your approach is the first step to success, and sticking with that approach to the long run is powerful. Stop chasing after the "holy grail" of trading and learn how to trade the right way. With the strategies and techniques in this book, you can take your trading to the next level and start seeing real results. So don't give up—the path to success is right here in front of you. Just open this book and start reading!

Have your game face on at all times and stay calm under pressure. Trading is not for the faint of heart—you have to be prepared to lose everything you put in if the worst-case scenario occurs. That being said, don't go overboard! Only gamble with what you can afford to lose. This may seem like an easy task, but it's quite difficult. Most people know a few well-known stocks, but they don't realize that if these two were being traded together, then one company could go up while the other goes down. Trading is hard because it's hard to control your emotions. Most of the time, traders are not able to stay calm and make good decisions. We all know that trading can be very profitable if you follow certain rules; but it's also risky if you don't play by the book. The problem is that most people don't have a proper system in place for managing their risk. To be a successful trader, you need to have your game face on at all times and stay calm under pressure. If you can do this, then you'll be well on your way to making a profit. It only takes one bad trade to wipe out your account.

Becoming a profitable trader is learning how to check your emotions at the door. We all know that trading is a risky business, but it's easy to forget this when you're in the middle of a trade. You need to remember that your emotions can get the best of you and cause you to make bad trades. This leads to losing money and missing out on potential profits. Understand that during trades, there will be times when you feel excited or angry with what has or hasn't happened, but emotions should not affect decision-making skills in any way. Traders often make emotional decisions and end up taking trades they shouldn't. It's always important to remain objective and think clearly about whether it is appropriate for you to take the trade or not. Becoming a profitable trader means making sound decisions based on logic, not emotion. So, the next time you're in the middle of a trade, take a deep breath and remember to stay calm and trade on!

To be profitable, you have to learn how to pick companies instead of just trading on stock symbols. Most traders don't know how to pick companies. They just pick stocks by their ticker symbol and hope for the best. This is like trying to find a needle in the haystack. It's much better to learn how to pick companies that are likely to be profitable. Then you can avoid being on an emotional roller-coaster. The Fortune 500 list is a great place to start your research. It provides stock tickers without having to spend hours upon hours researching different companies yourself. And don't spend countless months searching through numerous sources, including financial statements, news articles (including analyst reports), conference calls, etc. The Fortune 500 companies are a list of high-quality companies that are likely going to perform well. So, save yourself some time and start your research with the Fortune 500 list.

If you follow my advice, there will be no more guessing about which assets should be bought or sold next! You will finally understand how the market works and why certain companies move up while others fall in price. It doesn't matter if you're new at trading or an experienced veteran, everyone can benefit from these lessons. I have shown you how to read the market like a pro and make money doing it. Just remember, these lessons are for informational purposes only and are not a guarantee of success.

CLOSING STATEMENT

Early in the book we said that there is a general tendency to collect gains too early, especially by inexperienced traders. Often, they get blinded by the glare of the initial profits and forget the trading plan that they have established. There are also situations where new traders would set time-based profit targets to begin. Setting a weekly target of $100 profits does not help your overall game. Instead, it puts unwanted pressure on you and could possibly trigger you to make bad trades just to try and hit your quota. As you find yourself in a hole, these small, often bad, trades pile up and you end with more losses than gains.

We must remember that trading is not a sprint to the finish line. It is more comparable to a marathon where the right pace and focus will get you to the finish line. Success in trading does not come from doing more trades, it is a result of carefully planned trades that have more long-term impact on your profit margins. Many assume that trading is a get-rich-quick kind of thing. It is not. Yes, you can get rich, but it does not always mean you get there within a week or a month or even a year. Usually, the first few months of trading are about building experience and expertise in the craft. The results that you get now are not an indication of how you can successfully perform in stock trading five or ten years from now. Our overarching purpose (which I cannot stress enough) implies that we work for the long term and not be obsessed with the short-term gains. The more experienced you become in the market, the better returns you'll get in the long run. If you're looking to get rich quickly or make money fast, then it's better for you to gamble your money away instead of investing in the stock market. There are plenty of other ways that may seem easier and faster—such as working for McDonalds—but if you want to build up long-term wealth and create sustainable income streams, then this book showed you how with some great tips on how to avoid risk when trading stocks.

CONCLUSION

Even if you're not a businessperson, it's hard to not be at least a little interested in Warren Buffett. He's one of the most successful businessmen of our time and his story is fascinating. But what makes Buffett so successful? What can we learn from him? Warren Buffett's investment strategy is simple: find good companies and buy them at a fair price. You don't need to be a genius to invest like Warren Buffett, but you do need to be patient and have a long-term outlook.

He was born in 1930 in Omaha, Nebraska, USA. His focus on business courses and schools came from the books he read as a youth, such as the One Thousand Ways to Make $1000. He was schooled at Wharton School, University of Nebraska, Columbia Business School, and New York Institute of Finance, where he acquired the business philosophy of value investing. They influenced most of the decisions that he undertook throughout his career.

In fact, he's often referred to as the "Oracle of Omaha" for his keen insights into the world of business and investing. Buffett first made a name for himself in the 1950s, when he began working as a salesman for Buffett-Falk & Co. and Graham-Newman Corp. In 1956, he formed a partnership with famed investor Benjamin Graham, which would later be known as the Buffett Partnership. This partnership proved to be extremely successful, and helped to make Warren Buffett one of the richest men in the world.

He became and still is the chairman and CEO of Berkshire Hathaway. In the 1960s, Buffett began to focus on value investing, which is an investment strategy that emphasizes buying stocks that are undervalued by the market. Buffett has said that his investing philosophy is "to buy into a company because I think its intrinsic value is significantly greater than its market value." This approach has been very successful for Buffett, as Berkshire Hathaway's stock price has increased significantly over the years. Value investing requires a lot of research and analysis, but it can be very lucrative for investors who are willing to put in the work.

Over the years, he has acquired stakes in a number of companies, including Washington Post Company, ABC, Salomon Inc. and Coca Cola. These purchases have been attributed to his long experience in managing the stock market. For example, his 7% stake in Coca Cola triggered new levels of development and achievement for the company.

In 1990, Berkshire Hathaway started selling class A shares, which increased the value of the stock and made Buffett a billionaire. In 2002, he focused on forward contracts worth $11 billion, which delivered new profits based on the trade. During the 2007 financial crisis, Buffett had to deal with criticisms about the role he played in developing suboptimal deals. However, he has continued to be successful in the share market.

Despite his successes, he has experienced some major losses due to the stock market crash of 2008 and the ensuing economic recession. However, Buffett has bounced back from these setbacks and is currently worth an estimated $60 billion at this time. In 2014, the shares of his company, Berkshire Hathaway, reached $200,000 each, indicating that Buffett's strategic inputs and stock developments are once again yielding positive results. Some of the notable articles that Buffett has written include "The Efficient-Market Hypothesis" and "Super Investors of Graham and Doddsville." These articles demonstrate Buffett's deep understanding of the financial markets and his ability to generate long-term wealth for himself and his investors.

Warren Buffett is known for his disciplined approach to investing and his annual reports and inputs are highly respected by the investment community. Buffett continues to hold stock and shares in several companies, and his focus on stock trading has helped him maintain his position as one of the world's wealthiest people. Even in the face of the current pandemic, Buffett has remained calm and strategic in his evaluation of the stock market, and his insights have helped him develop solutions that favor his businesses. Buffett is a true master of the markets, and he continues to be a major force in the world of investing.

Warren Buffett is an American business powerhouse with interests in investments. He is a self-made billionaire who has amassed a fortune through smart investing and sound decision making. These experiences gave him a unique perspective on the world of business and finance, and he soon became one of the most respected investment advisers in the country. He is also a generous philanthropist, donating billions of dollars to charitable causes. Buffett is an American icon and an inspiration to us all.

Today, Buffett is still considered to be one of the smartest investors in the world, and his advice is highly sought after by both individuals and businesses alike. Most people don't have the time or knowledge to invest like Buffett. Even if you're not a business mogul, you can still make smart investments and grow your wealth over time. Through books such as this one, we can all learn a little about what makes Warren Buffett and others special in this world of investing. By understanding his investment philosophy and how he thinks about business, we can start making better decisions for ourselves.

THANK YOU

In this book, I taught you the dos and don'ts of stock trading and, I went in-depth about what strategies work and which don't. My goal with this book was not only to make you more knowledgeable about successful strategies, but also to provide helpful tools that will help you find success!

One of the most important things to know is that while there are many strategies out there, many of them are missing secrets for them to be profitable. After years of research, I have learned what does and doesn't work in the stock market. Now at the end of this book, you should be able to find a trading strategy that fits your needs so you're not risking your capital on unproven methods.

By understanding the journey that it takes, one can better appreciate its value in terms of both function and form. Similar to training for a sport, success is possible if you take the proper steps. From the beginning of the book. It is clear that the knowledge contained therein is vital to the understanding of how to best analyze Figure 0.1. By reviewing the figure from the start, one can gain a great deal of insight into what is happening in the price action. In short, the book provides a wealth of information that is essential to anyone wishing to make use of price action, as illustrated in Figure 0.1.

The stock market is a risky place. Although there are many ways to make money through it, you can also lose quite easily, too! I'm confident that by reading this book, you are now more knowledgeable about profitable trading techniques and better understand where opportunities lie as well as pitfalls within each strategy. Also, you have learned how to make the most out of any trade; and you also have found which risk management strategies are best for you.

As such, it should be required reading for anyone seeking to gain a fuller understanding of its potential. You can start with a smaller goal that will eventually lead up to your bigger dream. With that said, success in trading requires time and the right guidance to master. With targeted effort, if you have the right education, knowledge, and practice, it is possible to achieve profitability in the stock market.

Thank you for reading, and check out my online course <www.modernpriceaction.com>, about which information is provided on the about page. With that said, I wish you a prosperous trading and investing journey.

References

R. Garvey and A. Murphy, How profitable day traders trade: An examination of trading profits, working paper. University College Dublin, 2001.

S. Nison, Japanese candlestick charting techniques: a contemporary guide to the ancient techniques of the Far East. Paramus, NJ; London: Prentice Hall, 2001.

L. Sether, Dow theory unplugged: Charles Dow's original editorials & their relevance today. Cedar Falls, Iowa: W & A Publishing, 2009.

R. D. Edwards, J. Magee, and W. H. C. Bassetti, Technical Analysis of Stock Trends, Eleventh Edition. Milton: Chapman & Hall/CRC Press, 2018.

O. L. Velez, Tools and tactics for the master day trader: battle-tested techniques for day, swing, and position traders. New York: McGraw-Hill, 2000.

A. Brooks, Reading price charts bar by bar: the technical analysis of price action for the serious trader. Hoboken, NJ: Wiley, 2009.

S. Weinstein, Stan Weinstein's Secrets for profiting in bull and bear markets. New York: McGraw-Hill.

G. Capra, Trading tools and tactics: reading the mind of the market. Hoboken, NJ: Wiley, 2011.

B. Shannon, Technical analysis using multiple time frames: understand market structure and profit from trend alignment. Centennial, Colo.: Lifevest Pub., C, 2008.

J. J. Murphy, Technical analysis of the financial markets: a comprehensive guide to trading methods and applications. New York: New York Institute of Finance, 1999.

M. Douglas, Trading in the zone: master the market with confidence, discipline, and a winning attitude. Paramus, NJ: Prentice Hall Press, 2014.

G. Appel and E. Dobson, Understanding MACD. Greenville, SC: Traders Press.

About the Author

James Harris is an experienced engineer, stock market investor, and innovator with over fifteen years of experience in developing products with real value for people and businesses. He founded Smart Uncle, a brand with the goal of publishing books, media, and entertainment to educate, entertain, and inspire its audience. James is passionate about leveraging technology to bring innovative products to the market and create positive social change.

James received his degree in engineering from the Georgia Institute of Technology and his M.S. degree from the University of Iowa. During his time working at major aerospace corporations, he developed a strong passion for technology, data analytics, and automation. He believes that experiences and knowledge should be shared, and strives to do his part in making the world a better place. His endeavors have been successful in inspiring others to think outside the box, explore new possibilities, and contribute towards building a brighter future.

In 2023, he started his publishing company, Smart Uncle. Since then, he has been hard at work creating unique products and services to help people and businesses succeed. He has a vision to create an environment where everyone can have access to the same resources, regardless of their geographical location or socioeconomic status.

In his spare time, James enjoys reading, exploring nature, trading stocks, and spending time with his family.

About Smart Uncle, LLC.

The world of finance, investing, and the economy can be confusing and intimidating. It can be hard to know where to start when you're trying to learn about these topics. There's so much information out there, and it can be tough to determine what's worth paying attention to and what's not. Smart Uncle is here to help. Smart Uncle is a book publishing, media and entertainment company that is on a mission to educate, entertain, and inspire its audience with high-quality content. The company has published several bestselling books on finance, investing, and the economy. Its YouTube channel has many subscribers, and its videos have garnered millions of views. Whether you're looking to learn about the basics of investing or you want to be entertained by informative and entertaining videos, Smart Uncle has something for you. And because the company is always innovating, you can be sure that you're getting the latest and greatest information when you tune in. If you're looking for a new way to learn about the world of finance, investing, and the economy, then you need to check out <**www.SmartUncle.com**>.

About Modern Price Action

The stock market can be a confusing place, especially if you're just starting. It can be tough to know where to start when it comes to investing in the stock market. There are so many different options and strategies, and it can be hard to know which ones will work best for you. Modern Price Action is an education and community portal for stock-market enthusiasts. The site is a treasure trove of resources for anyone interested in learning about the stock market, whether they are a beginner or an experienced investor. The articles and tutorials on the site cover a wide range of topics, from the basics of stock market investing to more advanced concepts such as technical analysis and risk management. In addition, the Modern Price Action community includes a forum where members can discuss investment ideas and strategies. Whether you're just starting or you're a seasoned pro, <**www.ModernPriceAction.com**> is sure to have something to offer you.

Glossary

A

Accumulation: is a period when investors begin to purchase stocks, as they anticipate that they will increase in value. During this phase, stock prices start to increase gradually as more and more buyers enter the market.

Analysts: look at the company's financial performance, management decisions, and other factors to determine whether it is a good investment or not. They regularly recalibrate their outlook on certain companies by either "upgrading" or "downgrading" them based on the predictions for that company.

Ascending Triangle: signify that a current uptrend will continue, implying an imminent breakout at the point where the triangle lines meet.

Ask: is the lowest amount that a seller of an asset is willing to accept.

Average True Range: is used in technical analysis to measure market volatility by decomposing the entire range of an asset price for a specified period.

Averaging Down: is an investment strategy that involves buying more of a security when its price has dropped, in the hope that it will eventually increase.

B

Bear: are typically more sellers than buyers in the stock market, which leads to falling prices.

Bid: is the maximum allowable sale price that a buyer is willing to pay for an asset.

Blockchain: is a decentralized, distributed digital ledger that records transactions between two or more parties in a secure, verifiable, and permanent way.

Boom: is a period of economic growth accelerates, production rises, unemployment falls, wages increase, business profits surge, and consumption increases.

Breakaway: signify the end of one trend and a new start to another, making them an imperative technical analysis formation.

Breakdown: usually signals the start of a downward trend.

Breakout: is a rapid movement of a stock price through trend lines acting as resistance or support.

Brokerage: is a financial institution or firm that offers services for investing in the stock market. These services can include asset management, portfolio consultation, financial advice, securities trading, and more.

Bull: are typically more buyers than sellers in the stock market, which leads to rising prices. The opposite of a bear market is a bull market.

C

Candlestick: are a visual representation of stock market prices that help traders analyze market trends and identify potential trading opportunities. They display the open, high, low, and close price of a security over a given period.

Capitalization: is the total value of the outstanding common shares owned by stockholders of a publicly traded company.

Commodity Channel Index: is an oscillator that measures the historical average price relative to the current price over a given timeframe.

Consolidation: is after price stalls and fails to break through the resistance or support levels, a consolidation zone is formed. Price then reverses back in the opposite direction of where it came from within its trend channel.

Continuation: is the price surge that ignites from the pullback to continue in the direction of the primary trend.

Contraction: stage or recession, which is defined by a sharp drop in asset values and an economic downturn, is a process that frequently leads to a market crisis.

Cryptocurrency: is a digital currency that operates independently of a central bank or government. They are based on blockchain technology, which is a decentralized public ledger that records transactions securely.

Cup and Handle: is a popular bullish chart pattern that can be used by traders to identify potential buy signals. It typically appears as a "U" shaped pattern, with the "cup" representing the bottom of the trend, and the "handle" indicating a brief pause or retracement in price before continuing its uptrend.

Current ratio: is a liquidity ratio that measures a company's ability to pay short-term obligations.

D

Day Trading: is a trading strategy whereby investors buy and sell securities multiple times throughout the day to capitalize on short-term price movements.

Death Cross: is a bearish chart pattern that is formed when the 50-day moving average crosses below the 200-day moving average. This technical indicator is used by traders to identify bearish trends in the stock market, which can be a sign of a potential selloff.

Debt to equity: is a measure of the percentage of debt that a company uses for private financing.

Descending Triangle: is a bearish technical chart formation that is characterized by a horizontal support line and a downward-sloping resistance line. This pattern usually forms during a downtrend, as the stock price continuously encounters selling pressure at the declining resistance level. As the resistance line converges with the support line, it creates a triangle shape which signals a downward breakout.

Direction: If the price has crossed above the 50-day line, then it means that prices are likely to go higher over the next several weeks. Conversely, when price cross below their 50-day moving average line, it indicates that prices may continue lower. This moving average can help you to determine the primary direction of the market.

Distribution: is when smart money begins to cash out and take profits, prices typically peak during this phase, then begin to decline. It is typically accompanied by high volume and indicates a potential reversal.

Doji: is a candlestick pattern that indicates indecision, or uncertainty in the markets. It is usually represented by a single candle on a chart with the same opening and closing prices.

Dollar-Cost Averaging (DCA): is an investment strategy that involves buying a fixed dollar amount of an asset regularly over a specified interval of time. This strategy seeks to reduce the impact of market volatility on an investor's portfolio by spreading out purchases over multiple intervals and at different prices.

Double Bottom/Top: is a chart pattern that signals a potential reversal in the trend. It consists of two consecutive troughs and peaks that are at approximately the same level, which creates a "W" shape or an inverted "M" shape on the chart.

Dow Jones Industrial Average: is an index that tracks 30 large publicly traded companies in the U.S. It is also one of the oldest and most widely used measures of market performance in the world.

Downtrend: referring to lower lows and lower highs compared to previous periods, many traders tend to assume that the market will continue the trend until evidence of a reversal appears.

E

Electronic Communications Network (ECN): allows orders to be submitted and executed to trade securities through a computer-based broker, instead of routing them through an exchange floor.

Engulfing: is only one of the many tactics traders use to identify reversals. It displays that momentum is slowing down alerting investors to be mindful before taking trades on the wrong side.

Exchange Traded Funds (ETF): are a type of investment fund that is traded on the stock market, like stocks. They offer investors the opportunity to gain exposure to a range of different asset classes, such as stocks, bonds, commodities, and currencies without having to buy each underlying asset individually.

Exhaustion: are the result of a final burst of momentum, typically at the end of an extended trend.

Expansion: is a period that investors flock toward the asset; leading to a dramatic increase in trading volumes and prices.

F

Fade Trading: is a strategy that involves adding to a position moving in the opposite direction of the market's current trend. It is based on the idea that prices tend to overshoot and return creating an opportunity for traders to profit from price reversals.

Fibonacci: is a strategy based on the Fibonacci sequence and Fibonacci ratios. It uses the concept of retracements--that is, when prices temporarily pull back from their trend direction - to identify potential entry and exit points for trades.

Foreign Currency (FOREX): is the buying and selling of different world currencies on the currency market.

Fundamental Analysis: is a method of assessing the value of an asset by looking at underlying economic, financial, and other qualitative and quantitative factors. It helps investors identify undervalued investments and make decisions about when to enter or exit a position in the market.

Futures: are financial contracts that allow buyers and sellers to lock in an agreed-upon price for a certain asset to be delivered at a future date. These contracts can be used as an effective way for individuals and companies to hedge against the risk of price fluctuations.

G

Gap: are spaces in the chart of security that signify a large price move with no trading occurring in between. They can occur because of news events, economic data releases, or other announcements that cause traders to buy or sell quickly and forcefully.

Golden Cross: is a technical analysis pattern that indicates a long-term bullish trend in the market. It occurs when the short-term moving average (typically 20 days) crosses above the longer-term moving average (typically 200 days).

Head and Shoulders: is a popular chart pattern in technical analysis that signals a potential reversal in the trend. It consists of a peak, followed by a higher peak (the "head"), followed by another lower peak (the "shoulder"). The two shoulders are typically at approximately the same height - creating an inverted "U" shape. Once the neckline of the pattern is broken, it indicates that a downward trend could be in progress.

I

Intraday: is a method of investing that allows traders to take advantage of price fluctuations in a single day. It involves buying and selling financial instruments such as stocks, currencies, futures, and options within the same day. This means that all positions must be closed before the end of the market session.

Investor: is an individual who commits capital with the goal of generating a financial return. They can buy stocks, bonds, mutual funds, exchange-traded funds (ETFs), real estate, commodities, and other investments to diversify their portfolios and seek out potential profits.

L

Level I: is a type of trading that provides the most basic level of market data. This includes real-time bid and ask prices for stocks, as well as their volume.

Level II: is a more advanced form of market data that provides more information than Level I trading. Level II data includes the best bid and ask prices, as well as their volume, and provides this information for different price levels creating an ordering book.

Limit Order: is an instruction given to a broker or investment platform to buy or sell an asset at a specific price or better.

Long-Term: is an approach to investing in which investors hold onto their investments for longer periods, often years or even decades. The goal of long-term investing is to benefit from compounding returns over time, as well as the potential rise in the value of the asset with time.

Moving Average Convergence Divergence (MACD): is a momentum indicator used to identify potential trends or reversals in the market. It is calculated by taking the difference between two exponential moving averages (EMA): a short-term EMA and a long-term EMA. The MACD line is then plotted against a Signal line, which is a nine-period EMA of the MACD line, to generate buy and sell signals. These signals can be used by traders to identify when it may be time to enter or exit a position.

Margin: is a form of investing that allows investors to purchase securities on credit. It enables traders to borrow money from their broker or financial institution to increase their buying power and make larger investments than they would otherwise be able to. However, it also carries with it greater risks since the margin trader is obligated to pay back the borrowed funds plus interest.

Market Order: is an order placed with a broker to buy or sell a security at the current available price in the current market. It is usually used when an investor wants to execute a trade quickly, as the order is filled immediately upon being received. Market orders offer no price protection, however, so they may be filled at a worse-than-expected price.

Market Cycle: is a secular cycle. Sector rotation occurs during these secular cycles. This means that different groups of stocks do better at different times during the cycle. When a bull market begins, technology, consumer, and financial stocks typically outperform. Telecommunications, energy, raw materials, and industrials typically outperform during the middle stage of a bull market. Utilities, health care, and consumer staples thrive when the bull market ends, and the bear market begins.

Momentum: is an investment strategy that aims to capitalize on the tendency of a stock's price to continue moving in its current direction.

Moving Average (MA): is a technical analysis tool that shows the average price of an asset over a certain period. It is calculated by taking the average of a predetermined number of price data points, usually closing prices, to create a continuous line that best approximates the overall trend in the market.

O

One Cancels the Other (OCO): is a type of trading order that combines a stop order and a limit order. It is used to protect traders from having both orders filled if the price surpasses one of their set points. The OCO order instructs the broker to fill one order if it is triggered and automatically cancel the other. This allows a trader to enter a trade with predetermined exit points, minimizing the risk of loss while maximizing potential profits.

Options: are a type of derivative financial instrument that give the holder the right, but not the obligation, to buy or sell an underlying asset at a specified price on or before a predetermined date. Options offer investors the ability to take advantage of leverage and benefit from potentially lucrative returns for limited capital outlay. They can also be used to hedge risk, as well as for speculation. However, options also come with high risks if not used correctly and can expose traders to potentially large losses.

P

Pattern Day Trader (PDT): is a Financial Industry Regulatory Authority (FINRA) regulation that limits the number of day trades—defined as any trade opened and closed within the same business day—an individual can make in their margin account. The rule was introduced to protect unsophisticated investors from getting over-leveraged and incurring significant losses. Under the PDT Rule, any trader with less than $25,000 in their margin account is limited to three-day trades per week. Traders with more than $25,000 can make up to four times the number of day trades if they always maintain their minimum equity requirement.

Pennant: is a chart pattern used in technical analysis to identify when a stock or security is about to make a large price movement. This pattern is created when the price of an asset forms a symmetrical triangle shape. The two trend lines that make up this triangle form by connecting the highs and lows of the asset's price over a specific period. Traders use the Pennant pattern to identify potential reversal points and enter or exit trades accordingly. This strategy is particularly useful when trading volatile markets, as it helps traders anticipate large price movements before they happen.

Pinocchio: (also referred to as a Pinocchio bar) is a type of candlestick chart pattern that helps traders identify possible trend reversals in the stock market. It consists of a single candle with a long upper or lower wick, and a short body at one end. The long wick indicates that there was a battle between buyers and sellers, with the buyers pushing the price higher (in the case of a bullish pin bar) and the sellers pushing it lower (in the case of a bearish pin bar).

Price to book: ratio is comparing a company's current market value against its book value.

Price to earnings: ratio is a number that shows how much people are willing to pay for a company's stock compared to how much money the company makes. The ratio is used to see if a company's stock is worth more or less than it should be.

Pullback: is a temporary price retracement that occurs after an extended period of upward or downward movement. It is usually seen as an opportunity for investors to enter a more favorable price, allowing them to take advantage of the potential for profits from any continuation of price.

Q

Quick Ratio: measures a company's ability to use its cash or quick assets to pay off its current liabilities immediately.

R

Recession: is an extended period of economic decline and contraction, characterized by declining economic activity, higher unemployment, decreased consumer spending, and falling stock prices. During a recession, businesses generally suffer from decreased demand and increased costs. As a result of this reduced buying power, businesses are forced to lay off workers or reduce wages to remain profitable. A recession can last anywhere from a few months to several years and may be accompanied by deflation or inflation. Governments usually respond to recessions with measures such as increased spending and lower taxes to stimulate the economy, but if prolonged these policies can lead to an increase in public debt.

Recovery: is the process of economic growth and stability following a period of decline. It is characterized by increased consumer spending, increased business investments, improved employment levels, and rising stock prices. Recovery periods are often associated with government interventions such as increased spending and lower taxes to stimulate the economy. During a recovery, businesses may start to hire more workers and increase wages, allowing consumers to become more confident and spend more. While recoveries are usually seen as a positive sign for the economy, it is important to note that they can be short-lived if not properly managed. Therefore, governments must be prepared to react quickly to maintain economic growth over the long term.

Relative Strength Index (RSI): is a technical indicator used to measure the strength of a stock or other asset relative to its recent performance. It can be used to determine overbought and oversold levels, as well as identify divergences between price and momentum.

Resistance: is an area where it is hard for the price of a stock to move higher. This is often seen as a barrier that limits how much the price can go up because buyers do not want to pay more, and sellers do not want to accept less.

Retracement: is a temporary price decline that occurs after an extended period of upward or downward movement. It is usually seen as an opportunity for investors to enter at a more favorable price, allowing them to take advantage of the potential for profits from any continuation of the trend.

Reversal: is when the direction of a stock's price change changes. For example, when a stock that had been going up in price suddenly turns around and goes down.

Risk-to-Reward: is to evaluate the potential gains and losses on an investment. This tool assesses how much a possible return may be gained compared to any associated risks of loss.

S

Scaling: into a trade is a strategy where an investor gradually increases their position size over time as the price drops. This strategy can be used to mitigate risk and limit losses in volatile markets. It works by buying a fixed number of shares or contracts every time the price reaches a certain level, allowing traders to average out their entry points.

Short: is an investment strategy that enables investors to make money from a decrease in the price of a security. It involves selling a borrowed asset at its current market price and then buying it back at a lower price when the market corrects. Short sellers hope to profit from the difference between what they sold the asset for and what they bought it back for. This strategy is riskier than other strategies since investors can potentially face large losses if the price of the security increases in value.

Short-Term: is an approach to investing in which investors attempt to capitalize on short-term price movements in the market. It involves taking positions in assets that are expected to move within a few days or weeks, and then closing the position when profits are realized. Short-term trading carries with it significant risk, as there is no guarantee that prices will move in the intended direction.

Squeeze: is a situation in which a heavily shorted stock suddenly experiences a sharp increase in price, causing investors who have sold the stock short to scramble to buy it back to cover their positions. This often results in an even further rise in the stock's price due to increased buying pressure.

Stagnation: is a period when there is little or no growth in the stock market. It can be caused by economic factors such as slowdowns in consumer spending and business investment, reduced government spending, and weak global prospects. During such a period, stock prices may remain flat for an extended period, with investors delaying their buying and selling decisions until the market begins to show signs of improvement.

Stop Loss: is an instruction given to a broker to sell a stock when it reaches a certain price. Stop loss orders are designed to limit losses if a stock's price goes down. They are often used by investors who want to protect their investments in case the market takes an unexpected turn. Stop loss orders can be set at any price and they can be modified or cancelled at any time.

Stop Order: is a type of advanced order that investors can place with their broker to buy or sell a security once it reaches a predetermined price. Stop orders are often used to limit losses in case the stock's price drops and to take profits if the stock's price increases.

Support: is a level at which there is sufficient demand for the stock to prevent its price from falling further. This can be caused by investors buying up large amounts of the stock, or it can be due to positive news about the company that leads investors to become more confident. Once a support level has been established, investors may attempt to profit from any rebound in the price of the stock.

Swing Trading: is a form of investing that attempts to capitalize on short-term price movements in an asset. It involves taking positions in an asset that are expected to move within a few days or weeks, and then closing the position when profits are realized.

Symmetrical Triangle: is a technical analysis chart pattern that indicates a period of consolidation before the price of an asset either rises or falls. This pattern is formed when two trendlines slope downward and converge toward each other, forming a shape resembling a triangle. These trendlines represent support and resistance levels, which can be identified by price movement.

T

Technical Analysis: Technical analysis is an analytical method used to predict the direction of stock prices. It involves studying past data such as price movements, trading volumes and other indicators to identify patterns that can be used to anticipate future price movements.

Time and sales: Time and Sales is a type of data that shows the sequence of trades, their prices, and the number of shares or contracts that have taken place in real-time.

Timeframe: is referred to the period in which a trader can analyze price trends and other data. Different traders may use different time frames, depending on their trading strategy. Longer-term traders may look at a weekly or monthly chart, while shorter-term traders may use a daily or intraday chart.

Trader: is an individual who buys and sells stocks in financial markets. They use their knowledge of the stock market, fundamental and technical analysis, and financial analysis to try to make a profit from buying and selling stocks.

Trailing Stop Order: is an advanced type of stop order where the stop price is adjusted as the stock's price moves. It functions similarly to a regular stop order, in that it will trigger a sale if the stock falls below the specified stop price. However, with a trailing stop order, the stop price changes according to the movement of the stock. This allows investors to protect their profits while still giving the stock the chance to continue rising in price.

Trend line: is a line drawn on a chart to connect the highs and lows of an asset's price action over time. The trend line can be used to identify patterns and determine potential areas of support and resistance.

Tweezers: is a technical analysis charting tool used to identify potential reversal points in the stock market. It is characterized by two candlesticks with similar highs and/or lows that "tweeze," or squeeze together, forming a pattern that can suggest an imminent trend reversal.

Uptrend: is referring to higher highs and higher lows compared to previous periods, many traders tend to assume that the market will continue the trend until evidence of a reversal appears.

Volatility: is a measure of the amount of risk associated with investing in a particular asset or market. It reflects the degree to which price changes over time, with higher volatility indicating more uncertainty and potential for larger gains or losses. It is usually measured as the standard deviation of returns over a specified period. High volatility makes it difficult to predict future prices and can increase the risk of losses for investors.

Volume: is a measure of how many shares or contracts have been traded over a specific period.

W

Wedges: is a chart pattern that signifies consolidation in the stock market. It is created when two trend lines slope towards each other, forming a triangle shape. These trendlines are referred to as support and resistance levels, and they can be identified by observing the price movements of an asset. This pattern indicates that the price of an asset is in a state of indecision and could indicate a possible trend reversal and continuation.

Printed in the USA
CPSIA information can be obtained
at www.ICGtesting.com
LVHW050310060124
768269LV00004B/273

9 798987 391310